FLOWERS
of the
WORLD

FLOWERS of the WORLD IN FULL COLOR

by

ROBERT S. LEMMON

CHARLES L. SHERMAN

With Special Photography by

ROY GOIN · PAUL GENEREUX

HANOVER HOUSE · GARDEN CITY, N. Y.

LIBRARY OF CONGRESS CATALOG CARD NUMBER 58-10751

PRINTED IN THE UNITED STATES OF AMERICA

Introduction

THE variety of flowering plants in the world today defies calculation. Certainly there are many millions of different kinds. Some of their individual blossoms are almost microscopically tiny, while others can be seen a quarter mile away with the unaided eye. Their colors and tints run the entire gamut from white to black, and the multitude of their forms, structures, and functional ingenuities is immense.

Flowering plants as we know them are a superb tribute to the mysterious forces of natural evolution. Their remote ancestors were virtually formless slimes and molds whose only method of reproduction was to divide and subdivide their own sexless bodies. Those unlovely organisms originated when our earth was scarcely more than a chaotic mass of swirling vapors and endless rains. Yet they were the true forerunners of Roses, Orchids, and all the other surpassingly lovely blossoms of modern days.

Flowers, in a broad sense, are the plant world's most intriguing agencies of self-perpetuation. Their basic purpose is to produce seeds which, when they ripen and come in contact with the soil, will sprout and grow into plants similar to their direct ancestors. But ever since the dawn of recorded history flowers have strongly influenced mankind in ways that have nothing to do with their biological purpose. Painting and sculpture, literature and music, architecture, weaving, and designing of every sort are only a few of the arts and crafts in which their endless forms and beauties have been reflected for thousands of years. More subtly, but no less importantly, they have played a symbolic role in many religious creeds and services. With few exceptions all of the finer human emotions and concepts have their flower connotations.

The ancient Egyptians were among the earliest races who evidenced this appeal that flowers have for all mankind. When they abandoned their nomadic wanderings thousands of years ago and settled down to live in the Valley of the Nile, they began to raise cultivated food crops instead of depending upon such wild ones as they had chanced to find along their travel trails. From this beginning it soon became a major economic factor.

There is ample evidence that ornamental gardening often follows closely on the heels of successful food growing. Thus, as the Egyptians prospered, their leaders began to search for fine flowering plants to brighten their lands and homes. Hardy men were dispatched to regions of the Far East to find and bring back exotic plants whose blossoms were notably appealing. And largely through the success of these emissaries Egypt became an acknowledged pioneer in what we now call flower gardening.

Ever since that vanished era the quest for more distinctive flowers has continued unremittingly. Plant hunters, as we call the searchers today, have contributed enormously to our pleasure as we view the variety and loveliness of present-day cultivated flowers. Some of our benefactors were missionaries whose calling led them into remote regions. Others have been professional collectors sent out by horticultural firms or botanical organizations. Many have succeeded in bringing back quantities of valuable seeds, bulbs, roots, and entire living plants. But there have always been those who succumbed to the hardships and perils of the wilderness and never returned.

We should be grateful, also, to the skilled plantsmen at home and abroad who, with infinite patience, manually hybridize different blossoms of the same general race and thereby produce plants whose blossoms are delightfully new in color, fragrance, size, or form. Most of them work modestly and without fanfare. Some are almost hermits in their voluntary seclusion. They are true horticultural creators, utilizing the potentials latent in all plants and sometimes obtaining in the space of a few months such results as Nature unaided might not achieve for thousands of years.

In connection with the early beginnings of gardening in Egypt it is interesting to note that many of our favorite flowering plants were originally natives of the Old World. This was the case with Chrysanthemums and Daffodils, for example. Some, such as Dahlias and Marigolds, are of New World origin. And among the remainder there are those which have grown wild in both hemispheres from early times.

It is upon this basis of origin areas that the flowers have been broadly grouped. There is no horticultural significance in the order of their appearance on the pages except that members of the same genus are kept together. It has seemed advisable to arrange them on such a plan since this is a book of flower appreciation rather than flower growing.

We have also sought to present a considerable measure of authentic information about flower structure and habits in which the roots of your interest may thrive. These colorful, fragile creations are living, functional entities whose perfection no man can hope to match. It is only natural that the more one knows about them the greater their marvels become.

Robert S. Lemmon

Charles L. Sherman

Contents

Note: All the flower plates are numbered consecutively. To quickly locate any desired flower use the popular name index in the final pages. The scientific name will be found there as well. All text references to each flower will usually be found next to the flower-plate or on adjoining pages.

Flowers of the Old World

TEMPERATE ZONE

FROM the standpoint of plants the temperate zones in any part of the world are as variable as patches on a quilt. Geographically they are those areas which lie between the tropics and the Arctic and Antarctic circles. But in terms of temperature they present enormous extremes which result from factors such as altitude above sea level, ocean currents, and the direction of prevailing winds. Hundreds of regions within the North Temperate and South Temperate zones are virtually polar in character.

Similar temperature and climate variations exist in the tropics. There are vast regions where, on the high mountaintops, snow and thick ice are always present. This may occur even though the equator itself is only a hundred miles away. Yet a descent of three vertical miles is likely to bring you into a land where even the scantiest clothing feels burdensome.

Temperature and climate are major influences on the distribution of flowering plants. So when we say that this or that flower comes from a temperate zone it does not necessarily follow that it is found everywhere within that area. Frequently there are thousands of square miles which are far too hot or cold for its survival.

It is odd that, although these variations control the lives of flowering plants, they do not necessarily affect the charm of the actual blossoms. Some of the loveliest blooms are products of the cooler parts of the temperate zones. And there are certain kinds in the hot tropics which are as ugly to human eyes as their unrelated neighbors are captivating.

Among China's many contributions of shrubs to the blossom-seeking world the Glossy Abelia ranks among the leaders. It seldom exceeds six feet in height, but its countless funnel-like flowers open in a steady proces-

The finest of the **MORNING-GLORIES** (2) are products of the hybridizing genius of the Japanese. Their blossoms flare outward, often to six inches.

3

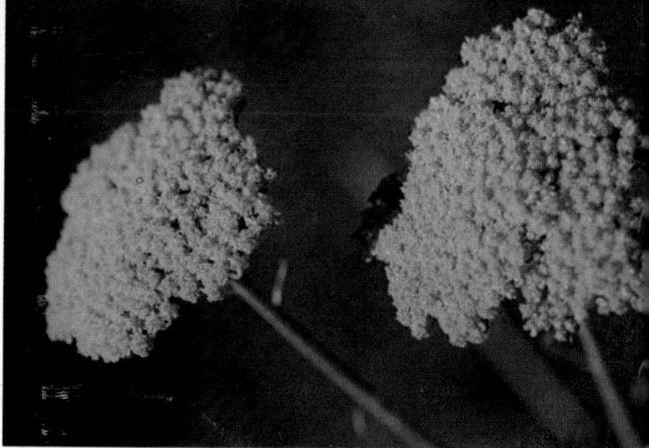

4

GLOSSY ABELIA (3) is a highly ornamental small shrub which keeps on flowering for four or five months. Slender branches, graceful blossoms and small, neat leaves mark it as a plant aristocrat. It is one of China's finest gifts . . . The **COMMON YARROW** (4) has spread so widely over American fields and roadsides that it is often considered a native weed, though it probably came from Europe. It demonstrates the impact of tiny massed individual flowers.

sion from June until November. Each of them is nearly an inch long, and there is usually a faint flush of pink in it which gives a warm tone to the otherwise pure white petals. When the sun strikes them, they show the same sort of translucent beauty that you see in the finest of thin porcelains. The whole effect is delightfully clean and attractive against the shining surface of the almost evergreen leaves.

In our Southern gardens, where this little bush is widely grown, it lives for many years. In that region it finds the sort of climate it knew at home. But in the North it is often seriously damaged, and sometimes killed outright, by the winter cold.

Common Yarrow, on the other hand, can stand almost anything in the way of cold weather. Its yellow and sometimes reddish blossoms are extremely small, but so many of them are massed together they occasionally form a flattened mat as much as three inches across. These colorful mats stand at the tops of slim stems whose lower portions are clothed with feathery, distinctively pungent-smelling leaves.

Most of the Yarrows, or Achilleas, hailed originally from Europe and Asia. But botanists are inclined to believe that the common species pictured here is also truly native in the northern parts of the New World. Certainly it is very frequent in sunny American fields and pastures. Often you see one or another of its varieties growing in gardens, too. A very close relative is known as Perry's White Achillea, and another thrives under the fanciful but quite descriptive name of The Pearl.

Yarrows as a group bloom more or less all summer. At the end of the season their stems, which first appeared in the spring and grew rapidly, die down to the ground. So far as you can see the plants are completely dead and gone.

5 6

The blossoms of **PERRY'S WHITE ACHILLEA** (5) are so large and double by comparison with Common Yarrow that the two plants look as if they belonged to different families. Perry's White is a noted garden favorite . . . Some species of **BUGLE** (6), or Ajuga, form almost solid ground hugging mats only a few inches high. The odd flower stalks of this one, however, are over a foot tall. The peculiar shape of the topmost blossom on the left side of the stalk is duplicated by all the others.

But beneath the surface their roots are very much alive despite their temporary inactivity. It is rather as if they were merely resting or perhaps sleeping. Their work will begin again even before the return of spring draws all the frost out of the ground. This annual period of coma followed by renewed activity often continues for several years. Meanwhile the wee flowers have produced multitudes of seeds to carry on the family line and spread it farther and farther afield.

There is no question about the North Temperate Zone of the Old World being the one and only homeland of the Bugle clan. There are scarcely more than a half-dozen different kinds in the whole group, yet their combined forces constitute an enormous population. All of them have the same characteristics of low, spreading leaves and stout, upright stalks carrying somewhat tapering heads of intriguing little flowers. As a rule the blossoms are some shade of blue or purple, but there is a white variety that is not often seen. Unlike many other plants, the Bugles are decidedly broad-minded about their requirements. They seem to be able to take moisture or dryness, sun or shade and really like each extreme.

Among trees, that striking ornamental one which is widely known as Mimosa, or Silk Tree, is actually a distant relative of our common Sweet

7 8

A full-face, close-up view of **MIMOSA** (7) flowers suggests a man-made sunburst rather than plant blossoms . . . The New World tropics try a variation of this impression with a **POWDER-PUFF TREE** (8).

Peas, String Beans, and numerous other familiar plants whose seeds are contained in close-fitting pods. It originated in the comparatively warm portion of the North Temperate Zone which extends from Persia to Japan. From there it has been introduced into many other parts of the world where suitable climatic conditions enable it to do its incomparable best.

A mature Mimosa may reach a height of thirty feet or so. The outer ends of its branches are crowded by slender, graceful sprays of ball-like pink blossoms with curiously long pollen-bearing stamens. The whole display is splendidly effective among the tree's countless dainty leaves.

Leaving the Mimosa to its odd ways, the opposite page begins the picture story of Azaleas, one of the largest and showiest groups of flowering shrubs in the modern world. There are literally hundreds of kinds now flourishing in the temperate regions of both hemispheres. A great many of these originated in the Orient. This surprising over-all number is due in part to the work of skilled hybridizers, in our own country as well as abroad, who for many years have devoted their time to developing new flower colors, forms, and sizes. Most of the basic material used by these geniuses came from the wild species of the Far East. But here and there some of the North American native kinds have been brought into the breeding experiments to contribute characteristics they alone possessed.

Mass plantings of **AZALEAS** (9) are superb in the warm days of spring. Almost any color scheme is possible. In the upper right are Dogwood blossoms.

10

11↓

Millions of small potted **AZALEAS** (10, 11, 12) like this are sold during every Easter season. All of them are hybrids of kinds which originated in China and Japan many centuries ago. There are scores of varieties today. Azalea blossoms vary widely in size, shape and color. All of them, however, have protruding stamens which often curve upward like those of Honeysuckles. Some are four or five inches wide.

12↓

Azaleas are fairly compact-growing shrubs that vary in height from three to a dozen feet or more. Their color range includes just about every conceivable shade of yellow, orange, red, pink, purple, and, of course, white.

The Azalea tribe falls into two general categories: those kinds which can survive cold winters, and those which cannot. With some exceptions the famous Azalea gardens in our Southern states are stocked with members of both these groups. The superb little potted Azaleas in full flower, however, which are so popular as Easter gift plants, are bred chiefly from Chinese and Japanese stocks, which are seldom practical for outdoor planting in the cold North. South of Washington, D.C., and in the mild climate of the West Coast, they are widely used out of doors.

Staggering numbers of these compact pot-grown beauties are produced every year by commercial growers in the United States and the Old World. A few years ago one of the large firms near New York was marketing about three million of them annually. Hundreds of thousands of these were forced so skillfully in huge special greenhouses that they would come into full bloom just in time for Easter. Retail florists depended on them to meet their holiday demand. Other thousands were shipped to the South for garden use.

That particular grower's establishment was a wonderland of flower beauty at any time of the year. Yet one of the key spots in it was never seen and seldom even suspected by the daily throngs of visitors. This was a small, quite dingy greenhouse hidden among the huge packing sheds and other utility buildings. No exterior could have seemed less important. But within those grimy glass walls dozens of new flower marvels were steadily creeping toward their ultimate public triumphs.

This was the hybridizing house. Its presiding genius was a gnarly, shy, taciturn old man who spoke scarcely above a whisper. As you watched him move slowly along the pathways between rows of benches filled with cryptically labeled Azaleas in every conceivable stage of development, you realized that he was an almost uncanny blend of dreamer, scientist, technician, and philosopher—a master hybridizer in the fullest sense.

There were only two keys to the locked single door of that glassed-in hideaway. One was always in a pocket of the old man's work trousers. The

A second color often appears in an **AZALEA'S BLOSSOMS** (13), frequently taking the form of small dots which begin deep in the throat of the bloom and fan outward as they emerge. It is a curious fact that these markings usually appear only on one or two of the uppermost petals. These are the ones toward which the stamens curve. Most kinds of Azalea flowers are about two inches wide, but a few species practically double that figure. A fair number of the American kinds are fragrant.

13↓

14 15

other never left the possession of the firm's president. Whenever either of these men entered or left the treasure house, he immediately locked the door behind him with his own key. Save for an occasional super-privileged guest those two were the only persons permitted to see the contents of that strange sanctuary. An important reason for this was that every precaution must be taken to safeguard the delicately contrived blend of humidity, light, and temperature necessary for the maximum well-being of the plants under test and development. Far too many future dollars hung in the balance for any sane person to take such chances. Also, there was a certain lurking thought that, without the best of security regulations, some inkling of the priceless new plants of the future might leak out and perhaps reach the ears of some ambitious rival grower!

Botanically it is a very far cry from Azaleas to Flowering Onions, but the comedown is not nearly as upsetting as it might seem. The fact is that this

16↓

The word onion is so closely associated with those odorous roots which we use for food that few people realize that they have dozens of cousins with such lovely blossoms that they are called **FLOWERING ONIONS** (14, 15, 16) . . . The little four-petal flowers of the **SWEET ALYSSUM** (17, 18) are the essence of primness besides being decidedly fragrant. The more closely you study them the more perfect their form seems to be . . . **BASKET-OF-GOLD** or Golden-tuft, and **SIBERIAN WALLFLOWER** (19) are close cousins of Sweet Alyssum. May is their month of months.

17

18

branch of the Onion group is definitely ornamental, with its lily-like leaves and sizable rounded heads of neat white, blush-pink, lilac, or bluish blossoms topping slender stems. Some of them are popular winter greenhouse flowers that are valued for decorative uses. And at least a half-dozen kinds are welcome members of a rock-garden community.

The best of these small charmers hail from the Southern European and Persian regions. There are some lovely ones in the American Northwest, although expert rock gardeners are about the only people who know much about them.

By contrast Sweet Alyssum, from the Mediterranean country, is everybody's garden delight. It has so much to offer in the way of fragrance, color variety, and neat habits that it has been a front-ranker for many years. It seldom reaches a height of more than a foot, although its show of clustered white to violet flower heads often continues all summer and well into the fall. Some of the varieties no taller than four inches make delightfully dainty mats over a foot wide before the end of their season. No other dependable plant is quite so desirable a provider of appealing cut-flower nosegays for minor accents in the house.

19↓

20

21

The modern **DOUBLE HOLLYHOCKS** (20) are as varied in size and color as those with a single set of petals. Whether this double-single distinction came about through man's efforts or existed among the wild plants is unknown. But the doubles have been improved . . . This member of the confused **ALKANET GROUP** (21) is the most popular for garden planting. It grows about a foot high and its blossoms are much like those of Forget-me-nots.

The same section of Southern Europe is the source of another, somewhat stouter mat-former appropriately known as Golden-Tuft, Gold-Dust, or Basket-of-Gold. In spring its glowing blossom mass seems to catch and heighten all the brightness of the strengthening sunshine. Small wonder that everyone who sees it becomes its enthusiastic friend.

Several centuries ago, when the Huguenots were fleeing from France to escape the religious persecutions which were the fashion of those days, they took with them a strange and showy flower known as the Outlandish Rose. Clearly it was not a true Rose, for its tall, straight stalk was thornless and the blossoms themselves were quite differently formed. Their petals were just as broad and colorful as those of Roses, however, so perhaps we should not be critical about such botanical differences. In any event, the popularity of that Outlandish Rose has survived until today and doubtless will continue far into the future. Few radical changes have occurred in the old plant. Only its name is really different. Nowadays we call it Hollyhock.

China was the original home of this universally beloved garden flower. The probabilities are that there was some variety in the color and form of its blooms even before the ancient Orientals paid much attention to it. Selection and saving of seeds from occasional individual plants which varied somewhat from their ancestors continued for centuries and have had much to do with the development of modern types. Diligent plant hybridists have now established strains that range from four to almost nine feet in height. Some have four-inch blooms so double that each one suggests a huge Carnation. Others have distinctly frilled petals, or are simple and

22 23

The popular name **POPPY-FLOWERED ANEMONE** (22, 23) is based on the form of the blossoms. In most instances they definitely do resemble those of Poppies. With us the plants are usually grown in greenhouses.

saucer-shaped. And the variety of colors, especially in the yellow, pink, and red tones, is literally bewildering.

Notwithstanding their centuries of human care, Hollyhocks seldom live for more than two years. They have the happy faculty, though, of producing such vast numbers of seeds that, given a fair chance, the plants may perpetuate themselves almost indefinitely and without any human assistance.

In contrast to the Hollyhock's spires the Anchusas or Alkanets are definitely mass formers. Asia, the Mediterranean region, and South Africa share the honor of being their native home. The tallest species reaches a height of five feet and a spread of somewhat less. Nurserymen, and occasional natural variants from Nature's own formula, have brought about several forms with blossoms in shades of blue and purple contrasting with white or yellow centers. There is even an all-white one, and another that is touched with red.

There appears to be a curious lack of relationship between the leaf and blossom sizes of the Anchusas. The tendency of their group is to produce coarse, hairy leaves, some of which are six to eight inches long. Yet none of them has blossoms broader than an inch, and some are nearly as small as those of Forget-me-nots.

The early history of some of our favorite cultivated flowers is a bit on the sketchy side. Documented proof of such matters was often a scarce commodity centuries ago. Nevertheless, competent and tireless plant researchers have uncovered numerous bits of evidence which, pieced together, lead to conclusions that appear to be quite definite.

A case in point is the Poppy-flowered or French Anemone, that gorgeous, multicolored beauty which is such a rewarding highlight in the better American florist shops and flower shows during the winter and early spring. It is a star member of a large and always charming clan that is widespread over the world. Originally, as well as today, it clothed the hills of Palestine

24

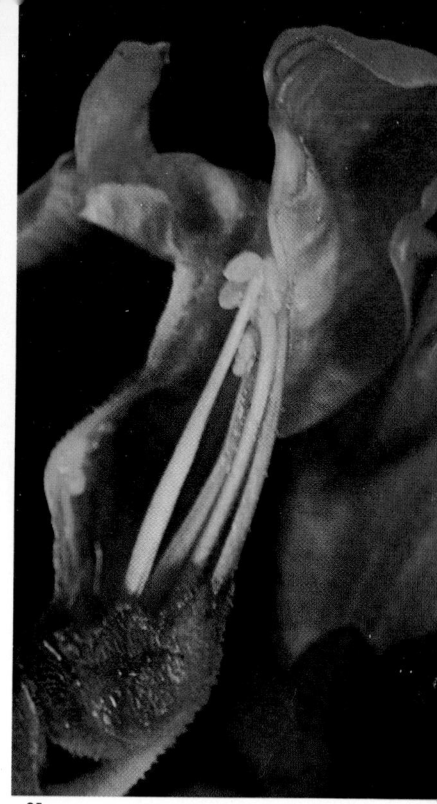

25

From a purely practical standpoint it may seem wasteful for a plant to live only six months after it begins life as a sprouting seed. Into this short span it has to pack all the miraculous effort of growing perhaps several feet, producing complex and ingenious leaves and flowers, and ripening hundreds of seeds. Yet this is what all **SNAPDRAGONS** (24, 25) have done for innumerable centuries.

and the Levant with indescribable beauty as an aftermath of each rainy season. There are those who believe that its hosts were the Biblical "lilies of the field." Here is the reputed story of its introduction into Italy.

In the days of the Second Crusade the Bishop of Pisa conceived the idea of having the empty troopships returning from the Holy Land bring good soil instead of worthless sand as ballast. This soil, he urged, would be doubly appropriate for depositing in the already consecrated Campo Sancta burial ground at Pisa.

These instructions were carried out, and one spring the Campo Santo miraculously glowed with great blood-red blossoms never before seen there. To the superstitious clergy they surely represented the blood of crusading martyrs who had lost their lives in defense of the Holy Land.

It is said that the name French Anemone arose from the fact that a Parisian florist came upon a particularly fine type in the seventeenth century. Its blossoms were so super-deluxe he vigorously refused to let anyone else have so much as a single seed from them. But the envious Burgomaster of Antwerp, who coveted at least a few, got around that restriction very neatly. While on a friendly visit to the florist's garden, during the season when he figured that the seeds would be ripe, he carried his fur-lined official robe over his arm. As he and his host passed by the Anemone bed he pretended to stumble so that the robe, fur side down, fell on top of the plants. Instantly his well-instructed servant snatched it up, folded it, and carried it to the carriage where he awaited his master's return. Of course the Burgomaster apologized profusely for the "accident" and, robeless,

26

27

PASQUE-FLOWERS (26) are delightfully exaggerated examples of the fact that the leaves, stems and sometimes blossoms of a vast number of unrelated plants have a covering of "hair." There are numerous possible reasons for this, but it is fair to assume that each one is concerned with survival . . . Like all the other thousands of daisy-like blossoming plants the true flowers of the **GOLDEN MARGUERITE** (27) are very small and closely packed.

continued the garden tour. But later, at a safer time and place, every seed was meticulously picked out of its hiding place in the fur, planted and zealously guarded, and that was the end of the florist's pet monopoly.

Southern Europe in general and the Mediterranean region in particular have given the world many of its most intriguing flowers. No doubt this is partly because of their wide variations in climate from the cold of alpine heights to the subtropical warmth of many of the lowlands. Another reason is that advanced civilizations have existed there for a longer period than almost anywhere else except the Orient. It is axiomatic that the greater the knowledge and discernment of a people the keener their activities on behalf of the finer expressions of life, such as flowers.

It is to these productive lands that we are indebted for Snapdragons, one of our most alluring garden and greenhouse flowering plants. There is scarcely a month or a week in the year when their spirey stalks of white, yellow, crimson, rose, lavender, bronze, or blended blossoms are not displayed out of doors or in florist shops. Perhaps it is not too extreme to say that there is at least one appropriate kind of Snapdragon for every conceivable occasion that calls for living flowers.

These Old World ornamental plants, and their several close relatives growing wild in North America, are called perennials because they are capable of living for several years after they sprout as seedlings. They may reach a height ranging from six inches to four feet, depending on the race and particular species involved. As a general rule their first full crop of bloom is the best, so it is quite customary for growers to keep succession

28

WALL ROCK-CRESS (28) can be counted on for early spring clusters of trim little white blossoms which are indispensable in limited but prominent gardening places. There is a double-flowered form of it in addition to this single type . . . A really colorful and satisfying **ROCK GARDEN** (29) is necessarily at its best in the spring, since not many suitably low plants flower freely during the summer except high in the mountains. It should also slope down to the point from which it is usually seen; this offers a view of all the plants in it. Big rocks look far better than small ones and help the plants grow.

crops of new plants coming along to maintain the magnificent display.

The somewhat fearsome name of Snapdragon derives from the peculiar construction of each blossom. A slight finger pressure on its sides causes its protruding lower portion to drop like an animated jaw and disclose a throat which, for one so small, is positively cavernous. The moment the pressure is removed the "jaw" snaps shut again. So Snapdragon is not such a far-fetched title, after all.

A short while ago we mentioned the fact that those magnificent Poppy-flowered Anemones have a considerable number of delightful if less brilliant relatives. One of these that has made a name for itself on both sides of the Atlantic is the oddly furry Pasque Flower, a native of well-drained and often rocky ground in various parts of Europe. It grows to a maximum height of a foot and often stops at less than that. Yet its blue or purplish blossoms about two inches across look upward into the spring sky with an air of quiet satisfaction that few other flowers can match. A rather similar but less impressive cousin, called the American Pasque Flower, grows wild in our North Central states and westward as well as in Siberia.

Many of the Anemones grow from peculiar underground parts known as tubers. These look somewhat like crosses between regular roots and true bulbs, such as those of Daffodils. They often have the ability to remain dormant and apparently dead for long periods until exposure to favorable conditions stimulates them to renewed activity.

In countless gardens here and overseas one of the prized features of the summer show is staged by the Golden Marguerite. It is a cheery, upstanding soul with dainty foliage and the brightness of sunlight gleaming in its two-inch blossom discs poised on slim stems as much as two feet above the ground. Cheerful and enduring, it demands nothing in the way of special favors. Perhaps this is one reason why it has persisted on its own for so many thousands of years in the untilled countryside of its native Europe and various parts of Asia.

The Rock Wall-Cress is one of those members of the Arabis group which, as someone has said, is best enjoyed when you are on your knees. This prayerful posture discloses the full charm of the softly downy, whitish foli-

30

31

In addition to their original purplish colors, the flowers of **BUTTERFLY-BUSH** (30) now come in several pinks, dark red and white. Probably others will be developed . . . Seeds from the finer varieties of **AUBRIETA** (31) cannot be trusted to grow into plants exactly like their parents.

age, which actually deserves a still-closer view through a magnifying glass. Of equal importance, it enables one to pick up the texture and amazing form of each blossom. And, perhaps the most rewarding experience of all, your nostrils will catch the flowers' clean, refreshing fragrance, which seems to embody the very essence of early spring.

This delightful little plant from the Caucasus, no taller than a foot, is widely used for edging along the front of flower borders as a sort of introduction to the taller flowers behind it. Its colors never clash with others, and it is always well behaved.

While we are on the subject of small, neat plants, the rock garden pictured on the opposite page is a demonstration of their possibilities when skillfully arranged. Too often American rock gardens are little more than collections of assorted stones from here and there. Such places justify a remark by that grand old master of plants, Dr. Liberty Hyde Bailey, to the effect that some rock gardeners really should have gone into geology instead of horticulture.

A rock garden at its best is an effort to achieve in miniature the spirit of a high alpine slope, ravine, or summit above the limit of normal tree growth. In such regions the shrubs and other hard-wooded plants are either absent or reduced to stunted, sprawling mats. No plant can safely raise its head much above the rocky ground because of the frequent fierce winds. But whereever there is a bit of sheltered, gritty soil there are groups and colonies of ground-hugging beauties whose blossoms are incredibly large for such harsh surroundings. In few other places does Nature succeed in achieving so much with so little.

Every now and then you come across a plant whose everyday name is especially appropriate. This is certainly true of the Butterfly-bush, one of the numerous outstanding ornamental shrubs which China has provided. In late summer, and often well into autumn, its pointed sprays of little lilac, purple, white, pink, or red blossoms are the favorite restaurants of the neighborhood butterflies. Big and little, brilliant or soberly clad, the long-tongued insects flit, hover, and perch as they satisfy their insatiable appetites for nectar. Among them an occasional fat bumblebee in yellowish fur jacket looks grotesquely coarse and clumsy.

The Butterfly-bush is one of those plants which demonstrate a weakness directly related to the climate in which they are known to have originated. Its roots can so well withstand winter cold which may freeze the soil to a depth of a foot or more that they will send up normal new shoots in the following spring. But those same frigid conditions usually spell death to the stems and branches which had been so gay with blossoms only a few months before. In our Southern states the winter temperatures are close enough to those in the Butterfly-bush's native home for it to attain an occasional height of fifteen feet after a few years.

Even a quick comparison of the little four-petal flowers carried by the Sweet Alyssum and the Aubrieta will suggest that these popular low plants are related. Actually they are rather close cousins and come from the same general Italy-to-Persia region. But whereas the Sweet Alyssum lives for only one season, the dense, spreading mat of Aubrieta thrives lustily for several years. Its blossom colors are gayer, too—blue, violet, purple, pink, mauve, and even white-eyed.

These cheery little plants, named after the French natural-history painter Claude Aubriet, are perhaps most effective in rock gardens where the beauty of their trailing, flower-sprinkled mats is not smothered by larger, ranker neighbors. Often their leaves are almost evergreen. Even on bleak winter days the plants give the impression of being on the verge of spreading just a little farther and thicker.

The **ASTILBE** (33), or Florists' Spirea, is at its best when in full flower, but in many cases the well advanced bud stage is more colorful. It is just as attractive in gardens provided the summer is not too hot and dry, and closely resembles the strong-growing **GOAT'S BEARD** (32).

32 ↓ 33 ↓

34

35

Theoretically the **ENGLISH DAISY** (34) is perennial by nature and therefore capable of living outdoors for several years. But many American gardeners grant it no more than one season . . . **POT-MARIGOLD** (35) or Calendula, however, by way of contrast, will grow almost anywhere. It is an out-and-out annual and a notably fast grower from seed. Incidentally, it is not a true Marigold.

There is probably no confusion quite as complete as the kind in which plant authorities sometimes become involved when they try to agree on a correct name for a controversial flower. Botanists, among themselves, are often as stubbornly far apart as Kipling's famous folk of East and West. The nurserymen are not much better off, because they have their individual preferences and, at times, very little patience with the bickering scientists. The amusing part of the situation is that the innocent flower which causes all the row keeps right on being its characteristic self and blithely proceeds to unfold its hereditary beauty for all to see.

Such is the case with the Astilbes, or Florist's Spireas, according to which school of thought you prefer to follow. The one which appears on page 17 hails from Japan and is often raised in greenhouses for sale as potted plants in full bloom. Knowing gardeners, however, plant them outdoors and, if certain requirements of soil and moisture are met, are delighted by their close-packed blossom plumes for several years. The most critical time often comes in early summer, just as the flowers are preparing to open. If the soil is then in the grip of a serious drought, only a toilsome job of prolonged watering will keep the show on the road. This stubborn choosiness is probably the main reason why many a good gardener says, "Astilbes are not for me."

English Daisies, at their best, are as trim and tidy as the most meticulous person could desire. They are only about six inches tall and their leaves grow in tight tufts that squat comfortably on the soil's surface. Their greatest charm, of course, lies in the two-inch heads of white, rose, or red blossoms poised jauntily on upright stems. Some of the flowers are single, while

36

37

In its native South Africa the **GERBERA** (36, 37) is probably the most popular and dependable member of the daisy tribe. Its exquisitely graceful and colorful blossoms last well when cut and are widely used in private homes, churches, banquets and all manner of occasions where flowers are appropriate. The original species which was the basis for the variously colored hybrids was a brilliant flame orange. Gerberas are choosy about where they grow. Large numbers of Americans have been unable to make them feel really at home.

others are so double they suggest oversize golf balls cut in half. No other miniature plant more truly reflects the primness which marks so many of England's smaller gardens. Yet for unknown thousands of years their ancestors, in practically identical form, have grown wild in many parts of Europe and the Mediterranean region.

On our side of the Atlantic, with its frequent droughts and baking summer days, the English Daisy is something of a problem out of doors. It just does not like the extremes of climate in which many of our gardens have to operate. Only in cool, well-regulated greenhouses is it likely to attain the winsome perfection for which it is so justly famous. But to a real flower-lover that goal amply rewards every effort.

Another notable foreigner, often called the Transvaal Daisy, or Barberton Daisy, is even more choosy in its demands. Botanically it is known as Gerbera, and its old home is southern Africa. That part of the world is likely to be rather warm and dry, which is precisely what this delightful flower likes. But this does not mean that it will flourish under the aforesaid baking conditions which English Daisies detest. In point of fact, we still have to learn more about the Gerbera's facts of life before we can welcome it to American gardens without reservation. Thus far our best outdoor results with it are apt to be in the South.

Most of the Gerberas you see in florist shops have been grown in greenhouses where all the important conditions from soil texture to temperature, humidity, and intensity of light are fully under control. They are crisply formed flowers with a considerable variety of colors including orange, white, pink, salmon, and ruby red. Some of their blossom heads are as much as four inches broad.

38

39

DOUBLE CANTERBURY BELLS (38), like the typical single form, have a wide color range . . . This is the **SINGLE CANTERBURY BELL** (39), reaching a height of three feet.

Any flower which grows wild from the Canary Islands to Persia can scarcely be called a purely local product. This is doubly true of the Calendulas, or Pot Marigolds, which are known far and wide outside of their original lengthy home territory. Hardly a flower-conscious region in the world is without its supply of these worthy stand-bys. In gardens, greenhouses, and private homes they rank among the best.

Nowadays, thanks to selective breeding and hybridizing by experts, there is a notable range of size, color, and form among Pot Marigold blossoms. Gold, apricot, cream, orange-and-brown, primrose, butter-yellow, and many intermediate tones are frequent. Some of the individual blooms are as wide as six inches. There are doubles, semi-doubles, incurves, downcurves, and singles. And nearly all of them, when cut and placed in water as soon as they open, last acceptably in house vases.

In the light of their homeland climate it is not surprising that Calendulas sometimes balk when it comes to accepting hot, dry summers outdoors. As a rule, though, they will come through if artificial watering can be applied to counteract the dry heat. And there is no denying the fact that when they are really happy they will blossom profusely from early summer until autumn frost cuts them down.

The Campanula tribe, to which the universally popular Canterbury Bells belong, has its main headquarters in the Mediterranean region. There are at least two hundred and fifty different species in it, plus great numbers of varieties which differ endlessly in size and conformation. A few of the high-alpine kinds are only two or three inches tall. In the lower lands, though, six feet is not an unusual height. Curiously enough, the blossoms of virtually the entire group are restricted to white and blue. There are numerous gradations of these hues, of course. Occasionally you may see a pink or rose-colored form in someone's garden, but such departures from the typical colors are in the minority.

Few flowers are more aptly named than Canterbury Bells. Their big blossoms, one to each short stem, are strikingly bell-like in form, although they face upward rather than down. Their edges are rolled softly outward, and a little imagination can easily liken the long central pistil to a bell's clapper. The whole bloom is about two inches long.

There are several natural variations of this basic form. One has flaring petals near the stem which have earned it the popular name of Cup-and-Saucer. Another is strikingly double—you might describe it as a long bell set inside a shorter and broader one.

All Canterbury Bells are members of a single species. Among their Campanula cousins there is a vast assemblage of kinds which, to non-

40

WILLOW BELLFLOWER (40, 41), like their Canterbury Bells cousins, are variously colored. They are often grown in rock gardens. All the flowers on these pages belong to the large Campanulas group.

41 ↓

42

43↓

44↓

botanists, may appear entirely different except for their prevailing blue colors. One of the loveliest is the famous Harebell, Bluebell, or Blue Bells of Scotland, a seemingly fragile, graceful delight that grows wild in the colder portions of the Northern Hemisphere on both sides of the Atlantic. Among the gaunt, dark mountains of the Gaspé Peninsula, in the Canadian province of Quebec, you see it nodding cheerfully in every crevice of the age-old rocks. Many an open New England hillside is literally blue with it in mid-spring, for it is unbelievably prolific when it finds a home entirely to its liking. No wonder that poets have sung its praises from time immemorial.

Another outstanding Campanula is the Carpathian Harebell, from the Austrian portion of the Carpathian Mountains. Usually it is no more than a foot or so tall, and its clear blue blossoms are held on wiry stems that lift them above the tufted leaves as if to make sure that no eye can pass them by.

Least, but by no means last, there is the creeping, four-inch marvel whose botanical title *garganica* is derived from Monte Gargano in Italy, one of its favorite strongholds. It is a rock-garden gem of the first water, for only in alpine-like surroundings can its personality be fully appreciated.

It is a long step from the clean simplicity of the Campanulas to the shaggy blossoms and bushlike growth of the Red Valerian, or Jupiter's Beard. Perhaps the latter title fits the plant better, for the general form of its flowers does suggest the flowing locks and whiskers of that wrathful old gentleman who ruled the mythical heaven of the early Romans.

This sturdy stand-by came originally from Europe and eastward into Southwest Asia. The British people have appreciated its ornamental value for centuries, and you still find it frequently in their gardens. In some parts of England it flourishes nowadays even among the limestone rocks of ancient walls that have fallen into disrepair. On our side of the Atlantic, unfortunately, it is seen far less frequently than it deserves. It will thrive for years in limy soil and bloom steadily through the summer. Few flowers last better when cut and placed in water-filled containers.

Most of our garden Centaureas, too, came from the same general part of the world which produced the Valerian. Their blossoms cover a wide range of blues, pinks, purples, and yellows, with now and then a white. One of

RED VALERIAN (42) is rather too coarse to fit into most garden borders, but by itself it is stunning . . . Perhaps the best of the **CORNFLOWERS** (43) is this perennial one with large, almost thistle-like blossoms. In addition to its obvious assets it is easy to grow . . . The silvery leaved coolness of **SNOW-IN-SUMMER** (44) persists all through the hot weather. It has a far less welcome cousin called Mouse-ear Chickweed, an immigrant lawn pest . . . The fantastically fringed and curled blossoms of this **CORNFLOWER** (45) measure four inches across. It is a native of Armenia.

45↓

46

49

Compact, hardy shrubs with attractive blossoms in early spring are none too plentiful in the United States. This is one reason for the popularity of the **FLOWERING QUINCE** (46). It used to be a rather obvious red, but nowadays there are pink, orange, apricot and white varieties . . . England's famous **WALLFLOWER** (47) likes the British climate so much that over here it demands mild winters and cool summers . . . **TRUMPET-VINES** (48) climb strongly by means of tough aerial rootlets scattered along their stems. The funnel-shaped blossoms are close to three inches in diameter and even more than that in length . . . The Cape of Good Hope has sent us a number of outstanding flowering bulbs of which the **CHINCHERINCHEE** (49) is a worthy example . . . Deep-frozen ground never worries **GLORY-OF-THE-SNOW** (50), a very early-flowering bulb.

47

48 ↓

50 ↓

the best known is the deservedly popular Bachelor's-Button, or Cornflower, whose sky-blue blossoms are a cheery sight in the sunny days of midsummer. The plants themselves reach a height of about two feet, and in their youth the leaves are a pleasant woolly white. Often it escapes from cultivation and takes care of itself, for its seeds have a way of sprouting in unexpected nooks and corners.

This same sort of leaf woolliness characterizes the European Snow-in-Summer throughout the growing season. In this case the over-all effect is silvery gray, a cool tone that harmonizes perfectly with the plant's creeping stems, which grow quite rapidly into flattish mats of considerable size. Spring days bring a flood of white blossoms, and when these subside the pale leaves take over effectively until the verge of winter.

When spring comes to countless rocky places among the hills and valleys of China the Flowering Quince is one of the first to respond with its abundant bright red to pink and white blooms. They are rather like miniature Apple blossoms in form, and are clustered together in little groups on rigid, half-thorny twigs. Some of them are the forerunners of incredibly hard, unattractive fruits which, if you have enough patience, can be converted into a fairly tasty quince jelly.

This sturdy but slow-growing, six-foot bush reached America about one hundred and fifty years ago. We quickly took a fancy to it, and planted it around many of the old houses of those days. It is still in steady demand, especially in some of its improved and softer modern colors that plant propagators have developed. One of its greatest charms is its willingness to serve as an indoor decorative note. When small branches of it are cut as their buds show a tinge of color, the flowers will open quickly in the house.

South Africa has provided us with many lovely flowers, among them the Chincherinchee, or Star of Africa. Its long clusters of intriguing white, star-shaped blossoms are too seldom seen in Northern gardens. But many florist shops have bunches of them during the winter months. Often these have come all the way from Africa after having been cut as buds and well refrigerated to retard their opening. This sounds like rugged treatment for any flower, but the Star of Africa does not seem to mind it. When the buds are provided with normal temperature they open readily and stay in good condition for weeks.

Among England's favorite spring-blooming garden plants the Wallflower has stood in the front rank for many generations. The year-round climate over there is neither too hot nor too cold, too dry or too wet for this native of the Canary Islands and the northern side of the Mediterranean. So the Wallflower's narrow, somewhat grayish leaves and yellow to orange blossoms have long been a sort of British tradition in gardens as well as the crevices among walls and rugged old stone quarries. Here in America the story often has a less happy ending, for the incurable reason that Wallflowers flatly refuse to accept many of the climatic insults to which they are exposed.

On the other hand, the Chinese Trumpet Vine, which came over here from the Orient via England in about the year 1800, has proved a complete

51 52

More than 700 varieties of **PAINTED DAISIES** (51, 52) have been recorded, each representing a different form of the same species. Botanists feel that this species is the most variable and important member of the whole Chrysanthemum tribe. Most gardeners think that Painted Daisies, because their official name is Pyrethrum, are not Chrysanthemums at all ... Numerous different types and colors are also available today among the handsome **SHASTA DAISIES** (53, 54).

success. Today, as for many years, its sturdy climbing stems cover innumerable walls and fences with lusty leaves from which scarlet trumpet flowers flame in August's hottest days. Sometimes the growth reaches a height of twenty feet, so that the mass gets quite out of control and requires severe pruning to return it to reasonable proportions. But even that effort is well repaid by the gorgeous display at a time of year when bright blossom color is often so scarce.

How different is the appeal of dainty blue or blue and white Chionodoxa flowers in the earliest days of spring! Glory-of-the-Snow, we often call them, for their opening often occurs while snow flurries are still a definite possibility. If flakes do happen to fall, the fragile little blossoms on their four-inch stems will not mind them in the least. It seems strange that these dainty midgets from the warmish climate of Crete and Asia Minor should be so tolerant of the rugged winters in our Northern states that they will live for years and even multiply rapidly by their own unaided efforts.

53 ↓ 54

55

The **CHINA-ASTERS** (55, 56) are top-flight favorites among garden and greenhouse annual flowers. They are not always easy to grow outdoors because they have a tendency to be attacked by a serious disease called "wilt," but scientific research has greatly reduced this weakness by the development of wilt-resistant strains. There is virtually no end to the forms and colors of their blossoms.

56

The multicolored Painted Daisies of our springtime gardens were among the finest of the floral beauties to reach Western Europe from the Orient nearly two hundred years ago. There is a good chance that the Dutch traders of those days, with their weather eyes open to the possibilities for a bit of extra profit, were largely responsible for introducing these worthy flowers to the Western world. All honor to them, for the Pyrethrums, as many of us call the Painted Daisies, have delighted countless folk for generations.

Botanically Painted Daisies actually belong to the far-flung Chrysanthemum tribe. Most of them grow a couple of feet tall, and their showy blooms are always poised singly at the tips of slender stalks that rise from neat, compact tufts of finely cut leaves. Practically all colors and shades, with the exception of blue and yellow, appear among them. Crimson, white, lilac, and pink are among the best of them. The blossoms are invaluable for cutting because of their splendid lasting qualities as well as their grace and invariable charm. It is good to know, too, that the plants themselves will live and bloom for several years if granted a fair opportunity.

Another cause for giving thanks to the Chrysanthemum group is the Shasta Daisy. You might take it for a glorified version of our wild Field Daisy were it not for the fact that many of its varieties produce double blooms instead of single ones. The blossoms are always white, or at least whitish, but this does not imply any monotony in their appearance. Some single varieties are flat platters as much as six inches wide. Among the doubles you will find fringed petals, crested centers, and compact, almost ball-like effects. Although the plants are not always easy to grow, they frequently thrive outdoors for several years where conditions are right.

No one could ever accuse the China Asters of lacking variety of form and color. The fame of these natives of China and Japan is now so widespread that most of us have forgotten the China part of their name and simply call them Asters. As such they are grown in countless billions every year for florist shops as well as in gardens.

There is virtually no end to blossom sizes, colors, and shapes of these one-season-only Orientals. Some flower early and others in summer. Singles, doubles, plumes, quilled petals, shaggy petals, twisted petals, tubed petals—these are some of the best. And their width may be anywhere from one to six inches or so.

Since florist flowers must be of maximum perfection, many of the cut Asters you buy in spring and summer have been grown under enormous cheesecloth tents which protect them from insects and the glare of direct sunlight. A group of huge cultivated fields covered with these ghostly shrouds is one of the oddest sights in the realm of commercial horticulture.

Chrysanthemums All Come from China

China has scored many triumphs in the production of flowers, but the world-famous Chrysanthemum is the greatest of them all. Even in those remote days when the power of ancient Rome was at its height, the Chinese plant wizards were well on their way toward creating the types of these autumn blossoms we know today. Starting with some of the common wayside flowers of their countryside, those inscrutable Orientals developed them amazingly by methods at which we cannot even guess with any degree of confidence. Even before the first contacts between the West and the Far East the growing of Chrysanthemums by rich and poor Chinese was a firmly established national pastime. Thousands of homes had special plots devoted exclusively to their favorite flower.

Through the centuries which followed those beginnings the beauty of Chrysanthemums has captivated the rest of the civilized world. The greatest interest, of course, is in those types which are suited to flowering in the garden during late summer and autumn, and those other forms which reach their highest perfection only when greenhouse-raised. In each of these categories there are now hundreds if not thousands of varieties distinguished from each other by blossom character, size, and a fantastic range of color.

The year 1754 seems to have brought the first Oriental Chrysanthemums into England. There were only a few of them, and these failed to arouse much interest. But in less than one hundred years thereafter the English florists were struggling to meet an overwhelming public demand for these outstanding cut flowers. Many of the wealthier citizens were grow-

The tremendous variety of blossoms among the **CHRYSANTHEMUMS** (57) is difficult to grasp. Even a flower-show exhibit like that on the opposite page can be no more than a cross-section of the whole story.

58

59

60

61 ↓

62

63

64

65 ↓

66

69

CHRYSANTHEMUMS. The modern hybrid chrysanthemums shown on this and the two preceding pages are labeled with the official type names based largely on the shapes and arrangements of their blossom petals.

58. **INCURVED**
59. **INCURVED**
60. **DECORATIVE**
61. **CUSHION**
62. **SPOON**
63. **DECORATIVE**
64. **QUILLED**
65. **ANEMONE**
66. **SPOON**
67. **DECORATIVE**
68. **CUSHION**
69. **DOUBLE**
70. **SPIDER**
71. **INCURVED**
72. **SPOON POMPON**

70

67

68 ↓

71

72 ↓

73

74

ing them in their own private greenhouses. The enthusiasm filtered on down to countless cottages where, in autumn, sunny windows were often banked with potted Mums in full flower.

Today, as for several generations past, the small-flowered Pompon Chrysanthemums are exceptionally popular. There is an immense variety of them, ranging in form from pure singles to tight little "buttons" no larger than a silver quarter. All of these were probably derived from original crossbreeding of only two old species. Both of the latter were brought back from the Orient in 1846 by Robert Fortune, one of the greatest plant hunters of all time. He had been sent on that particular expedition by the Horticultural Society of London.

During the past fifty years, especially, leading plant geneticists on both sides of the Atlantic have concentrated on immeasurably broadening the Chrysanthemum's range of size, conformation, and color. Only blue has escaped them, for the insurmountable reason that it has never appeared anywhere in the history of this astonishing plant group. Much has been accomplished, however, in building greater hardiness into the constitution of a

These **CHRYSANTHEMUMS** are: **INCURVED** (80)—petals curving toward center . . . **SPOON** (79)—long tubular petals with spoon-like tips . . . **ANEMONE** (73, 75)—many short petals ringed by larger ones . . . **SPIDER** (76)—thin tubular petals without flare at tips . . . **POMPON** (74)—very well rounded blossoms, large and small, with densely packed petals.

75↓

76↓

7

78

CLERODENDRONS (77, 78) are a group of climbing shrubs whose showy fruits are as interesting as their flowers.

flower which, at the outset, was unable to survive the rigors of northern winters. Two related species, the Korean and Arctic Chrysanthemums, were brought into the hybridizing picture with gratifying success. We now have hundreds of lovely varieties which, year after year, can withstand garden temperatures that would have been fatal to their ancestors. Even the Chrysanthemum's season of flowering has been notably lengthened. It is now perfectly possible to select a list of garden varieties that will furnish a succession of delightful blossoms from midsummer onward to the threshold of winter.

It is intriguing to realize that Chrysanthemum flowers have exerted a tremendous influence on the creative arts for many centuries. It is a moot question whether this impact is due to their basic resemblance to the outline and color of the sun, whose power over mankind's life and ways is so far beyond calculation. In any event, the appeal of these blossoms is all but universal. Tangible evidence of this truth came recently from the president of a large chain of American department stores who stated that the Chrysanthemum motif in damask tablecloths outsells all other patterns combined!

The Clerodendrums, or Glory-bowers, are only a moderate-sized clan of plants as compared with some of the others, but they are extraordinarily

79 ↓ 80 ↓

81

82

JACKMAN CLEMATIS (81, 82, 84) is an old-time favorite among the large-flowering group of this vine family. It climbs to a height of twelve feet or more and bears six-inch blossoms. The Ningpo Clematis is only half as tall but has flowers which are nearly twice as wide.

diverse in appearance and natural distribution. Of the fifteen or so best-known kinds, three hail from tropical Africa, three from temperate China and Japan, and the rest came originally from such far-flung spots as Australia, India, and Java. Their foot-loose nature extends beyond their homelands, too. Some are regular shrubs, others climb almost like vines, and at least one seems to have ambitions of becoming a tree. Also you will find among them broad, well-shaped leaves and leaves which are almost streamerlike in their length and waviness.

The most dependable everyday clue to a Clerodendron's family is its showy white, red, or sometimes violet blossoms. Customarily the slender petals of these blooms bend backward toward the flower-bearing stems. Most important of all, the stamens project far out into the wide-open spaces like dainty, somewhat stiffened threads.

Here in the United States and Canada the Clerodendrons are chiefly found in good-sized greenhouses, as might be expected in view of their warmish climate origins. In Florida and a few other parts of the Deep South, however, they are grown outdoors with considerable success. It is not unusual for a strong and perfectly satisfied individual plant to flower continuously for six months.

No plant of any kind is capable of continuous steady growth throughout its life. Even the sturdiest must have a period of rest during the year so that it may consolidate its gains, so to speak, before putting forth new growth. So, after its last flower has faded, a greenhouse Clerodendron has to be "put to bed" artificially for several months by cutting down on its water supply and reducing the temperature of the surrounding air. Out of doors in an acceptably warm climate, of course, it determines its own recuperative season and acts on it without the need of human persuasion.

It is chiefly to the Orient, also, that we are indebted for those magnificent climbing vines we know as the Large-flowering Clematis tribe. Most of them are in the blue, white, purple, pink, red range, and their ancestry involves a history of man-managed hybridizing that is almost untraceable. The end result is that the flower-conscious world of today has a priceless heritage in these climbers with their blossoms of breath-taking size and beauty. The individual blooms of some of these hybrids have a spread of five to as much as eight inches. And after they have gone they leave behind them dozens of silvery, curlicued seed clusters which remain delightfully decorative for weeks.

These blessings, however, are not for everyone. There is no escaping the fact that Large-flowering Clematis growing is an uncertain gardening project. To be sure, there are plenty of detailed, expert instructions for just when and how to grow them. Yet no honest authority would guarantee these precepts to be infallible, or be able to put his finger firmly on the reason for their occasional failure in the hands of even experienced gardeners. One is sometimes tempted to suspect that, like certain human prima donnas, the finest Clematises are just too temperamental for words.

When all goes well, some of these climbing marvels reach a height of ten feet or more and produce hundreds of blooms every year. Others, including several of the largest-flowered sorts, stop at five or six feet, as though they wanted to put all their remaining strength into staging a color show to end all color shows. These tendencies, of course, are primarily traceable to their ancestral backgrounds. And, as such, they persist for the duration of the plant's life.

Another hybrid form of the Jackman Clematis which suggests the number of different colors now available from growers . . . Without the cheerful, dependable **PARIS-DAISIES** (83) the winter-time florist shop would lack one of its most appealing offerings. These bushy little Chrysanthemums flower freely and last surprisingly long.

83 ↓

84 ↓

85

86

87

Year after year the **FEVERFEW** (85) tries to flower its pretty little heads off. It was one of Grandmother's favorites and is still welcomed for its success under difficult conditions . . . There is nothing else in the plant world like **LILY-OF-THE-VALLEY** (87). Its fragrance, daintiness and remarkably long life have won it international fame.

All the **COTONEASTERS** (86), whether seen close-up or at a distance, are unusually interesting. Few other shrubs can match the perfection of their small leaves, countless little blossoms and colored autumn fruits.

By comparison with these puzzling flowers the gay little Paris-Daisies from the Canary Islands are refreshingly free from complexes. Vast quantities of them are to be seen in our florist shops during the Easter season, usually with white, yellow, or occasionally pink blossoms. One seldom finds them growing in Northern gardens, largely because they are not constitutionally geared to withstand the winter cold. As you might expect from the formation and appearance of their flowers, they actually belong to the Chrysanthemum kingdom, to which picture pages 30, 31, 32 are devoted.

These trim, jolly flowers have an alternative name of Marguerite, which originated more than three hundred years ago and is now too seldom understood. It came about in this way:

In France, near the close of the sixteenth century, Marguerite de Valois became Queen of Navarre by marriage. Upon the occasion of her first visit to her kingdom she was given a gorgeous reception and presented with a bouquet of beautiful daisylike flowers. Being a lady of considerable political know-how, and a bit of a gardener as well, she promptly assured her subjects that she would adopt these blossoms as her very own. Thus they became known as Marguerites. And the noble queen was as good as her word, at least in this instance, for soon she was planning a magnificent new garden in which Marguerites played an important role. Shakespeare is said to have used it as the setting for his *Love's Labour's Lost.*

The old-time, all-time favorite Lily-of-the-Valley is one of the world's most widely distributed flowers. There is only one full species of it, yet with merely slight variations in color, size, and fragrance it grows wild in temperate Europe, Asia, and Eastern North America. In some forested areas of our southern Appalachians it is one of the common flower features of mid-spring. Yet few people except the natives of that region even suspect its presence there.

It appears to be a fact that the largest and most fragrant Lilies-of-the-Valley originated in the Old World. From there, also, may have come that faint tinge of pink you occasionally see in the normally white, pendent blossoms. This color touch seems to be firmly built into the system of the plants which are blessed with it, for as a rule it will reappear every season for many years.

Another gratifying aspect of Lily-of-the-Valley nature is the plant's prolific growth. Its whole root system is geared to indefinite expansion and the multiplication of buds and flower stalks. Thousands of homes have old "Valley" beds which cover many square yards and are still going strong. To be sure, they need regular stimulation with plant foods in order to maintain their best flower production. Yet actually the roots are so persistent they can hardly be killed by even the rankest neglect.

Feverfew, another rugged old-timer, originated in Eurasia. As if to prove that it belongs to that irrepressible Chrysanthemum crowd, its innumerable leaves have the unmistakable Mum scent in abundance.

There are several varieties of this one-time garden favorite, ranging in height from one to as much as three feet and all of them bearing either single or double white flowers. They are much more dependable than some of their sophisticated modern companions, which is no small advantage among gardeners in search of plants which can really take it.

China has contributed many worthy ornamental shrubs to temperate gardens the world over, as you will discover while you explore the pages of this book. None of these, though, surpasses the variety of form, flowers, fruit, and foliage offered by the group known as Cotoneasters—an odd name which, by the way, is pronounced *Cotone-ee-asters.* Some of them reach a height of ten feet or more, while others spread for an equal distance without rising more than a foot above the surface of the ground. The leaves of many species take on lovely autumn colors which handsomely complement the blacks, reds, and pinks of countless little dangling berries. The myriad little white or pink-tinged blossoms which precede these fruits are so exquisitely formed that they justify the closest examination. Indeed, the Cotoneasters as a group are so rich in varied and interesting details that only familiarity can disclose their full ornamental value.

In their homeland the dozens of Cotoneaster species are an unforgettable feature of shrubby mountain valleys and slopes where wind and sun and sometimes drought would make life miserable for less self-sufficient plants. We in America are not yet fully aware of what these picturesque shrubs can do for our own home landscapes, but we are learning fast.

Plant Names Have Strange Origins

The origins of everyday plant names are full of oddities. Defunct queens, statesmen, scientists, soldiers, explorers, sea captains, and mythological characters galore are commemorated today in countless blossoms large and small. Even the tools that men used in menial labors have their namesakes in the kingdom of fruits and flowers.

The name Scotch Broom falls in a combination of these categories. First, it grows wild not only in Scotland, but also in England generally as well as in many parts of Western Europe. So much for its first name. The second comes from the fact that dozens of its various ancestors were used as sweeping brooms by tidy housewives, butchers, and many other folk for the cleaning chores of simpler days. Their selection for this purpose, of course, was a highly practical one in as much as all the members of this wiry shrub group bear countless springy stems which are ideal for sweeping purposes.

Central and Southern Europe are the primary native home of these often showy bushes, with their multitude of yellow, white, red, or purple blossoms. They enjoy living in dry, sandy soil where many other plants would starve to death. But they definitely dislike low temperatures. This last peculiarity accounts for the fact that, although they reached America in early colonial days, you seldom see any of them growing outdoors in our colder Northern states except for experimental purposes.

Much less clear is the botanical history of those immensely popular Crocuses which brighten thousands of American home lawns and yards in the early days of spring. We often label them Dutch Crocuses, for it was in Holland that they were first developed commercially several centuries ago. However, there are no dependable records of what species of this variable bulb tribe were used in the creation of the colorful varieties we value so highly. Presumably their forebears came from somewhere in the Mediterranean and Southwest Asian regions, which are the native lands of practically every true Crocus species known today. But that is as far as we can trace them at all confidently.

Crocuses have been associated with spring bloom for so many generations that few people other than floral experts know that some of the loveliest species are strictly fall bloomers. These are dainty little things, far less ro-

88 **SCOTCH BROOM** (88), a dwarf, May-flowering member of a famous European shrub family.

89 **CROCUSES** (89, 90), always popular.
90↓

91 The incomparable florists' **CYCLAMENS** (91, 92).
92↓

93

Those tall accent points which add so much to the appearance of a deep flower border are splendidly provided by the numerous forms of **HYBRID GARDEN DELPHINIUMS** (93). Their best location is toward the rear of your garden . . . **CHINESE DELPHINIUMS** (94) are considerably less formal and statuesque . . . The long, nectar-bearing "spur," hallmark of the Delphinium clan, is especially noticeable in the blossoms of the annual species often known as **LARKSPURS** (95).

94 ↓

95 ↓

bust in appearance than their familiar Dutch relatives. Yet some of them, even in the Northern states, may spread their first slim-stemmed blossoms as late as the middle of November.

It is to the Mediterranean shore countries and the Middle East, also, that original credit goes for the stimulating beauty of the expensive potted Cyclamen plants which florists offer during the winter months. All of them are basically similar in type and general structure, for they all belong to only one original species. But the colors and other details of their leaves and blossoms differ rather widely as a result of planned crossbreeding of natural varieties that have cropped up among the wild specimens. The result is that the plants of today bear flowers that may be white and red, solid white or red, purple and blue, or red purple, to mention a few of the most frequent color schemes. Even the broad, heart-shaped leaves show considerable variety in their tones and marbled markings.

These unique Florist Cyclamens are grown primarily in special greenhouses, for they cannot survive bitter freezing weather. Yet they have a number of quite similar midget cousins, native in the Himalayas and other cold foreign regions, which can take severe cold without flinching. Avid rock gardeners quite justifiably treasure these sturdy mites inordinately, for they are almost too precious for belief. One of them is such a complete individualist that, even in New England, it blossoms outdoors in midsummer with no leaves at all, and then turns all its attention to producing almost circular banded and marbled foliage that stays fresh and green all winter.

Hybridizers Have Done Wonders with Delphiniums

The New World as well as the Old has furnished the background of the glorious garden Delphiniums of today. It is to Asia and Siberia, however, that the honors go for providing the species which hybridizers in Britain and the United States have built into those stunning blue, violet, white, or bicolored spires that tower above their lesser neighbors in our garden borders. Many of these strong, almost pillarlike flower stalks reach a height of six feet, and now and then you see one whose tip is a good eight feet from the ground. Even the individual single or double blooms are sometimes three inches across and tremendously interesting when closely examined.

These are the type which the word Delphinium most frequently brings to mind. They are distinguished, too, by the ability to produce a second flower harvest in autumn if their July and August stalks are cut off at the ground shortly before their blossoms fade.

The versatility of the Delphinium clan is well demonstrated by another section of the race with more finely cut leaves and flower stalks which branch gracefully instead of forming virtually solid blossom masses. Many people know these as Larkspurs, a name derived from the curious backward extension on each flower which suggests the rear toe and claw of the lark group of birds. Their general effect is far less dominating, and for this reason they are often more pleasing for cut-flower use as well as gar-

96 97 ↓

Close-up views of **HYBRID GARDEN DELPHINIUMS** (96, 97, 98, 99) furnish convincing evidence of the vision, skill and infinite patience of expert plant hybridizers. The individual blossoms, as well as their spacing along the main stem, vary enormously. There are fluted petals and rounded ones, singles and doubles and inbetweens. Every imaginable tone in the blue-purple range is represented, alone or in combination, often with a contrasting spot, or "bee," in the center of the blossom. Numerous pastel shades give an appealing softness to many of the varieties; some of these are definitely on the pink side, suggesting the possibility of really good reds at some future time. There may even be true yellows. Since red and yellow Delphiniums already exist among our native wild species it may seem like a fairly simple matter to breed these colors into our hybrid garden varieties. One important stumbling block would be to retain the blossom form of the latter, inasmuch as the wild species have simpler blooms. Other less obvious problems also enter the picture.

den purposes. The plants rarely exceed five feet in height and frequently they stop at three or four.

It is not surprising that flowers as breath-taking as the Delphinium should be a bit choosy about the areas where they will do their best. This is particularly the case with the steeple-stalk type, and much less so in the lower, more branching section of the family. Hot, dry summers are anathema to the giant ones. So, if you wish to be sure of seeing them in their full magnificence, there are few places on this side of the Atlantic that can equal the northern Pacific coast and those portions of the New England states which are near the coast and north of Boston. True, both these regions can be hot when they feel like it, but the nights are almost always cool and acceptably damp as far as the Delphiniums are concerned.

Our own Western highlands, from the edge of the Great Plains to the Pacific, are generously sprinkled with native Delphinium species whose worth is too little realized even today. Some are only eight or ten inches high, while others are as tall as an average person. In the former category there are kinds with blossoms in every imaginable tone from sky blue to pure white. One, at least, is almost startling when its buds open into dazzling red flowers of true Delphinium form. The stalk of another is so densely covered with fine leaves and crowded white to light blue blossoms that its form suggests a flower-mad miniature Lombardy Poplar tree.

Many of these little tads have comparatively scanty foliage, as if flower production were their overwhelming objective. But among the taller kinds there are those which in every respect would be worthy competitors with the famous garden hybrids. Most startling of the big fellows, perhaps, is a stately Californian, which unfortunately cannot survive the mountain

98 ↓ 99 ↓

100

102

101

103

SWEET WILLIAM (100, 101) is the best of that section of the Dianthus group whose blossoms are borne in large heads instead of singly. Unfortunately it is devoid of fragrance . . . **SLENDER DEUTZIA** (102) opens its myriads of blossoms in late May. It is one of the finest of its race . . . Exquisitely fringe-like double flowers mark the **SHOWY DEUTZIA** (103) during June.

winters farther north. Its big, trumpetlike blooms are an undeniably brilliant scarlet. And finally, as though to break the Delphinium-blue monopoly once and for all, there are Westerners with mixed yellow and blue flowers, others that are red and yellow combined, and even a yellow, blue, and white mingled together.

The usual garden forms of Delphiniums all have one great asset which is too often overlooked: they are ideal for pictorial house arrangements with many other kinds of flowers. Their blossoms, when cut fresh and placed in water indoors, last extremely well. The characteristic forms and colors, too, are excellent foils for blooms of numerous other types and hues.

Time after time they actually save the day for a room arrangement which otherwise would be baffling to the point of hopelessness.

Out in the garden, also, Delphiniums are among the planting arranger's most valuable allies. Tall clumps of them here and there provide the accent points needed to relieve any tendency toward monotony among the lower, denser masses of middle and rear areas. They are good harmonizers, too, for careful selection of their varieties and colors can lead to a highly successful transition between nearby groupings which would clash horribly if a peacemaker did not stand on guard to keep them apart. In fact, whenever and wherever Delphiniums grow normally they are one of Nature's greatest gifts.

The several Deutzias hold high rank among our favorite flowering shrubs of spring and early summer. They are of medium height and are quite upright-growing, with countless graceful sprays of white or blush-pink blossoms. Some of the blooms are single and others strikingly double, and all of them are completely charming. There are probably fifty distinct species, the majority of which came originally from Eastern Asia and the Japanese islands.

The Deutzia Is Named for a Dutch Patron!

The story of the Deutzia's introduction to the Western world goes back nearly two hundred years to the heyday of the revered Dutch East India Company. It was in 1778 that C. P. Thunberg, a surgeon and botanist employed by the company, visited Japan for a few months and returned with several strange plants. One of them was a shrub of exceptional beauty but no known designation. So Dr. Thunberg, to honor his friend and patron Johann van der Deutz, gave it the name of Deutzia. And Deutzia it has remained to this day.

Sweet William is of even earlier introduction. Three hundred-odd years ago it was still a novelty in English gardens. It had recently made its way across the Channel from such widely separated lands as China, Russia, and the Pyrenees and taken British gardeners quite by storm. As old John Gerard wrote in his famous *Herball,* which was published in 1597, this notable member of the Dianthus tribe was "kept and sustained in gardens more for to please the eye than either the nose or the belly. They are not used either in meat or medicine, but esteemed for their beauty, to deck up gardens, the bosoms of the beautiful, and garlands and crowns for pleasure."

Gerard was one of the greatest gardening authorities of his time. The accuracy of his appraisal of a plant's appeal has been well demonstrated by the prominent place the Sweet William still holds in the hearts of flower-minded folk everywhere. The early colonists brought it with them when they crossed the Atlantic to the new land of promise, and generations of their descendants have needed no urging to maintain its popularity. Today the original crimson and white of its blossom heads have been expanded to include numerous shades of copper and pink. There is virtually no end to the

104

105 ↓

In sunny, well-drained places the **MAIDEN PINK** (104, 105) forms dense, bright masses of color every spring. They come in both single and double forms ... Many **ALPINE PINKS** (106) are notably large-flowered.

106

107

108

The **GRASS PINK** (107, 109, 110) group is astonishingly varied in flower shapes and colors. Their petals are always fringed. They are delightfully scented, often with spicy flavor. Their slender leaves form dense mats of silvery bluish green. An especially deep-fringed Grass Pink variety is shown below . . . A good example of the florists' **CARNATIONS** (108), sometimes grown in gardens.

109

110↓

111

Every summer the **BLEEDING-HEART** (111) decorates its arching sprays with pink or white blossoms of rare beauty ... Individual **FOXGLOVE** (112, 113) flowers are two inches long and usually dotted on the lower inside.

112↓ 113↓

variety of dottings, massings, "eyes," and other distributions of these hues within the boundaries of the flower clusters.

At a casual glance the Sweet William does not seem to belong to the same Dianthus group as the Carnations, Clove Pinks, and other long-time favorites. Closer examination, however, discloses that each of the circular, domed flower heads is made up of massed individual blossoms, each of which is true Dianthus to the last detail of its four or five daintily fringed petals. In most cases these flowers are single and quite flat when fully open, but double forms have also been developed. The latter, when growing in the typical Sweet William masses, are crowded into a virtual ball of bloom.

On the preceding pages you will see a picture gallery of other notable Dianthus types. The first of them, the Maiden Pink from Europe and Asia, closely parallels Sweet William in its free-flowering character and its ability to perpetuate itself through scores of years. But it is not nearly as tall—usually its height is a matter of merely five or six inches. Also it has a delightful habit of growing in dense, ground-hugging mats composed of wiry creeping stems and narrow little leaves. Each stem tends to form its own roots as it goes, with the result that the mats sometimes become whole flowery carpets. Of the other two, Carnations hail from Southern Europe and Grass Pinks from Austria northeastward to Siberia. Both are universally loved for their delicious fragrance and amazing range of forms and colors.

Foxgloves, out of Britain, Europe, and Western Asia, play two major roles on the world's stage. First, they provide statuesque beauty to countless midsummer gardens. And second, their dried leaves are the source of that powerful heart stimulant we know as digitalis. There seems to be no clear-cut explanation of their peculiar common name. Perhaps it originated in

The accent value of **FOXGLOVE'S** (114) tall stems is one reason for the popularity of this odd, big-leafed plant . . . Generations of gardeners have been devoted to the **GAS-PLANT** (115) and its strange evening behavior.

114↓ 115↓

116

117

Most of the heather-like shrubs of the Old World are poorly adapted to America's northern climate, but the showy **SPRING HEATH** (116) can take it. There are several hybrid varieties . . . The short-stemmed **WINTER-ACONITE** (117) vies with Snowdrops for the honor of being the earliest flowering outdoor bulb. It grows best in well-drained places which are somewhat shaded during the summer.

the fanciful idea that the plant's large, woolly leaves suggest a good material out of which warm foxes' gloves could be fashioned!

Most of our garden Foxgloves raise their strong, straight spires of bell-like blossoms to a height of two to four feet, depending on how well the plants are satisfied with their locations. Flower-garden designers value them highly, for the strength which their clean vertical lines impart to other plant groupings which too often are confused and lacking in variety of form.

No one who has seen the Japanese-born Bleeding Heart in its early summer loveliness could doubt the appropriateness of its odd name. Those gracefully arching blossom sprays among the fronds of deeply cut leaves are sometimes hung with a dozen heartlike pendants apiece. Small wonder that at least one of these unique plants was a feature of every attractive old-time garden.

Along with the Bleeding Heart, in those bygone days, there was often another long-lived Far Easterner whose name of Gas-plant, or Burning-bush, was far less obvious. There is certainly nothing inflammable about the appearance of its cool, usually pure white blossoms. Yet on warm summer evenings they give off a volatile oil vapor which flashes like regular gas when ignited by a lighted match. One wonders if there is any limit to the strangeness of Nature's ways.

If we turn to ornamental flowering shrubs, the Spring Heath is almost unbelievable when its host of bright rosy or occasionally white flowerlets opens in the pale April sunshine. Its height seldom exceeds a foot, yet it is one of the hardiest of a famous Old World clan. Along with its fellow mem-

118

GLOBE-THISTLES (118) are a law unto themselves. They are coarse, homely plants so prickly that touching them with bare hands can be really painful. But their silvery, blue-tinted blossom globes are strangely appealing . . . The rather daisy-like **LEOPARD'S-BANE** (119) is an early spring favorite everywhere. Its heart-shaped leaves are a fresh, lively green and fit in well with the big blossoms.

119

bers it is often confused with the storied Heathers of Scotland, which are a group of somewhat similar cousins. The Spring Heath is actually a native of Europe, but because of its adaptability it has been introduced in many other parts of the globe where plants of its peculiar appeal are always in demand by gardeners and other flower admirers.

Heaths in general come from regions where the winter climate is relatively mild. But the Spring Heath is built of sterner stuff. It can even pull through some of our lower New England winters with little damage. It was introduced to us in America in 1763. But, oddly enough, it is probably less known now than its more tender pot-grown relatives which florists sell all winter under the more appealing name of Heather.

Early spring days are brightened in a different but equally welcome way by the golden-yellow daisylike blossoms of the Doronicum, or Leopard's-bane. Many of them are three inches or more across, and their habit of poising singly at the tips of straight, slender stems displays their beauty perfectly. The blooms are long-lasting, too, whether growing out of doors or cut and kept in water in the house. In the latter case they lend themselves to satisfying arrangements alone or in combination with other materials. Florists sometimes force them under glass for winter blossoms.

There are at least a couple of dozen species of this accommodating plant tribe. Their homeland is Europe and temperate Asia. Most reach a height of two feet, but one mountain midget stops at five inches!

Still earlier in spring—often hard on the heels of winter—the bright yellow single blossoms of the Winter Aconite unfold and face the sky. Each

120

121 ↓

122 ↓

Early spring is the season of **FORSYTHIA'S** (120) greatest glory. Then, against the sky's soft blues and whites, its golden blossoms and brown stems are matchless . . . **SNOWDROPS** (121) have been known to emerge unharmed after having their blooms snowed in for two weeks . . . All the **FREESIA** (122) varieties open their flowers in orderly sequence, beginning with those nearest the main stem. The tip blossom opens last. By that time the first ones are gone . . . Early April sun brings out the **GUINEA-HEN FLOWER'S** (123) curious blooms whose spotting accounts for their name.

123

of them is an inch or so broad and wears a curious leafy green ruff of larger size around its neck. Its otherwise leafless stem is sturdy but scarcely longer than is necessary to raise the flower and its collar clear of the ground.

The peculiar bumpy rootstocks of this hardy little European look completely dead when you plant them in the early fall. Dry, brown, and shriveled, they seem as useless as so many pebbles. Yet during the next few months they will plump up and, even before winter's end, be ready to start pushing their buds upward. This seeming death and resurrection will continue for many years, for such is another of Winter Aconite's oddities.

Out of Southern Europe has come the wholly different Globe Thistle, which has made quite a name for itself among American gardeners. It is a coarse, prickly-leaved giant sometimes five feet tall and broad in proportion. To this extent its principal value is to fill up vacant spaces and steadily broaden its domain as the years pass. But that is not the whole story. The plant's real appeal comes in July and August, when strange greenish-white knobs appear at the tips of the more upright stems. These grow slowly larger as the days pass until, quite unexpectedly, they fluff out into perfect silvery, steel-blue globes which may be almost as large as tennis balls. Many flower arrangers value these highly and make them key features of prize-winning displays. And others cut them in their prime, dry them indoors, and use them as decorations all winter.

There is little doubt that the Forsythia, or Golden-bell, is now the most widely planted spring-flowering shrub in the United States. Hardy, fast-growing, and incredibly showy in full blossom, it is used as hedges, windbreaks, boundary markers, foundation plantings, and about every other imaginable and unimaginable way. Yet it never lets its admirers down, except when its exuberant growth threatens to take possession of their entire property and perhaps the neighbor's.

The story behind this Chinese native's name involves a certain William Forsyth, once gardener to King George III of England. He was a canny Scot with a good eye for a fast pound sterling. Before he was fifty he had worked his way up the professional horticultural ladder to the high rung of being appointed Director of His Majesty's Gardens at Kensington Palace.

124

125

Most of the **BABY'S-BREATH** (124) plants used in American gardens are annuals and consequently have to be raised from seed every year. This extra work is repaid at flowering time by the delicacy which only these flowers can supply. Another reason for growing them is their cut-flower value. Many people even dry them for winter use in various indoor arrangements . . . All the true **GERANIUMS** (125) have single blossoms.

In the 1780s William Forsyth produced a new idea. It was a repulsive goo compounded of sand, lime rubbish, wood ashes, and several less mentionable items, and its name was Forsyth's Plaister. Its inventor claimed that it would cure tree diseases and arranged a demonstration of this in the palace gardens. An official inspection committee arrived to witness it and was duly impressed by the excellent health of the treated trees, whereupon Mr. Forsyth requested and received a reward of fifteen hundred pounds sterling (non-inflated) for his noble service to his country. Some years later a strong suspicion developed that the treated trees had nothing the matter with them in the first place and that Forsyth's Plaister was not exactly on the up-and-up.

Some weeks before our Forsythias start shaking out their glowing golden bells, the sheltered, sunny nooks on their south side are often dotted with the solitary, modest blossoms of the Snowdrops drooping above their setting of long, grasslike green leaves. With these, too, there may be the larger, curiously spotted bells of the Checkered-lily, or Guinea-hen Flower. Both of these little bulbous plants are natives of Europe and temperate Asia and frequently multiply steadily in New World situations that are well drained without being subject to dry summer baking. On their own account, no less than for their early appearance, they stand high on the list of our favorite early spring outdoor flowers.

Freesias, on the other hand, are strictly for greenhouse growing except in our lower Southern states. Their original home was South Africa, but nowadays many of the finer varieties are the result of hybridizing by Northern plantsmen in search of larger size and greater color range in the blossoms.

At present it is not difficult to obtain whites, yellows, lavenders, mauves, pinks, apricots, carmines, and coppers. And all without sacrifice of the dainty form and exquisite fragrance which have distinguished this famed Old Worlder for many flower-loving years.

There is no everyday name for the Geranium pictured on these two pages, unless you call it "one of the Cranesbills." It ranks among Eurasia's best gifts to discriminating Western gardeners who value it for its foliage as well as blossom effects.

Botanists say that the Cranesbill tribe has something over 250 members, practically all of them inhabitants of the world's north temperate lands; only a few come from the tropics. Europe and Asia are especially well supplied with them and one fine species, the so-called Wild Geranium, is widely distributed over North America in dry as well as damp locations which may be shaded or in full sun. Their Cranesbill alias is based on a fancied resemblance of the long, slender seed capsules to the bill of a crane or heron. Seed production is so generous that a well established colony of the plants may occupy many square yards which are warm with color in the bright spring days.

The name Geranium, by the way, is an oddly misleading one as used by most people. Actually it applies to these Cranesbills, not to the gorgeous house plants everyone knows so well. The latter, botanically speaking, should always be called Pelargoniums—a mouth-filling botanical word if ever there was one.

Fortunately no such confusion surrounds the Baby's-Breath tribe. Some of these universal favorites from Europe and Asia form mistlike masses of fine leaves and miniature blossoms in countless American gardens during the late spring. Others, such as the one shown here, trail along the ground

Where the winter cold is not too severe for them the **SUNROSES** (127) are top favorites among rock gardeners. In general they are dependable south of Philadelphia. They are principally neat, very low bushes with notably large and pleasing blossoms and leaves which are evergreen or nearly so. Abundant sunshine is one of their needs . . . Another form of the **TRUE GERANIUMS** (128) is shown below. It hints at the whole plant's grace.

127↓ **128↓**

129

131

130

132

The showy many-colored **HOUSE GERANIUMS** (129–132), so popular as winter house plants and outdoors in summer, are more properly called Pelargoniums. The ancestors of nearly all of them probably came from South Africa, but the modern varieties have very confused blood-lines.

and raise their airy sprays of white or rosy flowers only a few feet above it.

Another ground-hugging clan is the Sun-Roses. They are really dwarf shrubs with stems that are wooden instead of being soft and fleshy. The majority of them come from Southern Europe and the shores of the Mediterranean, and consequently are often unable to endure the winters of our Northern states. But farther south they are rock garden beauties.

House Geraniums, as the examples on these pages suggest, come in a bewildering array of colors and forms. Pink, deep red, white, scarlet, salmon, and crimson, sometimes with black markings, are frequent. Even the leaves, in many cases, are parti-colored—green and cream, bronzy red and yellow, for example. Plant hybridizers have worked on them constantly for more than a hundred years, with results that surely speak for themselves. So constant have been these crossbreeding activities that the species used in the beginning are probably no longer in cultivation. The chances are that even

133

135

134

136

Today's **PELARGONIUMS** (133–136) in this hybrid group are amazingly numerous. New ones are being added to the list every year, as in the case of Roses and Chrysanthemums. Sometimes they are disrespectfully called Fish Geraniums because of the peculiar odor of their broad, soft leaves.

those old-timers were highly variable in their own right, since this characteristic seems to mark the whole Pelargonium tribe. Their original headquarters was South Africa, whence they were introduced to England soon after 1700.

These extremely popular plants are almost shrublike in the hardness of their principal trunks and branches. They are capable of living for many years, too, where temperatures are suitable. In coastal California, and parts of the Deep South, they are grown as permanent outdoor bushes. But in colder regions they are limited to winters indoors and summers outside.

Expert hybridizing has also played an important part in creating the nearly four hundred varieties of Gladiolus we have today. Apparently the first of these mixed-bloods occurred in England between 1800 and 1840. Several wild species from the Cape of Good Hope region, which is the ancestral home of a major section of the Gladiolus tribe, were the basis of these early creations.

137

138

From such beginnings a fantastic range of size and type has been brought into being. The "Glad" of today sends up a flowering stalk from two to six feet tall, depending on the variety. The individual blossoms may be prim little "hoods" an inch or so broad, or flaring, ruffled, and waved giants that measure close to six inches from tip to tip. There is literally no color which cannot be found somewhere in the ranks of Gladiolus blooms.

These matchless garden stand-bys grow in a remarkable way. When planted in the spring they are merely circular, somewhat domed, and bulb-like lumps with a few whitish buds showing on their upper surface. Soon after planting each of these buds starts upward and begins forming a new corm, or "bulb," at its base. The new corms increase rapidly in size and send out roots of their own. These help provide nourishment for the whole young assembly. By autumn the new corms have produced not only full sets of mature leaves and flower stalks but also a few duplicates of themselves hardly bigger than pinheads.

Meanwhile the old corm originally planted has shriveled and died, for its job has been done. In a single season its offspring have reached such full maturity they can repeat the complete growth sequence next spring. At planting time each of them will be stocked with nourishment that will get the early growth off to a fast start. The net result of it all is that no individual Gladiolus corm ever produces more than a single crop of bloom. You might say that its motto is a short life and a gay one.

The blossoms and other characteristics of these corm-produced generations never change. So when a new variety is to be created the Gladiolus

139 140

It can be truthfully said that the **GLADIOLUS** (137–140) is everybody's flower. This implies upgrading the tribe rather than otherwise, for its members range from exquisite daintiness to almost overwhelming masses. And their appropriate uses in gardens and as cut flowers are endless.

breeder must fall back on hybridizing, or crossbreeding. His first step is to select two different varieties whose particular assets he wishes to blend. Then he takes the pollen from a just-opened blossom of variety 1 and transfers it to a fresh blossom of variety 2, at the same time snipping off the latter's own pollen-bearing stamens to prevent a possible mix-up. Both parent-flower spikes are covered with cheesecloth bags to prevent cross-pollination by insects.

If all goes well, a pod containing fifty or sixty brown, rounded seeds will start to form in the heart of blossom 2. After being planted these seeds will usually result in flowering-size corms after two seasons of growth. Only then will the hybridizer know whether his attempt at improvement has actually succeeded.

Whether hybridized or not, the individual buds strung along the blossom spike of a Gladiolus invariably open one at a time, beginning at the bottom. Thus, if a spike is cut and placed in water when its lowest flower opens, the bloom at the tip may not spread its petals until ten days or more later.

China, Japan, and Siberia share the principal honors of providing us with the rugged, long-lived, and deservedly popular Day-lilies. Actually they are not true Lilies, and they grow from masses of tough roots instead of bulbs. Their flowers, however, are shaped a good deal like those of Lilies. The fur-

141

Their origin in the northern part of Asia has endowed all **DAY-LILIES** (141–145) with a ruggedness which enables them to survive a wide variety of climatic conditions. Cold winters mean little in their lives, and most varieties are indifferent to baking heat.

142 ↓

143 ↓

144

145

ther fact that each bloom lasts only a little more than a day after it opens completes the reasons for the plant's odd name.

Yellows ranging to tawny reds were the only original colors of Day-lilies, and the great majority blossomed during the latter half of summer and into early autumn. But during comparatively recent years the busy hybridizers broke through these broad limitations quite surprisingly. It is now possible to plant varieties that will blossom successively in the garden from mid-spring until autumn frost. Their heights will range from one to almost five feet. And the colors of their blooms, although still basically restricted to the original categories, have been so intensified and combined that today there need be no feeling of monotony through the season. Even the forms and shapes of the individual blossoms have been appreciably broadened.

Day-lilies are far from being newcomers in the occidental world. At least two species had found their way to Western Europe by the year 1570. One of these appears to have been the same little Lemon Day-lily which thousands of gardeners still cherish. And doubtless there are still others undiscovered. This last fact, in view of the centuries during which indefatigable plant hunters have explored far corners of the world, is a tribute to the vastness of the Asiatic mainland and its wealth of floral treasures.

To a layman the language of science sometimes passeth all understanding. For example, if you ask a botanist to define the name Hibiscus, he could reply with complete truthfulness that it may mean a popular Southern vegetable called Okra, a foot-high ornamental plant that lives for only six months, a beautiful all-American garden giant called Rose Mallow, a regular bush, or a tree.

The Rose of Sharon is a sort of compromise between the last two of these categories. Its main original home was probably China, with perhaps a small annex somewhere in India. We in the United States were planting it before 1790 and are still doing so. Under some of our climatic conditions it forms a several-stemmed shrub. Elsewhere it frequently develops a single trunk and becomes a tree about fifteen feet tall. The most consistent things about it are the smallish triangular leaves and the four-inch

146

147

During comparatively recent years the blossoms of **ROSE-OF-SHARON** (146, 147) have had their faces lifted considerably in size as well as color. There are now more than a dozen varieties of them, including good doubles as well as singles. These tree-like bushes grow to fifteen feet.

flowers which seldom open before midsummer and pass their display peak rather rapidly.

In the early days these blossoms tended to be somewhat unpleasing, muddy red purples. But nowadays there are several varieties in excellent whites, pinks, violet blues, roses, and clean reds. Some of the most pleasing ones are five-petal singles, while others are generously double. This Rose of Sharon, incidentally, is the only one of the shrub-tree Hibiscus group that has even a fair chance of surviving a severe New England winter.

The gorgeous Hibiscus of our Deep South is the so-called Chinese Hibiscus, introduced long ago from China. This is definitely a shrub, but what a shrub! It grows rapidly and may develop into a broad, informal mass twenty feet high. Individual blossoms last for only a day, but new ones open each morning throughout the year so that the plant is never without good color. Some of the older varieties, singles as well as doubles, were scarlet,

148 ↓

ROSE-OF-SHARON (148, 150) buds are noticeably slow to open, but when the flowers finally decide to expand they are always at the tips of the short, new twigs. Severe pruning of the bush in early spring helps to produce larger blooms.

149

150

It is interesting to compare the **ROSE-MALLOW** (149) with its cousin **ROSE-OF-SHARON** (150). The blooms of both these plants have similar centers, and their petals are equally tissue-papery. **ROSE-OF-SHARON** is a bush that reaches a height of fifteen feet or so. **ROSE-MALLOW** is less than half as high and dies down to the ground every fall but comes up again in the spring.

pink, yellow, or salmon. But in fairly recent years several dozen new hybrids have been introduced in Florida from Hawaii, so the present color range is much wider. Unwelcome freezing weather, which occasionally pays a brief visit even to Florida, may seriously injure Hibiscus bushes. But the damage rarely reaches underground, so vigorous new growth soon starts making repairs.

A curious feature of all Hibiscus flowers is the stout, projecting column in the center of each blossom. This is formed by a group of pollen-bearing stamens surrounding a central ovary. Consequently fertilization is virtually guaranteed without the assistance of busy bees and other insects. Later the seeds form inside a green sectional capsule which ultimately dries, splits along the seams, and allows them to escape. Various members of the shrub-like group are sometimes grown in Northern greenhouses but seldom reach full potential size.

Although the Sidalcea is technically a native American member of the Hibiscus complex, it is included in this Old World section of the book because an overwhelming majority of its two hundred-odd kith are definitely Old Worlders in origin. Certainly there is nothing about its appearance which suggests that it is not of Oriental ancestry, for every inch of its six-foot height looks thoroughly and gorgeously exotic.

The original Rose Mallow, or Swamp Mallow, grows wild in the coastal marshes from Massachusetts to Florida and west as far as Lake Michigan. Occasionally it reaches a height of seven feet and its papery, light rose-pink blossoms may be as much as eight inches broad. Two other closely related species with darker flowers are found in the interior South.

151 152↓ 153

In 1898 American hybridizers began a series of crossbreeding experiments with these three species in an effort to develop strains that would be more free-flowering and carry new colors. Within ten years the first "Giant Mallows" were ready for sale. Their success among gardeners was immediate and long-lasting. Today there are well-defined whites, pinks, and crimsons that stage a marvelous display every August and September.

China has also given us the old-time decorative dooryard shrub which goes under the popular name of Kerria, Japanese Rose, or sometimes Globeflower. By the middle of May, usually, its five-foot mound is yellow with cheery single or double flowers an inch or so broad. These grow from green-barked twigs which, together with the smallish, pointed leaves, form a perfect color harmony with the gold petals. Strangely enough, the twigs remain green throughout the winter, an asset possessed by few other shrubs or trees.

The Popular Amaryllis Really Comes from South America

Among all the worthy winter house plants originally credited to South Africa the dramatic prize goes to the modern Amaryllis. Actually their origin is in South America. The typical old-time blossoms were plain red with a bit of white intermixed, but nowadays there is a wide range of considerably softer tones. Pronounced stripings in the petals give them still more variety. In addition to these improvements the individual blooms are much larger and frequently more numerous.

It is a general rule that the bigger a pot-grown plant becomes the more space it needs for its roots. This is not the case with the Amaryllis, which often does very well in the same pot for two or more years. Still more surprising is the fact that it much prefers to live with two thirds of its king-size bulb above the soil level and fully exposed to all the air there is. When the bulb starts growing it sends up leaves followed by the flower stalk. Then, as the flowers really open up, a swelling develops in plain view on the bulb's side. This slowly grows larger and produces leaves. Finally it separates from its parent and becomes an independent youngster equipped with its own roots and everything else necessary for growing up.

Those superbly fragrant small pillars of bloom we call Dutch Hyacinths have been a mainstay of the Holland bulb farms for more than three centuries. The first bulbs of them and of Tulips reached that thrifty country from the Mediterranean region and Asia at about the same time, and both are still being produced there in stupendous numbers. Many millions of them are shipped every year to other countries throughout the flower-conscious world.

Hyacinths are as versatile as they are magnificent. We Americans, as well as other nations, have long used them as formal massed plantings for early

The garden **SIDALCEA** (151) is a towering plant that lives for years in places where the soil is rather damp. Its petals vary considerably . . . so do those of the **ROSE-MALLOW** (153) . . . **KERRIA** (152), whether double or single, likes our year-round weather except in the coldest states.

154

From the botanical standpoint the background of the popular South African bulbs which we call **AMARYLLIS** (154) is quite confused. Apparently all of them have been hybrids for many years. Even the florist trade names assigned to them are often unreliable guides.

spring bloom. They are florist favorites, too, for use as late winter house plants in individual pots. And, especially in recent years, they have been serving as casual groups or scattered individuals on countless home properties where informality and color accents are important watchwords. One of their advantages for such purposes is their long life potential. Granted a well-drained, rich but light soil in a sunny location, they will carry on for years with little or no deterioration in their blossoms.

Almost every color preference can be met nowadays by these unique flowers, with their accompanying strong, straplike leaves. There are blues, reds, pinks, and yellows in amazing variety. Single flowers and doubles are numerous, too, and their impacts when in bloom are quite different.

Commercial growers have a most peculiar method of increasing their stock of Hyacinth bulbs. The old ones are taken out of the ground right after flowering. Two deep slashes are then cut across the bottom of each bulb, which is immediately replanted upside down. In two or three weeks the bulbs are again dug up and dried in the open air until October, at which time they

155

The modern cultivated forms of **AMARYLLIS** (155, 156) vary considerably in the shape of their petals as well as in markings and overall size. A few, such as the one on the opposite page, are decidedly graceful. But (156) below is a northern garden variety originally from Japan.

156

157

158 ↓

DUTCH HYACINTHS (157, 159) as they appear by the million in early spring from bulbs planted the previous autumn are the product of very special growing conditions in Holland. Their built-in vigor enables them to furnish the massive blossom heads shown on this page and opposite. . . . A year later the same bulbs, deprived of Holland's advantages, often have fewer flowers (160) . . . **GRAPE-HYACINTHS** (158) are not related to true Hyacinths, although the leaves of the two groups are somewhat similar. These odd fellows will live and spread almost anywhere for years without any loss.

159 160

are planted in the normal position. By the following June these cut bulbs will be completely dead, but each of them will have left behind twenty or thirty healthy baby bulbs exactly in its own image, color and all.

The so-called Grape Hyacinth from the Mediterranean region is not a real Hyacinth although it groups its numerous little blossoms in a somewhat club-like head. There are several species that range in height from four to eight inches and are variously colored from brilliant cobalt blue to white. These also are spring bloomers and remarkably long-lived. They form numerous seeds which often sprout on the surface of the ground where they fall. Then an astonishing thing happens: the young root pushes downward, gets a good grip, and starts pulling the infant bulblet down into the soil. By the time this new Grape Hyacinth is old enough to flower, it has been dragged to its proper permanent growing depth of two inches or so.

Once again the floral storehouse which is China and Japan comes through with a masterpiece known far and wide as the Japanese Snowbell, or sometimes Silverbells. It is a rather dense shrub or tree that may in time grow thirty feet tall. At maturity its breadth may equal twice its height, for its rather slender, twiggy branches reach out and out until you begin to wonder if they will ever stop. In early June the branchlets and twigs are strung with myriads of white blossom bells. These, although they do not open until after the dark green leaves have appeared, are not obscured by the foliage because they have the courtesy to dangle below the twigs, whereas the leaves grow upward.

The Snowbell family, called Styracaceae by the botanists, is a large one with representatives in many parts of the Old and New Worlds. Several species grow wild in our own Southeast and South. One of these, the Halesia or Mountain Silverbell, is native in the Great Smoky Mountains from Georgia northward into Tennessee. It has been known to reach a height of about one hundred feet—a mighty, well-rounded tree of superb proportions. On a sunny day, as you look up through it from a position near the trunk, it seems a complete fairyland of golden lights and green shadows and glistening, translucent, snowy blossoms.

161

THE FRENCH HYDRANGEAS (161, 162, 163, 165) are among our showiest flowering shrubs. They form a collection of hybrids based on a Chinese bush whose blossom heads measure as much as eight inches from side to side. White, pink, lavender and blue are their usual colors. A peculiar fact about them is that the pink ones will turn blue or lavender if grown in acid soil. Later they will return to pink if lime is added to that same soil. These handsome shrubs are extremely popular as potted house plants as well as outdoors in regions where the winters are not too severe. For the former purpose they are specially grown for spring florist-shop sale. The treatment they receive forces them to bloom splendidly while still very young.

162 ↓

163

164

In gardens north of Philadelphia the French Hydrangeas are likely to be seriously damaged by winter cold unless dead leaves or some other light insulating materials are piled high around their stems. In the Middle and Deep South, on the other hand, they have a good chance of growing to their normal height of ten or twelve feet. Cold weather never bothers the **CLIMBING HYDRANGEA** (164), a unique vine-like species from China and Japan that may reach upward for seventy-odd feet even in New England. Its flower heads contain tiny fertile blossoms and large sterile ones . . . A similar mixture marks another **HYDRANGEA** (166), a hardy bush with foot-long flower heads.

165 ↓ 166 ↓

167

The Evergreen Candytuft, from Southern Europe, is equally distinctive in a very different way. It grows only a foot tall, yet it completely hides the ground under a dense cushion of limber stems and narrow little leaves that may ultimately cover several yards. In mid-spring this flat pillow is thickly embroidered with trim, milk-white flower heads an inch or so across, each of them composed of numerous individual blossoms. On bright days the combination of dark leaves and glistening blooms is breath-taking.

Rock gardeners, especially, often value this unique shrublet despite the need of curbing its growth to save less assertive plants from being overrun. And many other garden folk use it to cover broad, flat, sunny areas whose decorative planting would otherwise be a problem.

Torch-lily, Flame-flower, Red-hot-poker-plant—take your choice of a name for the astonishing South African red-yellow oddity which appears on the opposite page. Its flowering time is from midsummer into autumn, but it is not easy to grow satisfactorily in our Northern states. Farther south, in milder climates, it will flourish in the flower border for many years.

The Irises, with more than a hundred distinct species and probably thousands of hybrid and other varieties, rate high on the list of indispensable flowering plants. Primarily they are native to large portions of the North Temperate Zone of the Old and New Worlds, particularly the former. Our most popular garden forms are descendants of wild species in Central and Southern Europe, North Africa, Northern India, and China. Many discriminating gardeners also grow other types from Japan, Siberia, and a few that are found wild today in various sections of the United States.

168 169

The way to see the **JAPANESE SNOWBELL'S** (167) dainty blossoms at their best is to look up at them from underneath the tree, as the photographer did when he took this picture. The individual flowers are about three-fourths of an inch wide . . . When **EVERGREEN CANDYTUFT** (168) spreads its white sheet in May it is hard to believe that the plant is a shrub . . . Apparently the name **TORCH-LILY** (169) is just one of those things, for this plant's picturesque flower spire, perhaps three feet above the ground, neither looks nor behaves like a lily.

Apparently the influence of Irises on human events began at least fourteen hundred years ago. Ancient tales have it that early in the sixth century the armies of King Clovis, ruling monarch of the Franks, were pinned down on the bank of the Rhine by a superior force of Goths. There seemed to be no escape for them until Clovis, who must have had something of a naturalist's seeing eye, noticed yellow swamp Irises in bloom far out in the stream. To his resourceful mind this proved that the river was shallow enough for human wading, so he and his followers took off into the water, splashed their way across, and lived to fight another day.

Be all this as it may, it appears to be a fact that Clovis made the Iris his personal emblem, an honor that the royal family maintained for many years. This may have been the reason why, centuries later, Louis VII of France chose the Fleur-de-Louis—our modern Fleur-de-lis—as his patron flower during the French Crusades in the Holy Land.

The Iris tribe is so variable and versatile that it contributes greatly to the effectiveness of every kind of flower garden regardless of its size. It is entirely possible, by careful selection of types, to arrange for an almost unbroken succession of bloom from April until October. The most obvious feature, of course, is the blossoms. These range through many stages from the classic simplicity of the Siberians and others of the old Fleur-de-lis persuasion to the great complex blooms of the modern garden hybrids. Practically every known color is represented in a list headed by blues, pinks, whites, coppers, purples, golds, burnt oranges, and rich browns. In numerous instances several colors are combined in a single blossom, always

harmoniously and sometimes linked together by exquisitely fine traceries of dots and pencil lines. To cap all this, the strong, upright stems, which often produce three or four successive flowers apiece, are anywhere from four inches to four feet tall.

Tall Flowers Dramatize a Garden

This upstanding growth habit is obviously valuable in garden arrangement through its provision of strong vertical lines in places where there is too great a tendency toward lax, spreading masses. In the case of most Iris types these accents are supplemented by stiffish, quite upright leaves either swordlike in character or, in the case of the simpler blossom forms, suggestive of rapiers or even fencing foils. In all instances the foliage tends to remain in good condition for weeks after the flowers have gone by.

In addition to their usefulness in mixed garden compositions these self-respecting, universal favorites adapt themselves readily to other landscaping uses. Entrance walks and garden paths can be lifted out of mediocrity into striking beauty with edge plantings of any desired width and devoted entirely to Irises. Any of the dwarf types can be used to finish off these strips on the sides nearest to the pathway.

Isolated group plantings of the taller, showier kinds can be tremendously effective in keying up distant corners of the lawn, garden lounging areas, and other spaces which are in need of a bit of face-lifting. Water-garden margins, too, are ideal for occasional groupings of the exquisite tall Japanese Irises, which welcome an extra supply of moisture in their soil. And there is no better way to soften a rigid wall angle than by giving it a special clump planting of Irises suited to it in height and color.

All of the large, stout-flowered kinds of Irises have most peculiar roots. The foliage and flowering stalks come out of fat, pale, fleshy blobs that are shaped somewhat like huge, very chunky caterpillars. These lie flat on the ground with their backs fully exposed. At intervals of an inch or more they contract in diameter and produce one or two side branches which quickly develop in size and sprout leaves of their own. Thus the original planting spreads farther and farther in all directions.

This whole system of rhizomes, as botanists call the outsize "caterpillars," sends many strong, rubbery roots deep into the soil from its hidden undersides. These are the food gatherers which keep the rhizomes fat and able to carry on their duties year after year.

All Iris types are potentially long-lived and often far more enduring than you might expect. As an illustration of the latter characteristic, many gardeners who have become overstocked with rhizomes have dug up the surplus in the fall, shaken the soil from them, and left them fully exposed

A curving brick walk bordered with tall **BEARDED IRIS** (170) and lightened here and there with Columbines and the slender leaves of Day-lilies can well lead the eye to a peaceful scene beyond.

171

174

172

173 ↓

175

176 ↓

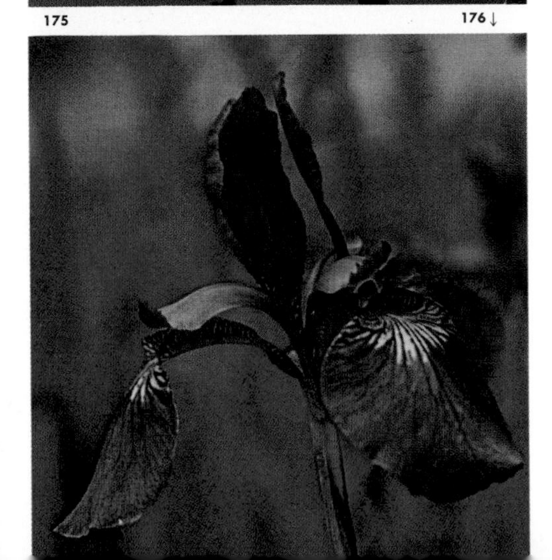

177 178

Some of the most popular flowers in American gardens are the **BEARDED HYBRID IRISES** (171, 174, 175, 177, 178), five examples of which are shown on these pages. Their massive blooms open at the top of strong stems from two to four feet high. After the big show ends in June their sword-like leaves take over as a ground-cover for the rest of the season . . . For less dominating effects the **SIBERIAN IRISES** (173, 176) are old favorites. They are not quite as tall and their leaves are more slender . . . Recently a third group, the **DUTCH IRISES** (172), has gained favor in fairly warm regions. These and the very similar Spanish type are also forced in greenhouses for sale by florists. They grow from bulbs, not just roots.

on top of a trashpile to dry out and be killed by the freezing winter weather. In spite of such rough treatment the banished beauties merely bided their time, sent out new leaves early in the following spring, developed new roots, and by midsummer were well on the way to establishing a trash Iris garden of their own.

This never-say-die spirit meets more than its match in certain insect pests and diseases which specialize in Iris destruction. Another factor which normally weakens the compact and free-flowering effect of a new Iris planting within two or three years is the tendency of the original rhizomes to quit working after their branches have taken over a larger area. The only remedy for this situation is to dig up the whole planting after it has flowered, discard all but the most promising of the young rhizomes, and replant these so as to make a completely fresh start.

Irises, like people, have their true aristocrats—species which, for one reason or another, stand out from the general crowd. The Roof Iris from Japan, seldom exceeding a foot in height but delightfully refined and lovely

179

182

A definitely oriental note appears in the unique beauty of the **JAPANESE IRISES** (181, 182, 183). There are scores of varieties as a result of many years of hybridizing, but the fancy names assigned to them are completely unreliable from the purchasing standpoint. One can be confident, however, that every Japanese Iris is a delightful garden prize. It usually blooms in July . . . The **VESPER IRIS** (180) flowers several weeks after the Japanese. No other iris can match the exotic appearance of its blossoms on their two-foot stalks. It is not difficult to grow but often dies after a year or two . . . **ROOF IRISES** (179) also are delightfully different.

180

181 ↓

183

in every way, is clearly in this special group. In its native land the Japanese people, with their instinct for simple yet exquisite artistry, grow it by thousands in the thatched roofs of their cottages—hence its intriguing name. Since its first appearance in Europe in 1872 it has gradually become known in America, yet few of our gardeners except the connoisseurs are familiar with it. True, we have no thatched roofs to beautify by its presence. But it will thrive perfectly well in the right sort of garden surroundings.

Another choice Oriental, this time from Russia, Manchuria, and China, is aptly called Vesper Iris because its numerous delightful blooms open only in the afternoon and last for but a few hours. Its two-foot stalks have many flowering branches with the result that, while the blossom show lasts, it is outstandingly generous and effective.

The Japanese Irises, native to Eastern Siberia as well as Japan itself, are outstanding in several ways. Some of them open their nearly foot-wide blooms a good three feet above the ground, while other forms are comparative dwarfs. The general shape of the flowers is rather flat on top with a tendency for the ends of the broad petals to droop earthward. There is an almost endless range of colors and color combinations. Some of these are white with lemon throat, all deep blue, blue with white stripes, white with gold bands, light and dark blue with orange center, and pink blended with violet. All of them are revelations to anyone familiar with only the average Iris types.

All of these slender-leaved Japanese Irises follow a quite conventional growing habit. Instead of having fat, exposed rhizomes they develop a sort of hidden "crown" from which unusually long roots head downward to be sure of reaching the generous moisture supply they require during the growing season. This crown gradually increases in breadth, of course, and may eventually need to be divided and replanted. But that will not happen for a number of years.

Central Europe has furnished us with many notable flowers, yet among its smaller treasures there are few whose charm excels that of the Spring Snowflake. This is a small bulb of ironclad hardiness whose delightfully modest blossoms pick up the early spring story where the better known Snowdrops leave off. It grows about as tall as its predecessor and persists for years after it has become well established. There is a Summer Snowflake, too, with cool-looking flowers which are more than welcome during those later days when the temperature soars skyward and most of the garden feels hot and dry.

Dr. Ernest Henry Wilson Named the Beauty-bush

In the year 1901 the late Dr. Ernest Henry Wilson, who subsequently became keeper of the renowned Arnold Arboretum in Massachusetts, returned from a collecting expedition in central China with a remarkable new shrub. Shortly thereafter he gave it the popular name of Beauty-bush, a title it still bears. To the best of our knowledge it is a complete lone star

184 185 ↓ 186

Soon after the Snowdrop has finished its very early flowering the equally welcome **SPRING SNOWFLAKE** (184) comes into bloom. It is taller than Snowdrops and its belled flowers are tipped with green . . . There are hundreds of **SWEET PEA** (185) varieties covering an enormous range of colors, petal display and degrees of fragrance. They are not always easy to grow in gardens, for most of them dislike hot weather. But progress in overcoming this quirk is marching on . . . **BEAUTY-BUSH** (186) is almost the only popular ornamental shrub that has no relatives. It always retains a suggestion of feathery softness.

without a single relative. Certainly no other shrub of any kind can match its masses of soft pink, almost fuzzy blossoms in the early days of June.

Tall, upright-growing, and with a tendency for its branches to arch gracefully outward, the Beauty-bush is decorative through half the year. First come the innumerable blossoms and then the curiously twisted, feathery seed heads whose subtle lavender tones sometimes persist into early winter. Even after these are gone the wee brown cups from which they grew continue to tip the twigs throughout the cold weather.

Again from the Orient, the first Japanese Flowering Cherry came to the United States about a century ago, long after it and its numerous relatives had achieved undying fame in their native land. Trees of their clan have grown wild in Japan from time immemorial. In 1735 an avenue near Tokyo was planted with them for a distance of three miles. Many of those old-timers eventually reached a height of seventy-five feet and a spread of almost as much. For many generations others have been cultivated in Japanese castle and temple gardens and the small plots of the peasants. It is no wonder that emperor after emperor decreed a national holiday every year when the spectacular Cherries came into the fullness of their bloom.

If we move now to Western Asia and Southern Europe, the spectacular Golden-chains reached us in colonial days. They grow readily to a height of thirty feet and are unforgettable when their branches are draped in late spring with foot-long yellow pendants of pealike blossoms. Unfortunately most of their several forms are so sensitive to cold that our Northern winters may prove fatal. South of the national capital, however, their success is virtually assured. Strangely enough, the leaves and all their other parts are said to be poisonous if eaten.

About two hundred and fifty years ago, while Queen Anne reigned as the titular head of Britain, a certain Father Cupani, in Palermo, Sicily, sent some small black seeds from his monastery garden to a schoolmaster near London who was known far and wide for being "a curious collector and introducer of many rare exoticks, plants and flowers." Little was heard of this gift until, twenty-odd years later, flowers of a new kind were placed on sale in London. They were small, purple and blue, and extremely fragrant. "Sweet-scented Peas" was the name given to them by their vendors. Today we would have called them insignificant. Yet, thanks to the initiative of old Father Cupani and his schoolmaster friend, they became the ancestors of all the fabulously popular Sweet Peas of modern gardens and greenhouses.

For several centuries the Common Lilac has been a favorite shrub in gardens of the Western world. Yet even today comparatively few people outside professional growing and botanical circles are aware of its puzzling early history.

The **KWANZAN JAPANESE FLOWERING CHERRY** (187) is magnificent in May . . . This is also the month when **GOLDEN-CHAINS** (188) lower their graceful flower streamers from every twig and gray-green branchlet.

187 ↓ 188 ↓

189

An enormous variety of colors and cluster shapes marks the **LILACS** (189, 190), especially those of the French Hybrid group represented on this page. Selection of the best depends on personal preference.

190

191 192

Hardy and strongly preferring shade to sunshine, the large leafed **PLANTAIN-LILY** (191) from China and Japan lifts graceful blossoms a couple of feet above the ground during the summer months. It is completely hardy and will live for many years . . . The famed **LOTUS** of Egypt and the East has its American counterpart (192). Both are aquatics, like the rest of the Water-lily group.

It seems that one of our Lilacs' ancestors was brought from Constantinople to England in Queen Elizabeth's days. Its true homeland remained a mystery until, about a century ago, identical wild specimens were discovered in the mountains of Bulgaria.

Another of the ancestral types, the Persian Lilac, appeared in British gardens during the middle of the seventeenth century. In those days little was known of its source or background except that it had been cultivated in Western Asia as far back as records could be found. Not until the 1890s was an almost similar plant found growing wild in Afghanistan, a strangely recent discovery, as plant matters go.

A hybrid between these two species, known then as the Rouen Lilac, showed up toward the end of the nineteenth century in the Botanic Garden at Rouen, France. From it, apparently, the large number of forms and colors, sizes and degrees of fragrance present in the Lilacs of today were developed during the past fifty-odd years by outstanding hybridizers of whom the most important was the world-famous Lemoine horticultural firm in Nancy, France. It is to Lemoine that we owe many of the greatest flower improvements of all time.

From late June into August the huge, fragrant, white to red blooms of the renowned Lotus give evidence that once again the Orient has come through with a unique ornamental. It originated primarily in the region that

195

Hundreds of **LILY HYBRIDS** (193) have been developed over the years and given obscure names by their introducers. This lovely form is a case in point . . . The **CANDLE-STICK LILY** (194) has been cultivated for two centuries in its various forms . . . The **DAY-LILY HYBRIDS** (195) grow from two to four feet tall, some are fragrant. It is an easy lily to grow and a great many hybrids have been developed. It differs from all true lilies in having its leaves at the base of the stalk instead of along the stem.

193 194↓

The immensely popular **EASTER LILY** (196) is actually a variety of a somewhat smaller species native in Japan. In our northern States it has to be raised in greenhouses, since it cannot survive bitter winters. Vast numbers of it are grown in Bermuda.

19

lies between the Caspian Sea on the south and Japan on the north; it has been considered sacred by the Hindus from earliest times. Normally we see it growing only in botanical water gardens and occasional private ponds, for we in America still consider it an exotic and therefore in need of special attentions.

However, in at least one of our middle Atlantic states it has escaped to the wild and apparently succeeded in getting along perfectly well on its own. There is nothing else quite like it in the flower kingdom, and one can readily understand the worship and religious status which have been accorded to it by so many millions for so long.

Many of the Lilies are peculiarly susceptible to diseases when removed from their homeland. An example of this in America, unfortunately, is the really spectacular Tiger Lily, otherwise one of the best.

Plant pathologists have made great progress in the prompt detection and control of the ten or a dozen known kinds of Lily ailments, but there is still much to be learned before Lilies as a whole can be considered as trouble-free. Perhaps, as time goes on, science will be able to determine whether the uncertainties of Lily health are constitutionally built into the plants or are induced by man's activities in moving the bulbs to unaccustomed, far-away places. There is already some evidence pointing toward increased susceptibility due to the chemistry of certain soils. The whole problem is a challenge which every lover of flowers hopes can be truly met.

Nearly all of the land areas in the Northern Hemisphere, excluding the polar regions, have provided us with Lilies. East and West have indeed met in the matter of these stately and well-loved flowers. But if there were such an oddity as an impartial plant enthusiast he would probably admit that the East emerged from that meeting as winner by a fair margin.

Such a victory would be won partly on the basis of numbers and, more importantly, because of the obvious glamour of certain Old World kinds. Leaders among these beauties are the stunning Gold-banded Lily from Japan; the widely known white Easter Lily, also a Japanese species; the white Madonna Lily, native to Southern Europe and Southwest Asia; and the incredibly tinted and perfumed Regal Lily from the mountains of Western China. The record of this last species' discovery and introduction to the outside world is so revealing of the plant-hunting profession as to merit summarizing here.

In August, 1910, Dr. Ernest H. Wilson, whom we have previously mentioned in connection with the Beauty-bush, reached the valley of the Min River near the northern border of Tibet. On all sides were rugged mountains between which the Min roared and foamed toward its juncture with the mighty Yangtsze and so to the East China Sea two thousand miles away. Blazing hot in summer, bitterly cold in winter, and always subject to swooping winds and violent storms, the whole of that back-of-beyond land is incredibly harsh and forbidding. Yet Dr. Wilson knew, from unsuccessful experience, that here was the home of the fabulous Lily he sought. He was determined that this time he would win.

197

REGAL LILIES (197) . . . **CENTIFOLIUM HYBRID** (198), since their introduction from the interior of China by Dr. Ernest H. Wilson, have won the gardening world. Free-flowering, fragrant and sometimes reaching a height of eight feet, they are superb from every standpoint. Few if any other Lilies are so dependable and long-lived in a variety of situations.

198↓ 199

For seven days Dr. Wilson and his Chinese coolie pack bearers wound their way down a narrow, dangerous road through the Min River gorge. Then he made camp, located vast quantities of Regals growing on the mountain slopes, and spent several days in making arrangements to have six or seven thousand of their bulbs collected at the proper time in October and shipped to him at the Arnold Arboretum in Massachusetts.

Finally, with all these preparations completed, he and his followers set out for the comparative civilization of Chengtu Fu, four days farther on. They had scarcely started when, without warning, a rock slide crashed across the trail and plunged downward to the river three hundred feet below. Wilson, struck by a leaping boulder, lay helpless in its wake with his right leg badly lacerated and broken in two places below the knee.

The next four months were a nightmare of suffering and doubt for the plant hunter. Yet eventually he won through and returned to Boston only a few days before his precious Regal Lily shipment from the Min Valley arrived at the Arboretum in perfect condition!

A happy ending to the adventure, you say? Yes, in a way, for the Regal Lily has prospered mightily in America and delighted countless numbers of people here and in other Western lands. Yet the story of that Min River expedition may have had its tragic sequel. Dr. Wilson's accident had left him with a permanently shortened right leg and an appreciable awkwardness in using it. Many years later, in October 1930, he was driving quietly with his wife down a winding, rain-soaked Massachusetts road. At a curve the car left the road, plunged into a rocky ravine, and both the Wilsons were killed. The cause of the accident apparently was never determined. Dr. Wilson was far from being a reckless driver. It seems possible that the awkwardness of his right leg might have caused some fumbling of the car's accelerator and perhaps an undue pressure on it at just the wrong moment.

Many authorities think that the Tiger Lily, a long-time favorite in American gardens, has been cultivated in China and Korea for more than 1,000 years. In the beginning it may well have been grown principally because of its supposed medicinal merit. This was the original value attached to several Lily species in that part of the world. Even after their ornamental fame had spread to other lands this reputation persisted. Thus, centuries ago,

The basic **JAPANESE LILY, PINK SHOWY** (199) is often grown in forcing greenhouses to bring it into bloom for florists. It is equally good in gardens provided its bulb is planted about nine inches deep. The Chinese Lily to the right is **HENRY'S LILY** (200).

200↓

201

204

It may well be that the oriental **TIGER LILY** (202, 205) was the first flower to be brought under cultivation . . . There are many hybrid varieties of **ORIENTAL LILIES, HENRY'S** (203) . . . **JAPANESE HYBRID** (204) . . . **LILY MACULATUM** (206), some of them with blossoms facing skyward . . . The so-called **DAY-LILY** (201) is not actually a Lily, despite its appearance. Popular flower names can be misleading!

Europeans believed that Madonna Lily bulbs were helpful in healing human wounds.

Within the last thirty years or so spectacular progress has been made in mastering the unique problems involved in crossing different Lilies and thereby creating scores of magnificent new varieties. A large part of this advance has occurred here in the New World, especially in the Northwest where climate conditions are ideal for large-scale growing on an experimental basis.

Lilies as a group have a simple dignity and beauty that have appealed to all people from time immemorial. They are probably the oldest of garden flowers, although even today their species and varieties are far outnumbered by the Roses and several other famous plant tribes. It is a curious

202 ↓

203

205

206

fact that, despite their loveliness and universal appeal, they have never aroused those hectic stampedes of popularity which have marked the history of Tulips and Pansies. Perhaps their influence on mankind is too solid and deeply rooted to be subject to mass hysteria.

Some years ago a group of American florists launched a promotion campaign under the slogan "Say It With Flowers." Their effort was a marked success and did much to increase the public demand for a variety of flowers which hitherto had not received the attention they deserved. Lilies, however, had little need for such stimulated popularity. For hundreds if not thousands of years they have served man's deeper thoughts and emotions on a greater variety of occasions than any other flower. Spiritually, white Lilies are the living symbol of purity throughout the Christian world. Easter would lack one of its most precious expressions were it not for the Easter Lily. Countless churches value Lilies above all other flowers for altar decoration through the year. Many thousands choose the Lily as a symbol of their enduring devotion to the memories of the dead.

There are not too many fine flowering plants capable of making unqualified successes of their lives in two radically different environments. Nature's general rule is to tailor her worthiest representatives to particular sets of conditions, and there is not much that mere Man can do about it.

The cheerful little Edging Lobelias, nevertheless, take readily to window box as well as regular garden planting. There are several different types of them, none more than a foot tall and the majority considerably smaller. Although they live for only one season, they make it a gay and lavish one with their wide variety of blue, rose, white, and occasionally crimson blossoms over a period of weeks. Some of their larger, longer-lived cousins from other parts of the world are incurably temperamental!

The Flaxes, by comparison with the Edging Lobelia's ground-hugging habits, are the essence of airiness. There are several forms of them, all with upright, wiry stems and small, narrow leaves. One could not hope for more graceful supports to carry the delicate, inch-broad blue or white blossoms. The most prevalent garden species in the United States reached us from Europe and lives for several years. Others, including red-flowered and

207

There is an **EDGING LOBELIA** (207) for every sunny spot where low, free-flowering annual plants of neat habits are needed. Their varieties include many different blues, crimsons and white . . . The **BUSH HONEYSUCKLES** (208) offer a considerable variety of blossom size and color. They are rounded, substantial shrubs and make excellent backgrounds . . . **TRUMPET HONEYSUCKLE** (209) is a climbing species that may reach a height of fifty feet. Its blossoms, two inches long, continue through July . . . There is no match for **PERENNIAL FLAXES** (210).

208

209 ↓

210

yellow-flowered species, are native in North Africa, New Zealand, the Mediterranean country, and our own Southwest. The last one is very similar to our garden favorite.

The most interesting of the Flax group, in some respects, is the one which has been cultivated for its linseed and fiber since earliest recorded times. It has run wild in many countries, so that its true origin is uncertain. The probabilities, however, are that in the beginning its fatherland was somewhere in Europe and Western Asia.

Honeysuckle Varieties Number over 175

Believe it or not, there are about one hundred and seventy-five different species of Honeysuckles and an undetermined number of additional varieties. Many of them are shrubs of various sizes, while others are twining vines or plain weeds. There are even a few treelike Honeysuckles. All told, probably two hundred or more kinds are known to be grown under cultivation somewhere.

It takes a lot of space to accommodate a plant tribe of that size. So it is no surprise to be told by the botanists that wild Honeysuckles are distributed throughout the Northern Hemisphere except up toward the North Pole. One especially adventurous kind even lives on the island of Java, well down in the Southern Hemisphere.

Our best-known Honeysuckle is the climbing, semi-evergreen vine whose tubular, deliciously scented blossoms turn from white to yellow as they grow older and eventually are followed by glossy, black little fruits that serve as welcome food for winter's wild birds. It reached us from Eastern Asia more than a century ago and immediately began making itself right at home.

At the start, of course, the newcomer was merely a cultivated vine—and a fine one, too. But you just cannot keep a good Honeysuckle down, so this one quickly took to spreading itself all over the landscape. Today Hall's Honeysuckle, as we call it, covers countless thousands of idle acres with a tangled blanket several feet thick. When it comes to a tree it climbs the trunk and in a few years often occupies every branch and twig to a height of fifty feet or more. Actual measurements show that a single stem of it can grow fifteen feet in the course of a single season. Come hot weather or cold, Hall's Honeysuckle never says die.

How can any plant take over so much territory in such a relatively short time? Well, those little black fruits were what turned the trick. Wild birds eat them greedily, as we mentioned. So the seeds they contain simply hitchhike around inside the birds' crops and digestive tracts and sprout wherever they happen to fall. It is just as simple as that.

The Loosestrifes, too, are a widely distributed crew, although the kinds most likely to be seen in American gardens are Old Worlders. Unlike Honeysuckles, nearly all of them die down to the ground in the autumn and come up again in the spring. They will continue doing this for years; hence their designation as perennials.

211

212↓

Some gardeners are inclined to scoff at **DUSTY MILLER** (211) or Mullein-pink for its common looks. But its eye-catching blossoms and odd felted, almost white leàves are full of character. Incidentally, the name Dusty Miller is also applied to various plants with pale, felt-like foliage . . . There is certainly nothing mediocre about **SPIRY LOOSESTRIFE** (212), from the Orient. Its individual blossoms are only a half-inch wide, but they form a fantastic spire.

213

Loosestrifes run to purplish blossoms despite the fact that some of their first cousins with the same name are white. The majority grow two or three feet tall and have a definite preference for damp or even marshy soil.

The so-called Purple Loosestrife is the showiest of the lot. The date of its first arrival on our side of the Atlantic is problematical but apparently was not too far in the past. Since then it has spread into uncultivated places with an enthusiasm suggestive of Hall's Honeysuckle, though happily without the latter's smothering of other plants. Some of the finest wild colonies are in our coastal river valleys. They are really a sight to see when the heat of August and early September closes in.

Another escapee from Europe which has almost eye-searing scarlet flowers is the Maltese Cross, or Scarlet Lightning. This two-footer from Russia has truly scarlet blossoms about an inch wide which fairly blaze during June and July. Many an old-fashioned garden contained its quota of Maltese Crosses, but nowadays these dependable plants are not too often seen.

The closely related Dusty Miller, or Mullein-Pink, flowers at the same time but presents a quite different appearance. Its blossoms are a curiously intense light crimson, or cerise, and are perfectly displayed against their background of felted, white-woolly stems and foliage. Dusty Millers are self-reliant fellows, too. More than one gardener whose color sensitivity finally rebelled against their insistent hue has sought to banish them forever by pulling them out and heaving them away. Perhaps for the next year or two there were no further signs of the horrid things. And then, behold, they blazed forth again in various untended nooks where their executioner believed that not even the lowliest weed seed could gain a fair foothold.

When Apple trees open their superb blush and white flower show every spring, it is hard to believe that they are charter members of the far-flung Rose family. So, indeed, are Peaches, Plums, Cherries, and Apricots, to mention a few other hard-to-believe surprises.

Tracing the origin of our modern Apples makes the proverbial needle-haystack search seem like child's play. Apparently Adam and Eve knew Apples when they saw them, and acted accordingly. There is good botanical evidence, also, that points toward Europe and Asia as ancestral Apple homesteads. That was long, long ago, as indicated by the fact that charred

Dusty Miller has a fiery relative which is known to some people as **MALTESE CROSS** (213) and to others as Scarlet Lightning. Both of these names are appropriate enough, especially in consideration of the petals' peculiar form . . . The tall aromatic **NEPETA** (214) is grown for medicinal purposes and the creeping variety for ground cover. Catnip is one of the sweet herbs of this family.

214↓

215

A national poll of America might prove that **CRABAPPLES** (216) and **APPLES** (215) produce the favorite tree flowers. Their appeal is universal. By the time an Apple's petals have fallen the forms of the future fruits appear as slight swellings just below the stamen tufts.

216↓

217

218

Most kinds of **FORGET-ME-NOT** (217) bloom at about the same time as the Apples do. The one usually seen in American gardens has stems about eighteen inches long and often semi-horizontal. It is native in Europe and Asia . . . Gardeners who sometimes wish that Gladiolus stalks and blossoms were more graceful and informal are sure to like some of the **MONTBRETIA** (218) group. Both of these plants grow wild in the Cape of Good Hope region and are easy to manage . . . At first glance **BELLS OF IRELAND'S** (219) blossoms look like flowers within flowers. Actually the true flowers are small and confined to the center of the deep cones which surround them. Each cone is a calyx; in other words, the covering of a flower while the latter is still in the bud stage. This intriguing annual plant is still a novelty in America . . . Another delightful plant group from the Old World is the **STOCKS** (220). The one shown opposite is the Common or Brampton Stock, an old favorite of gardeners and florists alike. They grow to two feet.

219

220

remains of these fruits have been found in Switzerland's prehistoric lake dwellings. Could it be that these were the world's first baked apples?

Once in a while the color harmonies of the Apple's blossom time are enriched by a scattering of the earliest Forget-me-nots. We have our own wild species of these delectable pixies, but the ones most frequently seen are Europeans which have been here for many, many years.

Among the "Cape bulbs" (garden lingo for flower immigrants from Africa's Cape of Good Hope region) the Montbretias immediately suggest their Gladiolus relatives. They are definitely more graceful, however, and their colors are surprisingly varied. Red, orange, yellow, and copper in numerous tints, proportions and combinations give them top billing.

How very different are the blossoms of the quaint Bells of Ireland, an oddity from Western Asia which rated only as a curiosity with us until its recent enthusiastic vogue among flower arrangers. Its actual blossoms are whitish and far from impressive. Their chief interest lies in the peculiar bell-like, chartreuse calyxes from which the name is derived. The plants grow a couple of feet tall and their curving, leaf-studded stems are highly effective.

The Stocks of Olde England's days and our own colonial gardens have never lost their poignant fragrance and appeal in all the passing years. Their colors run from white through yellow, lavender, blush, rose, and red to purple. In some forms the blossoms do not open until late afternoon, as if they seek to save their perfume for the evening hours, when it will be most effective. The origin and significance of their strange name are obscure, at best. But there is no doubt that the true homeland of these perpetual garden and greenhouse favorites was Southern Europe.

221

In all the gardening world there is no more effective spring display than quantities of various **DAFFODILS** (221) massed irregularly in spacious, informal surroundings. Even on a smaller scale they are glorious.

Many Gardeners Specialize in Daffodils

For a thousand years and more the Daffodil, or Narcissus, has held an unwaveringly high place in mankind's affection. The early Greek poets wrote of it effusively. To the Chinese it has been the emblem of spring from time immemorial. Few indeed are the flowers which have meant so much to so many human beings through the centuries.

There are believed to have been about fifty "original" wild forms which were the foundation of the thousands of daffodil types and varieties we know today. These range all the way from perfect miniatures only a few inches high to two-footers whose individual trumpet blooms spread to five or six inches. White, cream, gold, apricot, buff—these are the principal colors which, alone or in numerous combinations, are now present in available varieties. All of them, when suitably handled, can be forced for winter bloom indoors in addition to serving as permanent garden residents. Thus, by wise planning and moderate effort, it is entirely possible to have Daffodils in bloom from January to June. Most of the true species and varieties have at least a fair trace of fragrance, and many of them have the supreme touch of delightful perfume.

Once they have been properly planted outdoors, the Daffodils are all things to all gardeners. They increase their own numbers with such ease that an original planting of six bulbs may become sixty or more in three years. This is not done by seeds, or even by mirrors. It is a straight case of self-multiplication by bulb splitting and resplitting until each original one becomes a jam-packed mass of new and independent offspring in its own precise image. The first thing you know, you will have an ever-increasing surplus to give away, since these crowded hatfuls will not bloom to capacity and so should be taken up in early autumn, separated, and replanted farther apart. If your supply of friends gives out and in desperation you are forced to throw away the excess bulbs, they may come up anyhow where-ever they fall!

Severe winter cold makes little difference to a Daffodil bulb provided it has been planted several inches deep and at the proper time. Consequently these astonishing flowers can be grown dependably in the North, South, East, West and all way stations between. Few insect pests or diseases are likely to attack them, by comparison with other fine flowers.

Evidence points toward the Daffodil tribe's arrival in America with the early colonists. At least three types of them—the Doubles, Trumpets and Short-cups—were probably among those pioneers in the New World. It is interesting that all three are still immensely popular. At the present time the Short-cups seem to have even increased their appeal. This may be due in part to their striking purity of form and colors.

When early summer comes the permanent flower garden faces the first of the season's full tests of its quality. Practically all of the early spring blossoms have gone by and their places must be taken over by later blooms.

222 224 223 225

One of the numerous varieties of **LARGE-CUP DAFFODILS** (222) so called because of the cup-shaped central portion . . . A **DOUBLE-FLOWERED DAFFODIL** (224) . . . **TRUMPET DAFFODILS** (223, 225) are appropriately named.

On the other hand, the major summer stand-bys such as the Hardy Phloxes and Physostegias are still no more than mounds of growing green. So, all in all, there is no better time to examine some of the important principles which underlie the art of outdoor plant arrangement.

The first order of business is to notice how the lowest growers are placed in that portion of the area nearest the position from which the garden is normally viewed. Behind them are the medium-height kinds, and at the back the tallest ones. This graded arrangement gives every plant a fair opportunity to display its special assets. The height lines, however, are not rigid or unswerving. Rather they are pleasantly flowing in nature, each of them receding in some spots and advancing in others.

Secondly comes the question of grouping or not grouping. The wisest policy on this is to use no less than three plants of the same kind and color

226

Many of the **LARGE AND SMALL-CUPPED DAFFODILS** (226), are bicolored. In some cases the cups are darker than the petals, and in others this color relationship is reversed.

in any one place. Every such group, of course, should have immediate neighbors whose colors either directly harmonize or, in some instances, serve as a pleasant visual transition to still other colors farther along the line. The over-all result, of course, is a series of small or larger masses which merge easily into each other, never clash in color, and give the whole planting an impression of movement and entity. Often, especially in a long border, sectional groupings can be repeated at intervals with excellent results on the overall effect.

Monotony, however, is every artist's enemy. So, to be sure of avoiding it, garden planners place strongly dominating plants at strategic points

where they will immediately catch the eye. Their purpose is not to belittle their near neighbors, but rather to accent and enhance their pictorial value as an exclamation point brings out the full significance of the words in a written sentence. This they may accomplish by their greater size, strong color, character of growth, or all three combined. A perfect demonstration of such garden emphasizing is provided by even a single clump of tall Hybrid Delphiniums.

To give the whole picture greater cohesiveness, as it were, a narrow band of a compact, very low-growing plant is often stretched along the forward edge of the entire planting. This has the same effect of unifying the various elements that a frame has on the painting within it. Here is the place of all places for Sweet Alyssum, Pansies, or some of the lower-growing Ageratums.

All Gardens Change from Year to Year

No good flower garden, fortunately, is ever a static thing, unchanging as the years go by. Some of its plants inevitably die out while others spread far beyond the stations originally allotted to them. A gardener's ideas and special interests change too, which is quite as it should be. So it is entirely understandable that outdoor plant arranging often becomes an absorbing and pleasantly rewarding hobby that never ends. Even in midwinter, when outdoor work is necessarily at a standstill, there are new plans to work on, fresh combinations to dream about, broader fields to explore. It is of such experiments and pleasant labors that true flower gardens and the gardeners who create them are so often made.

Yellow, pink, white, rose, orange, blue, crimson, purple—just name your favorite color and the chances are that the Monkey-flowers can supply it. Most of them grow from one to two feet high and live for only one season. But if the summer nights are cool and the daytime air is seldom humid, the plants will continue flowering profusely for weeks. The structure of the individual blooms, which usually are about an inch broad, suggests that of the much more widely known Snapdragons.

Although these remarkably showy plants have been familiar to botanists for more than a century, European gardeners showed little interest in them until the 1890s when some were imported from America. Then a stampede of hybridizing swung into action and is still pushing ahead at full speed. The two photographs were taken in England.

The Nepetas, by way of contrast, are specialists in blue blossoms and strong-smelling leaves. The latter characteristic points clearly to their membership in the Mint family. Probably the most famous of their tribe is the Catnip, or Catmint, whose pale green, heart-shaped leaves have such a peculiar stimulating effect on domestic cats.

Gardening styles come and go, much as do those in human clothes. The pendulum swings from formal to informal, both tested and proved for centuries. Here is a splendid example of an **INFORMAL GARDEN** (227).

228

There is no escaping the fact that **MONKEY-FLOWERS** (228, 229) live for only one season and therefore a new batch of them must be grown from seed every year. However, once they decide to get going in a suitable climate their crop of colorful little flowers is prodigious.

229

230

The **CATNIP** (230) or Catmint tribe's best-known asset is the attractiveness one of its members has for cats. Only gardeners appreciate the fact that the species known as Nepeta Mussini is wholly desirable for its soft blend of foliage and blossom colors.

The gardening fraternity, however, concentrates its enthusiasm on the one-foot *Nepeta Mussini,* which apparently lacks a non-botanical common name. Countless spikes of mauve blossoms rise above its grayish leaves in May and off and on through the summer. Persia and the Caucasus have the honor of originating it, and we have carried on from there.

The history of gardening is filled with anachronisms. One of the oddest of them is that foreign wars have served to introduce many of our most cherished flowers. These plants played no part in the actual fighting, of course; if they even saw any of it they were merely innocent bystanders. The real point is that even the sword-swinging warriors of Ye Olden Days were human beings who, in the intervals between battles, sometimes thought of their womenfolk in the castles and hamlets back home. So when all the slashing and spearing was over they often gathered choice roots or seeds of strange foreign flowers they thought would please some Lady Godiva

231

233

232

234

LOVE-IN-A-MIST (231) comes through with something new by having leaves so narrow that they look like stiff threads. These give the whole plant a hazy appearance which, combined with the delicately fringed blossoms, accounts for its odd name . . . Originally the **STAR OF BETHLEHEM** (233) came to us as a garden flower from the Old World. Our climate apparently suited it so well that it soon began spreading its seeds so widely that nowadays it is often thought to be a native American wildflower. It normally blossoms in mid-spring . . . **CHASTE TREES** (232, 234) from the same general region as Wisteria, preceded the latter into the West by some fifty years. They have a double distinctiveness—midsummer blossoms (rare in small trees) and pointed, strongly aromatic leaves which grow star-like clusters. Under certain light conditions the foliage shows a delightfully grayish overtone. The second of these photographs shows a very close-up view of the blossom spire at the left.

or Miss Trottwood and toted them back to her as a sort of domestic peace offering.

The Nigellas are far less climate-conscious, partly because they come from the Mediterranean lands instead of the Far North. The best-known one, Love-in-a-mist, is remarkable for its threadlike leaves, among which the delicate blue or white blossoms nestle as if for protection. Generations of American as well as Old World gardeners have valued it highly, despite the fact that the flowering period of each plant is brief. On the other hand, the seeds sprout and grow rapidly, so if a new crop is sown at monthly intervals in spring and early summer the show will stay on the road until autumn frost arrives.

No such fleeting handicap bothers any of the Star-of-Bethlehem clan, whose early headquarters were around the Mediterranean and in South Africa. They grow from bulbs, somewhat after the fashion of a Crocus or a Tulip, and there are at least a hundred different kinds of them. In every case the starry, six-petal blossoms are white and greenish and the leaves are almost as slender as large blades of grass. Several of the species, despite their relatively mild home climate, can thrive during our cold northern winters. One of them, indeed, which reached us many years ago and was a prime favorite in Grandmother's garden, has escaped from cultivation and cheerfully established itself in many a dampish country meadow.

Fine Orientals that Live for Years and Years

It was in this romantic fashion that the old red Peony, which still flourishes in many an American farm garden and occasionally a sophisticated suburban one as well, first reached France and probably England about the middle of the thirteenth century. It had come from some part of Eastern Europe or the Orient, although details on this matter are far from being clear and adequate. There is little doubt that some of its blood, together with that of another species native to Siberia and the Far East, formed the basis for many of the hundreds of garden Peony varieties we value so highly today.

The term "garden" Peony does not mean merely that it grows in gardens. Rather, it signifies that portion of the tribe whose stems die down to the ground every fall but whose roots are capable of living healthily for fifty years or more. There are a great many hybrids in this group, some of them delightfully fragrant and others completely scentless. Singles, doubles, semi-doubles, anemone-flowered—these are the chief physical forms the blooms assume. Their breadth may be almost anything from two to six inches, and in some instances they are practically as high as they are wide. Mere size, however, is not the overwhelming goal that it was some years ago. Indeed, there is now a growing emphasis on form as distinguished from bulk. Perfection of design, especially in the direction of simplicity in lines and details, is now increasingly important. Perhaps we are beginning to realize that true beauty is often based on delicacy rather than physical size.

Pink, red, and white, with numerous intergrades, are the primary blossom colors among these hybrid Garden Peonies. In many cases, though, the prominent central group of stamens is yellow, and yellow is beginning to creep into the petals of a few of the newer varieties. One of the finest and oldest of the hybrids, the matchless Festiva Maxima, is a pure white double of great size whose central portion is tantalizingly touched with a few crimson flecks.

All of the garden Peonies are excellent for cut-flower use as well as outdoor display. One of their advantages indoors is that they provide their own foliage accessories. Their blossoms often last for a week if cut in the early morning, just as they are opening, and then immediately placed in deep, cold water in a dark place for a few hours before going into the regular vases, jars, or other display containers.

For centuries the Chinese and Japanese have cultivated what we in the Western world now call Tree Peonies. These constitute a second important section of the Peony group. They are not really trees in the usual meaning of that term, but rather shrubs or bushes. Occasionally they reach a height of six feet, which is about twice the size attained by the majority of the garden division. Comparatively few American gardeners are familiar with them and their rather special requirements for becoming established and then doing their marvelous best. This may well account for their reputation of being extremely difficult to grow in this country.

Potentially these shrubby Peonies are completely unique. Unlike their garden cousins, which die down to the ground at the end of each season, their stems remain as hard and vigorous as any other shrub's throughout the year. When well established they flower profusely and put on a tremendous display. Some of the varieties produce blossoms six inches in diameter and as exquisitely designed and perfumed as any connoisseur could ask.

These shrubby Orientals have brought a welcome note of pure yellow into the petals of the over-all Peony picture. In some varieties this yellow stands completely on its own, although in most instances it is blended softly with many of the other hues found in the more numerous Garden group. There is also a strong tendency toward petals of varying lengths, widths, and shapes. This results in delightfully informal blossoms, each of which may be slightly different from its companions on the same or an adjacent plant.

Peonies, as a whole, form roots which are distinctly different from those produced by other common flower-garden plants. Their character is quite suggestive of a regular tree's roots; this is true even in the case of the group that dies to the ground every autumn. All of the stems and main shoots originate in a roughly circular central "crown" whose top is normally a couple of inches beneath the soil surface. From the sides and bottom of this crown several heavy, almost woodlike roots grow out and somewhat downward like the anchor and buttress roots of a full-sized tree. As they progress in

Many of the **DOUBLE-FLOWERED GARDEN PEONIES** (235) have rounded blossoms four or five inches thick. When the plants are well grown they become magnificent features of gardens except in the far South.

236 238 237 239

Typical **DOUBLE PEONY** (236, 238) blossoms in the process of opening . . . Double Peonies specialize in petals of many shapes . . . **FESTIVA MAXIMA** (238) one of the best . . . Many gardeners like **SINGLE PEONIES** (239) for variety . . . An **OPIUM POPPY** (237) that looks like a Peony!

length, they divide and redivide, losing a little of their diameter each time but building up an astonishing system of small, active feeding rootlets which gather abundant liquid nourishment for the crown and stems in addition to holding those vital parts very firmly in place.

A root system of this sort is exceptionally efficient and long-lived. Its one weakness, if you can call it such, is that it serves only its own central headquarters and never initiates a new one. Thus all numerical increase of any given Peony must come from planted seeds or, in the case of most practical home gardeners, by occasional division of large crowns into two or more sections, each of which has a few stem buds and enough attached roots to sustain it when properly planted by itself. Every division will have flowers exactly like those of the plant from which it came, and consequently is of no use to those growers who are trying to create new varieties. So the hybridizers, patient souls that they are, must rely on their full technique of hand-pollinating the parent flowers, frustrating the bees and other insects which instinctively could upset the whole plan, and eventually planting some carefully guarded seeds with the hope that one or two of them may eventually become plants whose blossoms will be a little different from all the rest that have preceded them.

The Peony tribe is sometimes criticized for providing only a limited period of bloom. This is not quite fair, inasmuch as a little searching among the types and varieties readily available from American nurseries specializing in them will disclose a list which will furnish a succession of blossoms from mid-spring until well into early summer—a span of some five or six weeks.

The cultivation of garden Poppies reaches far back into the past, quite possibly to the first recorded plant-hunting expedition, which was sent out by an Egyptian queen about the year 1570 B.C. Quite surely the famous Opium Poppy, of Mediterranean origin and progenitor of some of our loveliest modern garden forms, was one of the rewards of that search along the African coast. Even as early as A.D. 1597 there are authentic records of several double as well as single forms of this species with white, red, purple, scarlet, and mixed-color blossoms. All of these hues are embodied in our modern varieties.

Oriental Poppies Are now Grown Everywhere

Perhaps the stunning Oriental Poppy was also among the old queen's treasures, although its principal home was farther north in the wilderness valleys along the Persia-Afghanistan border. By the early part of the eighteenth century this tall and somewhat flamboyant beauty had become a favorite in European gardens. As for the completely delightful Shirley Poppies of today, they are descendants of the European Wild Poppy, a common field pest in its native home and therefore of questionable popularity in that region.

There are more than 100 species of Poppy, most of them natives of the Mediterranean region, Persia and eastward. Probably the most famous of them is the three-foot Opium Poppy, source of the world's supply of opium. This ill-famed drug incidentally, is made from the plant's milky juice, collected as it oozes from shallow cuts made in the sides of the young seed pods. The seeds themselves contain nothing of a narcotic nature; in fact, they are widely used as cage-bird food under the name "maw seed." A valuable oil is also extracted from them.

All of the Poppies bear flowers which are surprisingly large for the size of the plants. These blooms are also very colorful as a rule, with the result that they are famous although temporary eyecatchers in any garden where they are grown as ornamentals. Invariably they stand well above the leaves, which serves to accentuate their impact. A large mass of them, as demonstrated on the following page, is overwhelming.

240

241 242 ↓

243

The sight of a whole field of **ORIENTAL POPPIES** (240) in full bloom can be an event of a life-time. Many of the plants are three to four feet tall and at the top of each stem is a blossom several inches wide. Close-up views of the blossoms disclose the peculiar almost tissue-paper quality of the petals. Many of the blooms begin falling apart in a day or two after opening. Then the central seed capsules clearly show their developing form. At maturity each capsule splits open in a dozen or so places to permit scores of tiny seeds to escape.

The **ORIENTAL POPPIES** (240, 241, 242, 243, 244) of today show a far greater variety of size and colors than their ancestors of thirty years ago. They are true perennials and grow strongly in almost any sunny place provided it is well drained. One may wish occasionally that they were less space-taking, partly by means of their own roots and partly through the myriads of tiny seeds contained in those peculiar striped cases in the centers of the blossoms.

244

It is not easy to reconcile the apparently fragile loveliness of the Iceland Poppy with the often savage climate of Iceland and other parts of the arctic and subarctic regions around the world. No flower could be more delicately formed from top to toe or quite so subtle in the satiny luster and color variety of its fragrant, sometimes two-inch blossoms. The majority of them are in the yellow-orange category, with some whites, pinks, and ambers. The wiry stems, from a few inches to a foot or more tall, are completely leafless and so slender that one marvels at their ability to withstand a windy day.

In its home surroundings this most delightful of the Poppies is a true perennial that lives for a number of years. Regrettably it seldom shows such persistence in temperate lands, so most gardeners who grow it sow seeds every year to replace those older plants which have died.

Comparatively few Americans give much thought to Peach trees except as producers of delectable fruit, yet there are several double-flowering forms of them which are strikingly decorative when in bloom. All are of Chinese origin, and the first specimens probably reached us prior to the year 1700. Their large blossoms justify the name Flowering Peaches.

With luck, and rather special care, these smallish trees are among the first of early spring bloomers in our normal Fruit-Peach regions. Their great misfortune is their susceptibility to damage by insect pests, a weakness which calls for control spraying and often heavy pruning. Only in this way can they be induced to provide abundant, large-size blossoms year after year. Sometimes they remind you of the little girl in the nursery rhyme who "When she was good she was very, very good, but when she was bad she was horrid."

245

246

247 ↓

248

249

Many an experienced American gardener has reached the reluctant conclusion that the incomparable **ICELAND POPPY** (245) is only for those who sow fresh seeds of it every spring . . . **JACOB'S LADDER** (246) is the best-known cultivated member of the Polemonium clan. Its modest blossoms are borne at the top of stalks as much as three feet tall . . . The **CHINESE LANTERN** (247) plant's orange "lanterns" are at once odd and decorative . . . There are so many different sizes and shapes among the **BALLOON FLOWERS** (248) that it is difficult to believe they all belong to the same family . . . The several various forms of **JAPANESE FLOWERING CHERRIES** (249) are world-famous for their springtime blossom display . . . **JAPANESE ANDROMEDA** (250) is a long-lived evergreen shrub whose delightfully drooping blossom sprays open in early spring.

There is only one species of Platycodon, which we often call Balloon Flower or Japanese Bellflower. It grows two or three feet tall and through most of the summer its dense, bushy form is well decked with blue, whitish, or variegated blossoms as much as three inches in diameter when fully open. Gardeners who are blessed with well-drained, productive, and somewhat sandy soil rate it highly on their long-lived and dependable-flower list. Some of its varieties are considerably smaller and therefore less popular.

The official name of this Oriental is Platycodon, a composite of two Greek words meaning "broad-belled." This is certainly descriptive of the fully open blossoms, but why the gardening synonym of Balloon Flower? The reason here is equally valid, for in the advanced bud stage, just before opening time, the tips of all five petals are joined together so that each flower does look like a small, half-inflated balloon.

Another Asian oddity, this time with bright orange "balloons," is the Chinese Lantern-plant, or Strawberry-tomato. These adornments, however, are the fruits instead of the flowers. Inside each one there is a peculiar seed-stuffed gadget which looks somewhat like a miniature Tomato. The whole combination is often cut and dried for indoor decoration before it is ripe enough to open and lose its obvious appeal. The blossoms themselves are whitish and yellow and seldom attract much attention.

The Polemonium or Jacob's Ladder tribe is really a two-hemisphere group with one particularly hardy member that lives in the arctic regions of the world. Probably the most popular kind in New World gardens is the tallish plant shown on Page 112 immediately above the Lantern-plant. This is a common European wildflower, hardy, upstanding, and cheery with somewhat tufted leaves and clusters of blue or occasionally white blossoms about an inch broad.

250↓

Returning again to superplants from the Far East, the Japanese Andromeda would be a top-ranking evergreen shrub in any gardener's estimation. With us it seldom exceeds a height of nine feet, yet there is not a month in the year when it fails to be eye-catching. In mid-April it is incredibly lovely as its hundreds of cream-white blossom sprays sway among the lustrous, dark green leaves. Then, a little later, the color scheme changes completely as the flowers go by and the new young leaves, exquisitely graceful and rich bronze among their older green companions, come creeping out.

Flower Fashions and Primrose Paths

Fashions in flowers are sometimes as notional as they are in clothes and coiffures. To be sure, there are always the old faithfuls, such as Tulips, Roses, and Primroses, which never go out of style. But there are plenty of other worthies which have never elicited more than a nod except from an occasional broad-minded enthusiast.

No sane person can complain that Primroses have ever been neglected! They are primarily natives of the cooler parts of the North Temperate Zone with an especially heavy concentration in China and the Himalaya Mountains. There are well over three hundred species of them, plus an additional host of varieties resulting from natural crossings as well as controlled hybridizing. New kinds are being discovered every year, and no man can say when a final total will be reached or what it will be.

Primroses are predominantly spring bloomers whose flowers are bright with almost every color and color combination imaginable. As a rule they will live and multiply for years out of doors provided the ground is dampish rather than dry and the summers are not baking hot. Their flowering stalks, which rise from a group of broad, thick, and often wrinkled leaves, may be anywhere from three inches to more than a foot tall when growing in the garden. In many cases the blooming period continues for weeks.

One group of them in particular, the Chinese, provides most of the potted Primroses American florists raise in large numbers for the winter trade. A peculiar and literally irritating fact about this group is that some people are allergic to their leaves and may develop severe skin itching from too much direct contact with them.

Rounding out the complex Primrose picture, there is the case of the golden-flowered Sundrop, a lovely North American which is widely planted on both sides of the Atlantic. Botanical authorities include it in a group which they call Evening Primroses, although it is not a true Primrose and opens its blossoms in broad daylight!

The Stachys tribe, as compared with Primroses, is rather like David and Goliath. There are only a half-dozen kinds, one of which is a remarkably widespread weed. The most worth-while ones are Europeans which have long been called Heal-all because of a centuries-old German belief that they are helpful in curing human ills, especially quinsy.

251

The **SWAINSONA** (251) is a native of Australia and may be propagated by cuttings. There are innumerable hybrid varieties of **GARDEN PRIMROSES** (253, 254, 255, 256), many of which can be depended on to pull through our northern winters. They show to best advantage when planted irregularly in naturalistic surroundings. May is their usual flowering month. The **CHINESE PRIMROSE** (252) (below) is a standard florist plant.

252 ↓

253

254

255

256 ↓

257 259

Gardeners in search of smallish novelty plants that will never fail them might well consider the **BETONY** or **STACHYS** (257), which is a one-foot member of the Heal-all clan. It has purple and white varieties, also . . . **FLOWERING ALMOND** (258) from China is among the best of our spring-blooming shrubs. It may grow ten feet high unless its branches are pruned shorter as soon as the flowers have gone . . . The **SUNDROP** (259) well deserves its popular name when its large golden blossom cups look upward to the sky. There are several kinds of it which make up a small division of the much larger group called Evening-primroses. Sundrops are day-blooming versions of the others . . . This pair of cultivated **BUTTERCUPS** (260, 261), often called Ranunculus, demonstrates the sharply different impressions created by single (260) and double (261) flower forms of a species . . . The **HIGAN WEEPING CHERRY** (262), as we find it today in good American nurseries, has usually been grafted on a different species to keep it from becoming too large a tree.

258 ↓ 26

These enduring, low-growing plants are unique in the peculiar form of their blue, purple, or occasionally white flower heads. The individual blossoms are slightly suggestive of small Snapdragons, and when they stop appearing in summer the maturing head, with its numerous seeds, looks not unlike a brown, upright-growing pine cone.

In early May the pale pink flowers of the double Flowering Almond all but hide the twigs with their welcome masses. Only China could have originated such a delightful shrub, which has been with us Westerners for more than a century. It is one of the easiest shrubs to grow despite the extreme slenderness of its young twigs. And rarely indeed does it fail to put its best foot forward every spring. Incidentally, it is a cousin of the Peaches, Plums, and other stone fruits, including the Higan Weeping Cherry.

This particular Flowering Cherry, with its pendulous branches decked with dainty blossoms, seldom grows taller than fifteen feet. It is a variant of a much taller species said to be the most common Flowering Cherry in China and Japan. It appears to have reached America more than a hundred years ago, for it was listed by a New York nursery firm in 1846.

People to whom the name "Buttercup" signifies only the winsome wild species whose small glistening blossoms spangle our damp spring fields and meadows may well be astonished by the Middle East and Asiatic members of this almost world-wide race. Florists and most gardeners know them as Ranunculus, which is the generic part of their scientific name. They are far more compact in growth than the plants we are accustomed to seeing in the wild, and the blossoms are much larger. Many are so fully double they seem half spherical. And there is practically no limit to the number of their colors.

With us the garden forms of these impressive Easterners are decidedly more showy than their greenhouse relatives. The blooms are not only larger, but so very double they look almost like full-blown Peonies.

The Evergreen Rhododendrons, whose huge flower trusses are so magnificent on both sides of the Atlantic in early summer, belong to a truly believe-it-or-not family whose Greek-inspired name stands for "Rose Tree." There are hundreds of wild species distributed through the Northern Hemisphere, with the greatest concentration probably in the Himalayas and

261 ↓

262 ↓

263

266

Occasionally a **RHODODENDRON** (263, 264, 265, 266, 267, 268) opens its top bud first. This is the reverse of the normal procedure whereby the lowest ones commence the show and the others follow as the central stem of the cluster lengthens. Flowers (263, 264, 265) are Rhododendron Maximum from the New World shown in comparison with varieties from the Old World.

264

265 ↓

267

26

Southwest China. Their sizes run from a high-alpine shrublet two inches tall to sixty-foot trees, and their blossoms come in whites, pinks, reds, yellows, blues, and what-have-you. Together with their non-evergreen but closely allied Azalea cousins they rate as the most ornamental and diverse flowering shrubs in the modern world.

The origins of the large-flowered, incredibly spectacular Rhododendrons with which we are all familiar are as obscure as objects in a London fog at midnight. They are often called Catawbiense Hybrids, in honor of a species that grows wild in our own country. But hybrids between this Catawba Rhododendron and what? The true answer to this question would test the persistence of the F.B.I. The story may have begun with a cross between a Catawba and a shrubby species from Asia Minor, followed by a breeding of that offspring, about 1820, with a forty-foot tree type that is native in the Himalayas. From then on who knows? It does seem probable that our present-day forms have more Old World than New World blood in their veins, as it were.

Regardless of their family history these hybrids constitute the bulk of the Rhododendrons in cultivation today. They love to live in crowds where the ground is well-drained and free of lime. Full sunshine and light shade suit them equally well, especially if their home is on a slope. And when the thermometer drops below the freezing mark they will roll their leaves into cigar-like tubes so as to reduce the evaporation loss of that supply of internal moisture needed to carry them through the long winter months.

This habit of mass community living is convincingly demonstrated wherever Rhododendrons grow wild and undisturbed. The vast Rhododendron thickets below snow line in the Himalayas are famous the world over. Nearer home, if you climb the slopes of our southern Appalachians in late May you will hardly believe the immensity of the Catawba colonies and the blaze of their countless blossoms. And on some of the high plateaus where trees are scarce and distances unending there will be flowering hosts of the Catawbas' first cousins, the matchless native Flame Azaleas, in the full glory of their gold, lemon, orange, and subtle shades of red.

Roses of Today and Long Ago

"Among all flours of the worlde the floure of the rose is cheyf and beeryth ye pryse. And by cause of vertues and sweete smelle and savour. For by fayrenesse they fede the syghte; and playseth the smelle by odour, the touche by soft handlynge." So wrote a scribe in the thirteenth century, quite probably in tribute to the Cabbage or Hundred-petal Rose, a type that is as beloved today as it was before the time of Christ.

It has been well said that the history of the Rose is the history of humanity. From earliest recorded time this flower, in one or another of its numerous natural forms, has been part and parcel of mankind's expanding interests.

There are at least one hundred definite species of Roses which are known to grow wild in one or several of the temperate and colder parts of the

Northern Hemisphere. They fall into two distinct types in terms of blossoms: singles and doubles. A high percentage of them are naturally fragrant, and virtually all have at least a trace of perfume. Many of these basic kinds are so variable in character and have been so widely used in breeding experiments for so many centuries that it is impossible to be specific about the full ancestry of most of our modern Garden Roses. It seems probable that the major credit belongs to Asia and parts of the Middle East inasmuch as they were the chief cradles of human civilization.

Today there are well over five thousand recognized species and varieties of Roses, most of which are grown under cultivation somewhere in the world. The smallest one stands about four inches high and the largest, a climber, is capable of spreading over a horizontal distance of thirty feet along a wall or fence top.

The majority are more or less bushlike in character. These are the ones that most of us call Garden Roses, for the simple reason that their size and general character fit them superlatively for life in highly cultivated and often restricted areas. It is within this somewhat specialized yet highly popular group that the plant breeders have wrought their greatest and most appealing triumphs of blossom color, texture, type, and abundance. Years ago Garden Roses bloomed only in early summer. Today, however, nearly all of them have a second flowering season in early autumn—a sort of extra dividend, as it were, which adds immeasurably to our pleasure.

Just to indicate the multiplicity of modern cultivated Rose types, there are now ten major classified groups based on growth and blossom characteristics, and about thirty minor ones. To these may be added another twenty-odd wild species, with their numerous variations, which are cultivated fairly often by specialists. All of which suggests that the Rose is in no grave danger of losing the phenomenal popularity it has so long enjoyed!

With us the favorite type for garden-bed planting is still the Hybrid Teas, a curious name which indicates to Rose-wise folk that the blooms are exquisitely formed, good- to large-sized, fragrant, strong-stemmed, and embodying every color known to Rosedom.

Hybrid Tea bushes are rather compact, upstanding, and fairly tolerant of our cold northern winters. They come through the chilling season with sufficient vigor to display a superb June burst of flowers, an occasional blossom during the hot summer months, and another good show in September, which is sometimes stretched as far as Thanksgiving if the weather remains unusually mild and summer watering was not neglected.

Another group of bushy-type Roses, known as the Floribundas, has come rapidly to the front in recent years and is now a strong contender for first place in gardening circles. Their smaller but more numerous blossoms are borne in clusters rather than singly, and the plants which produce them are sturdier, more cold-resistant and less demanding of special attentions than

GARDEN ROSES (269) are so varied in type, size and habit of growth that they are equally adaptable to grand-scale and small-scale planting. But they should always have ample sun and well-drained soil.

270

273

HYBRID TEA ROSES (270, 273) have many attributes which make them outstanding for use in regular Rose gardens. Their blossoms are immense, often fragrant, and cover a tremendous color range. They also flower almost as freely in early autumn as in June when properly cared for. Some varieties are so hardy that they can withstand the cold of even our upper New England winters . . . In comparatively recent years a new type of Garden Roses called **FLORIBUNDA** (271) has gained deserved popularity. The plants in this group are somewhat smaller in all respects than the Hybrid Teas, but they flower more freely and have a tendency to mass their blossoms in groups. This of course makes them remarkably showy. They are stocky, informal bushes which fit well into such casual places as border corners, garden entrances and along the sides of garden walks . . . A third and very important Rose group consists of plants whose main stems sometimes reach a length of fifteen or more feet. They are collectively known as **"CLIMBERS"** (272, 274) although their stems are unable to support themselves by twining as regular vines do. They are unequalled for training on fences, walls or arches.

271

272 ↓

274 ↓

most of the Hybrid Teas. One reason for their fast-rising popularity is their suitability for mass plantings along walks and driveways and in other key landscaping places as well as informal close-up beds. Their best-known representative, perhaps, is the beloved Sweetheart Rose, whose wee pink blossoms are the soul of daintiness. No Rose lasts longer when cut or provides flower arrangers with more profound satisfaction than does Sweetheart.

Informal Roses and Their Garden Uses

The Climbing, or so-called Rambler Roses, are still more versatile in landscaping qualities as well as blossom variety. Some of them bear single flowers several inches wide. Others have doubles or semi-doubles, often produced in clusters of varying size which open one at a time or quite simultaneously. At least one, the old reliable New Dawn, comes closer to being actually ever-blooming than perhaps any other variety. Its large blush-pink blossoms, unfortunately devoid of real fragrance, begin opening in early June and continue on until the very threshold of winter.

From the practical homeowner's standpoint Climbing Roses have many uses. They are excellent for trellis training to frame doorways, cover broad exterior spaces between windows, or mask outdoor utility areas such as enclosed drying and play yards. Garden entrance archways are also choice locations for them, and so are summerhouses of many types. Stone walls and other boundary structures are often blanketed with them from end to end. All in all, they are one of gardening's best-paying investments.

An odd variant of the Climbers is the trailing, or ground-cover, Rose group, importantly represented by the old white Memorial Rose, especially dear to the hearts of Southerners, and the much more recent variety known as Max Graf, a related hybrid with pink, three-inch single blossoms. The former has smallish fragrant blooms and glistening, half-evergreen leaves, while Max Graf's flowers display cheerful golden centers. Both these kinds are perfectly contented to trail along on the ground, taking care of themselves and soon covering large areas with their enduring mats which, here and there, mound upward in pleasant billows to a height of a foot or so.

The Memorial Rose is a true wild type from Japan and may well serve as an introduction to the whole group of what are believed to be original Rose species. Gardening sophisticates often refer to these as Shrub Roses or Species Roses, the latter being a rather more accurate designation inasmuch as some of the group are far from being shrublike.

The ancient Cabbage or Centifolia Rose, from the eastern Caucasus, is the most famous of the Species group. Probably no other Rose, as we have already mentioned, goes farther back in human history. But it is by no means the only true species deserving of modern admiration. For example:

On many parts of Cape Cod and other seashore regions of Massachusetts and southward the sandy, impoverished soil is a friendly host to the Japanese Rugosa Rose, toughest of the tough. Fierce winds, salt spray, and bitter cold alike fail to affect its sturdiness and long life, although their combined at-

275

278

276

POLYANTHA (275, 277) or Baby Roses are prime favorites among the smaller types of regular garden kinds. The plants themselves grow only a foot to eighteen inches tall, but they blossom profusely in a broad range of colors. Most of their petals are rather loosely arranged. Some varieties, however, bear flowers almost as ball-like as those of a double Ranunculus . . . Among the **FLORIBUNDA ROSES** (276, 278) there are several varieties whose petals are attractively variable and informal in effect. The sale of this hybrid group has skyrocketed since its members first became available a few years ago . . . The opening stages of a typical **HYBRID TEA** (279) blossom are an object lesson in the mechanics of flower behavior. The outside petals emerge first from the swelling bud, curve outward and then down toward the ground as they expand. The next layer follows suit but does not turn downward quite as far. At this stage the petals at the very heart of the blossom are still rolled together snugly. The petals which expanded first may be almost ready to drop from old age before the innermost ones are fully unfurled and the flower is complete.

277 ↓

279

tack may reduce its potential six-foot height to a yard or so. By mid-spring its stout, bristly frame is well clothed with wrinkled, dark green leaves an inch or two long, and in early June there will be pink or white single blossoms as broad as your palm. By the time the season closes the latter will be replaced by brick-red "hips" or roundish fruits an inch across, which many a flower arranger cherishes as color spots in compositions.

Another leader of the shrubby Species tribe is the far more graceful Multiflora Rose from China and Japan. It is not quite as hardy as Rugosa, but with age its numerous arching stems may reach a length of ten feet or even more. Such a veteran is superb in early summer, when its great mound is all but blanketed with clusters of little white single blossoms. There is a pale pink variety, also, and another that has been dubbed the Seven Sisters Rose because the flowers in a single cluster often show seven distinctly different colors.

Besides being strikingly beautiful as a landscaping feature, Multiflora has great utilitarian value. It is probably the most vigorous of all Roses and so is widely used by nurserymen as a stock on which to graft choice varieties of Hybrid Teas and other Garden Roses. When you buy new young bushes of such kinds, the chances are that all their roots really belong to good old Multiflora!

Harison's Yellow Rose, probably a hybrid variety of the Austrian Briar species from Western Asia, is somewhat similar to Multiflora, but its double, bright yellow blossoms give it a totally different effect when great quantities of them open in mid-June. We have had Harison's Yellow in this country since 1830, and through all those years it has held every atom of its unique appeal.

In the same yellow-flowered class, although of somewhat smaller overall size and with single instead of double blossoms, there is Father Hugo's Rose. It was discovered in Central China long ago by the plant-hunting priest whose name it bears and has been with us for nearly sixty years. One of its many distinctive assets is the deep scarlet color of its fruits, which are such welcome highlights in otherwise bleak autumn days.

Although we are still in the Old World portion of this book, it would be unfair to the matchless Rose genus to omit mention of our native American wild species. Their flowers are all singles and predominantly pink in color. There are several swamp dwellers among them and others whose preference is for high, dry, and often impoverished fields. All are heartwarming in their simplicity, despite the handicap of irregularity and often sparse and straggly growth. One rarely sees them in cultivation, largely because of their habit of sending out far-ranging underground rooting stems which insist upon popping up in all manner of unwanted spots. But few flowers fill a more cherished nook in the souls of observant folk who discover in country byways a quiet charm which can never be found in the midst of our vaunted civilization.

In view of the thousands of years during which Roses have been known and grown it seems strange that their kind could still hold any surprises. Yet

280 282

281 283

The constant public demand for more kinds of Roses keeps the professional hybridizers hard at work. Among their major achievements has been the development of numerous varieties of Climbing Roses which, in addition to growing vigorously, produce blossoms of such unusual size and substance that they have become known as Large-flowering Climbers. In many instances this involved eliminating all but a trace of fragrance in order to incorporate the requisite vigor and character of growth necessary in a real Climber. But certainly there is no doubt of the size and beauty of the blossoms and the fabulous number of them on each well-grown plant. The investment of time, land, labor and equipment necessary to develop just this one new group suggests the fact that commercial Rose growing in the United States alone is a multi-million-dollar business. Another example of the inborn charm which characterizes so many of the individual Floribunda Rose varieties. Even the clustered stamens in the center are delightfully dainty . . . Six more of the large **HYBRID TEAS** (281, 283, 284, 285, 286, 287) in various stages of expansion . . . An example of Hybrid **POLYANTHA** (282) . . . An old variety of **TEA ROSE** (280).

284 286 285 287

occasionally they still do, at least as far as the general public throughout the world is concerned. Did you ever, for instance, see a green Rose blossom? Well, there is such a thing, and it is of enormous size in relation to the rather dwarf bush which bears it. Botanists call this oddity *Rosa viridiflora,* which of course may be freely translated as Rose with Green Flowers. For hereditary reasons which apparently are still obscure all of the numerous petals in its blooms have been transformed into small, narrow green leaves.

And finally, consider the case of Rosa Rouletti, or Swiss Rose, a pink-flowered native of the Swiss Alps which, in its wild homeland, is sometimes so small that the whole plant, including one or two blossoms, can be covered by an inverted teacup. Here is the tiniest of all flowering-age rosebushes, as intriguing in its diminutive way as the sprites of a favorite fairytale.

The St.-Johns-Wort family, like the Roses, is widely distributed through the temperate regions of the Northern Hemisphere. It is a much smaller

288

290

289

291

It is quite possible that credit for the world's smallest **MINIATURE ROSE** (288) goes to Switzerland where, high among the Alps, there is a wild species only three or four inches tall and bearing blossoms the size of a dime . . . The clean simplicity of **MULTIFLORA ROSE** (291) . . . One of the world-wide bramble group (290) to which Blackberries belong . . . **ST. JOHNSWORT** flowers (289) have tufts of delicate filaments.

group numerically, yet it contains hardy garden perennial plants as well as a good supply of flowering shrubs with hard, woodlike stems. The baby of the tribe merely creeps along on the ground, while the biggest boy of the lot sometimes is a good fifteen feet tall.

It would be unjust to judge these golden-flowered plants by the rather weedy species we often see growing wild along our roadsides and in other unkempt places. True, this self-sufficient customer is a native American, but it is also far less personable than many of its foreign relatives. One of the latter is a true rock-garden prize, hailing from the Himalaya Mountains. It

92

293

The majority of **SCABIOSA** (292, 293) species have blue blossom heads, but individual variations and professional hybridizing have greatly broadened the color range. Today there are white forms as well as lavenders, roses and purples. All have the same general shape.

is a genuinely dwarf, creeping shrub that forms a trailing mat of small, bright green leaves topped by large golden blossoms all through the summer months. Its only fault is that it may succumb to a bitter winter anywhere north of New York City. This is also the case with a closely related beauty from Asia Minor which makes a tuft of six-inch stems whose narrow little leaves are a soft blue gray. Against this subtle background the groups of two-inch, bright yellow blossoms are as spectacular as though a spotlight were playing on them.

Southeast Europe and Asia Minor have furnished us with another fine shrubby St.-Johns-Wort of somewhat greater stature which we often call Aaron's Beard. Its evergreen leaves are as much as four inches long and the bright golden blossoms, either solitary or in heads, are about half that much in width. This showy fellow, seldom more than a foot tall, spreads steadily by means of underground stems and eventually blankets much of the nearby ground.

There is also an exceptionally handsome shrub hybrid between Aaron's Beard and a Japanese species. Some gardeners know it as Goldflower and value it highly for its two-foot height, drooping branches, and extra-large flowers.

Scabiosa, Mourning Bride, Scabious, Pincushion-flower—these are four of the popular names which have been bestowed on the one- to three-foot South European plants whose lavender, blue, rose, red, mahogany, white, or nearly black blooms are so superdouble they do look like pincushions stuck full of pins. They are as perfect for outdoor mass plantings as they are for supplying cut flowers to use in the house. And they are as easy to grow in a sunny place as any worth-while flowers you are likely to find.

Several variations of this general Scabiosa theme have been developed by hybridists in quite recent years. Some of them live for only one season,

294

When Early **SQUILLS** (294) are left undisturbed in suitable places they will multiply amazingly . . . The **SCILLA** (295), another of the Squill group, reaches a height of more than a foot. There are two color forms of it . . . Stonecrop, one of the brightest of the complex and worldwide **SEDUM** (296, 297, 298) genus, thrives practically anywhere in the sun. Some of the Sedums lift slender stems above their leaf mats (297) others have showy blooms in late summer (298).

295 ↓ 296 ↓

which they contrive to make exceedingly busy with their constant supply of blossoms. Others are true perennials, provided only that in the North their location is given some winter covering that will serve to keep the roots from freezing to death.

The northern half of the Old World has furnished all of us with a vast array of flowering bulbs in an all but limitless range of size and colors. Many of these, such as the Tulips, Lilies, and Daffodils, are spectacular in their size and vigor. Yet the impact of their beauty can never quite match the thrill which comes when the first Squills, or Scillas, unfold their slender little petals in the early days of spring.

There are several dozen species, plus many varieties, of these European, Asian, and Mediterranean bulb plants. Nearly all of them have straplike leaves of surprising length by comparison with the flowering stalks and their sometimes pendent blossoms. The basic colors, often combined with white, are blues, pinks, purples, and a true red.

The majority of the Squills we plant in the New World are hardy, dependable little tads who can take a large dose of neglect and apparently like it. To be sure, an occasional application of some plant nutrient is appreciated if the soil is impoverished, but outside of this they will pretty much take care of themselves. One experimental soul tried planting them in his well-kept lawn, where they held their own for several years in spite of losing most of their leaves to the mower before they had completed their job of restoring the bulbs' expended energies.

It is a curious fact that some of the most attractive flowering plants contain an element of danger. The Deadly Nightshade is one of these, and so is Foxglove. Right now the case in point is a very close Squill relative whose bulbs harbor a substance that is widely used as an emetic and cathartic. In comparatively recent years it has even been developed into an effective preparation for killing rats, although it is not a poison in the usual sense.

The full story of Sedums would easily fill an entire book. Even expert botanists are uncertain about some of the details, although it is generally agreed that there are almost three hundred distinct species. For the most part they are natives of the temperate and colder portions of the Northern Hemisphere, and with few exceptions they prefer sandy soil,

297 ↓

298 ↓

299

300

Most garden Spireas blossom in the spring, but the variety **ANTHONY WATERER SPIREA** (299) holds back its flattened six-inch flower heads until the latter part of June . . . Other spireas have double as well as single-flowered forms **VAN HOUTTE'S SPIREA** (300).

rocks, and all the sunlight there is. Despite their customarily low stature they are unbelievably persistent and enduring against heavy climatic and nutritional odds.

All Sedums have fleshy, succulent leaves that help to serve as water-storage reservoirs for safety in dry weather. These leaves are amazing in their variety of shapes and sizes. Some of them are nearly as narrow as stubby-pencil lines, although the leaves of one species, the Showy Sedum, are from two to three inches long and half as broad. This Showy is about the tallest of the group, as its upright stalks with pink or occasionally white blossom clusters at the top are often twenty or more inches long. It comes from Japan and blooms in late summer and early fall.

Most Sedum species either spread flat along the ground or grow in crowded clumps only a few inches high. The old-time, yellow-flowered Stonecrop, or Wall Pepper, is the best known of the spreading group. It came originally from Europe, North Africa, and Eastern Asia but has made itself so completely at home here in the States that it pops up in many rocky, wild areas. No soil seems too worthless for it or discourages its cheery springtime carpet of gold. Once started, it is so persistent it can almost be called everlasting.

Many of these horizontal-growing Sedums, which root as they go, are all but indestructible. Even a small scrap of stem, tossed away in a bare, barren spot, is likely to take root and grow into an invasive carpet. About the only certain way of killing them is to grub out every last bit of root, stem, and leaf and throw the whole collection into the middle of a hot fire. Even at that it is well to watch for stray pieces which may have eluded you.

One cannot help admiring determination like this, even in a small plant. Perhaps this is one reason why many a discriminating gardener is a rabid fancier of Sedums and gladly overlooks the occasional shortcomings which accompany their unquestionable merits.

The beloved Van Houtte's Spirea is undoubtedly the Spirea of all Spireas in American gardens. It comes from China and Japan, and one springtime glimpse of its gracefully arching branches laden with little white, double blossoms is enough to make a new friend for life. A large old one may be nine feet tall and as much in breadth—a compact yet airy mound of beauty ideal for countless spots along lawn edges, beside driveways, or in informal gardens. Many other forms of this shrub genus have come to compete with it since those days, but good old Bridal Wreath still carries on serenely.

The great majority of Spireas lack special distinction after their brief flowering period is over, but Bridal Wreath is not among them. All through the growing season its dainty foliage is a lustrous green. Then, as autumn comes, the color changes slowly to red or orange, often exquisitely blended on the same plant. And later, whenever a light, damp snow falls, its maze of slender twigs becomes a wonderland of white.

How very different is Bridal Wreath's hybrid cousin, Spirea Anthony Waterer! Here is a rather stocky little shrub only a couple of feet high whose leaves are tinged with pink when they first appear in spring. Few people would give it a second glance then, but that situation changes radically as the flower buds begin to appear in the early part of June. They are grouped together in flat, surprisingly large clusters which grow broader and broader until, toward the end of the month, the first ones expand into stunning crimson platters often six inches wide. Even these are only the beginning of Anthony Waterer's annual flower show, which continues intermittently for several weeks.

There are other cultivated and wild Spireas—quite a host of them, in fact. They can be roughly divided into spring-flowering and summer-flowering groups, together with a few which delay their bloom until autumn. Yet, despite their numbers, the only flower colors are white and varying shades of pink and red. One of them, a pink-flowered American "weed" bush, is

There is almost no end to the spectacular variety of the Florist **CINERARIAS** (301, 302). All of them have leaves of substantial size and blossoms which are rather daisy-like in form. But some of the plants are low and compact while others are much taller.

301 ↓ 302 ↓

303 304

so tough to eradicate from wastelands that generations of back-country folk have grown up to know it only by the realistic name of Hardhack.

Nearly two centuries ago, during the reign of King George III, His Majesty's Garden at Kew was England's center of truly horticultural knowledge. All manner of new plants were tested there and old ones often improved. Even in those years Kew was well on its way to the international fame it holds today.

In the spring of 1772 Kew sent its first plant hunter, a young Scot by the name of Francis Masson, on an expedition to South Africa. He returned from this assignment with such a wealth of notable botanical discoveries that a couple of years later he was dispatched on a second Kew mission, this time to the Canary Islands and other more tropical lands. During both of these journeys Francis Masson gathered the original wild plants from which the many lovely Cinerarias of our time were subsequently developed.

Among us Americans today the Cinerarias are predominantly florist plants grown in greenhouses by skilled professionals who give them the precise conditions of light, temperature, and humidity they demand. Vast numbers of them in full bloom appear in the shops during the Easter season, but their glory usually vanishes a few days after we get them home because modern living conditions simply do not suit them. There is little that most of us can do about this, however green our thumbs may be. Before the age of thermostats and steam radiators the story was sometimes different, partly because householders of those days did not mind if their room temperatures stayed at the fifty-degree level, which is the Cineraria's ideal.

305

306

CAPE HONEYSUCKLE (303) from South Africa, is a luxuriant garden feature of many gardens in Florida and along the Gulf Coast . . . All parts of the amusing **LAMB'S EARS** (304) really do look soft and woolly. The small, tightly bunched blossoms are borne on upright stalks about a foot above the ground . . . A very close-up view of the blossoms of any **SEA-PINK** (305) species brings out the innumerable short "hairs" which mark the group . . . **SEA-PINK** (306) sprays are often dried for indoor arrangements.

Out of the region from the Caucasus to Persia comes another unusual plant which goes by several odd names including Woolly Woundwort, Lambs-ears, and Rabbit-ears. The last two of these make perfectly good sense in view of the dense white "hairs" which cover nearly all of the plant from top to bottom. The chances are that the nickname Woundwort also sprang from the same source, since the sizable woolly-surfaced leaves do look as though they might make nice absorbent dressings for a wound.

The small, purplish flowers of this rugged creeping plant are nothing special to look at, but the foliage is splendid for mat-edging a garden border provided the 1½-foot stems are cut off before they develop fully. Many a gardener, too, has discovered that a sprig or two of the leaves can add a priceless final touch to an arrangement of cut blossoms in a well chosen indoor container.

The Woundworts (or Stachys, if you are a botanist) are really quite a versatile crew. One species, the Chinese or Japanese Artichoke, produces numerous crisp, rather slender tubers just under the ground. These make excellent eating, whether raw or cooked. They soon shrivel when exposed to the air, so it is just as well not to dig them up until you are hungry.

Sea-pinks, or Thrifts, are certainly superior to Woundworts when it comes to attractive blossoms. They are cute little things, often only a few inches tall, with tufty evergreen leaf mounds or mats and compact, rounded heads of tiny blush-pink or lilac blossoms.

Practically all of the Thrifts are rugged individualists in that they ask few favors and do well in almost any sunny spot that is not noticeably wet.

Many of them are excellent rock-garden plants in addition to their suitability for edge-planting along the front of a flower border. The majority of them come from European mountain regions, which accounts for their alpine plant habit of packing great charm into minimum space.

Another worth-while branch of the Sea-pink clan contains a very popular European-American species called Common Thrift. It reaches a height of a foot or more, and although its blossoms are not so tightly clustered they have a somewhat wider color range. These colors hold rather well, too, when the stems are cut with the flowers still in their prime and immediately brought indoors for careful drying preparatory to serving as winter-long "everlastings" that will be far more attractive than most other dust catchers.

The Tulip Family Is Truly Spectacular

If there were a Who's Who of Garden Flowers, it would devote a whole page to Tulips because of their dignity, fantastic variety of blossom shapes, and colors, and the impression of aristocratic ancestry which invariably characterizes them. Tulips by the untold millions are planted every autumn in many parts of the temperate world, while other millions are proving that, given a fair chance, they will endure for years. Although there is a widespread belief that their flowers are scentless, there is a whole group of early bloomers with thoroughly delightful fragrance. These doubly gifted beauties represent two of the ten official types into which our modern Tulips are divided by the experts.

Like other plants which grow from bulbs rather than run-of-mill root formations, Tulips are exceptionally interesting in their annual behavior underground. When you plant them they appear to be little more than inert lumps, rootless and apparently as dead as last year's maple leaves. Yet within each dry brown skin there is the embryo of every stalk, leaf, and bloom which will be so captivating next spring. All preparations for launching that spectacular display have been completed within the body of the bulb. Nourishment, new roots, every detail for future success—all these are there, poised and waiting only for the word to go when the right time comes.

If the bulb is of top quality in size and built-in vigor, it will work still another miracle in the active season which lies ahead. Besides sending out new roots from the flat plate which forms its base it starts preparation for the future. Within the many fleshy layers which compose most of its body new replicas of itself commence to form. At first they are mere dots, but as time passes they increase in size until finally they separate from their parent and are fully on their own. By the time the largest of them is old enough to bloom their parent is only an empty, shriveled husk, its life mission accomplished.

Fine modern **TULIPS** (307) are available in so many different heights and colors that they may be planted in a wide border in such a way that they will slope upward from front to back when in bloom.

It is not generally realized that Tulip blossoms can be enjoyed at home in the North almost continuously for three or even four months. The first half of this period, to be sure, is restricted to indoor pleasure. It is assured by special planting and handling techniques which, when employed by florists and many experienced home gardeners, force the bulbs to come into flower by mid-January. Successive batches of these bulbs will keep the show going until, along with the first of the early Daffodils, the cream or yellow Tulip species known as Kaufmanniana begins flowering in the garden. This is followed by the single and double Earlies which keep blooming until a group of medium-early hybrids steps in and bridges a gap which otherwise would exist until the tall Cottage, Darwin, and Breeder Tulips open and carry on to the end of the season in late May.

The names of these last three types have an intriguing history. Cottage Tulips commemorate the cottage folk in the old European countries who have maintained them with little change ever since the collapse of the astounding "Tulip madness" which we will come to in a few moments. The Darwins, on the other hand, are named after Charles Darwin and have been in existance only a little over sixty years. As for the Breeders—well, here is the gist of their peculiar record as the horticulturists have analyzed it:

When a Tulip has been grown from a seed instead of a small new bulb produced by an older one, its blossoms usually show only a single color. However, after a few years this same bulb often drops its one-color habit and "breaks" into several colors which frequently show up in feathery markings. Actually the one-color state is a "breeding" stage for new and different Tulip kinds. But, wonder of biological wonders, no specific "breeder" will ever break again provided its numbers are increased solely by the young-bulb method which we have already described. In this way the new variety can be propagated indefinitely. For still another surprise, if some of its *seeds* are planted, they will grow into bulbs whose flowers will have the same old one-color tendency!

Original Tulips Came from the Eastern Mediterranean

The early history of the Tulip as a garden flower is buried somewhere in that vast Eastern Mediterranean region we know as the Levant. It may well have been there that the ancient Turks, who kept few if any records of such happenings, first brought into cultivation some of the wild Tulip species whose identity we cannot even conjecture with any confidence. It is quite certain, however, that many varieties of domesticated Tulips were locally popular in the neighborhood of Constantinople as early as A.D. 1554. That was the year when O. G. de Busbec, Austria's ambassador to the mighty Turkish Empire, saw them in full flower and, a little later, bought a few

Delightfully varied spring displays of **TULIPS** (308) can be achieved where there is ample space for informal landscaping. They can be replaced by annual flowers when their leaves have turned yellow.

As with many other popular flowers, the full ancestry of most modern Tulips is impossible to trace. The blossom types on this page are: **PEONY-FLOWERED TULIP** (309); wild species (311); Biflora (310); Darwin (312).

bulbs for what appears to have been a fantastic price and took them home to plant in his own garden in Vienna. He could not have been more jealous of their welfare if they had been his own children.

This was the forerunner of one of the Western world's strangest developments in the long history of ornamental gardening. Central Europe in those days had many wealthy merchants and landowners who competed vigorously to outdo each other in the beauty and lavishness of their estates. As word of the ambassador's new Tulips spread through Germany and eventually into Holland, these worthies hastened to import their own Tulips from the Levant. The more of them they brought in the greater became the variety of blooms. Tulip enthusiasm skyrocketed and so did the prices for bulbs. By the year 1634 the craze for Tulips was sweeping through the Netherlands like a prairie fire, engulfing first the people of wealth and then the ordinary

Tulip pistil and stamens; the specks on the pistil stalk are pollen grains from the brown stamen tips (313) . . . Darwin Tulips opening (314) . . . a fragrant Single Early Tulip (315) . . . Breeder Tulips (316).

citizens, farmers, seamen, and even household servants and old-clothes peddlers. Almost everyone, regardless of age or social position, got into the act with a vim. Truly "The gaudy Tulip was an object which . . . drove the grave, the prudent and the ambitious Dutchman as wild as ever did the South Sea Bubble the gullible John Bull."

Reckless mass speculation in these wonder flowers from the East became the order of the day. Tulip bulbs were bought and sold sight unseen and with the scantiest of credit. Many of these deals were purely paper transactions relating to actually nonexistent bulbs. The moneylenders, often deeply involved themselves, upped their charges higher and higher as their customers dug their own financial graves deeper and deeper. One Amsterdam dealer is reported to have had a single extra-choice bulb which he sold for 4000 guilders (about 1200 uninflated dollars), a new carriage, and two gray

317

318

319↓

320

321

horses with complete harness for both. One bulb of another variety, believe it or not, brought its lucky owner 8000 pounds of wheat, 16,000 pounds of rye, 12 fat sheep, 2 hogsheads of wine, 1 complete bed, 4 oxen, 8 swine, 1000 gallons of beer, 2 large tubs of butter, 1000 pounds of cheese, and 1 silver drinking horn.

Many bizarre tales have come down from those hectic days. One of the oddest concerned a Dutch importer who was restlessly awaiting the arrival of a shipment of goods from the Levant. At last a sailor rushed into his warehouse office with the glad tidings that the vessel had come. The overjoyed merchant thereupon presented the seafarer with one red herring for his supper and turned his own thoughts to the new riches so near at hand.

On his way out of the warehouse the sailor spotted what he thought was an onion lying on a pile of expensive silks and velvets. An onion would certainly make that lone red herring taste better, he thought, so he slipped the object into his pocket and departed. Shortly thereafter the merchant set the whole warehouse echoing with his screams that his cherished bulb of Semper Augustus, an extremely valuable Tulip variety, had been stolen. During the ensuing confusion somebody recalled having seen the prize shortly before the seaman left the building, so rescuers rushed out in mad pursuit of him. By the time they caught up with the poor fellow he had eaten all of Semper Augustus as well as the red herring, and that was that. It was probably the most expensive meal he ever ate, since a magistrate sentenced him to several months in jail for his perfectly innocent mistake.

Oddly enough, the beginning of the Tulip bubble's end took place in Britain during the year 1636. While the mania was still racing along at top speed in the Netherlands, Tulip bulbs were offered for sale in the London Exchange. But the English public was cagey. Vainly the worried dealers strove to match the fabulous prices prevailing in Holland; the British were unimpressed. Then they switched their efforts to Scotland but soon discovered that the Scots kept an even firmer grip on their purses. Tensions mounted and about a year later the whole bottom fell out of the speculative Tulip market. Word had spread around that some of the shrewdest dealers, knowing that every boom must have its bust, had quietly slipped out from under while the slipping was still fairly good. As soon as this became really known in the Netherlands there was a shattering panic followed by the inevitable slump. Many Dutchmen who had believed they were on Easy Street awoke to find that their only assets were some Tulip bulbs nobody wanted to buy. The whole country was stunned by the completeness of the catastrophe. Countless legal actions were taken for broken contracts, criminal deceptions, and heaven knows what else.

Opposite page. In many instances the interest of a **TULIP MASS PLANTING** (317) is substantially increased by intermixing a variety of blossom types. This is especially true of the late-flowering groups . . . **PARROT TULIPS** (318, 319) are characterized by irregular, feathery petals often with numerous stripings . . . **PEONY-FLOWERED TULIP** (320) blossoms are doubles with petals of various shapes and sizes . . . A **DARWIN** (321) variety.

322

323

The most graceful and spectacular of all the **VERONICAS** (322) is a three-footer from Europe and Asia. Every one of its flower multitudes is a marvel of perfection. This perennial beauty blossoms in August and September . . . Soon after the ground becomes frost-free in the spring the **TRAILING MYRTLE** (323) begins to open its jolly blue flowers.

Those were indeed prolonged, dark days for the Dutch. Yet, strangely enough, the clouds which had once been so storm-wracked eventually showed their silver linings. After the Netherlanders had quieted down, they rolled up their sleeves again and began to salvage what they could from the wreckage of their dream. And as they worked they gradually realized that their particular kind of soil and climate could well be made the literal basis for the greatest and soundest of all bulb nurseries. The city of Haarlem would be its center, they decided, and they would grow and grow and sell and ship throughout the world. This time there would be no miscalculations, no hallucinations of sudden riches—and there were none. In 1940, when the German troops invaded Holland, she was selling 100,000,000 fine Tulip bulbs annually to the United States alone. And since that devastating gale which carried away so many of her vital dikes a few years ago she has rebuilt the barriers still more strongly, reclaimed her salt-ruined soil, and is again forging rapidly ahead.

Perhaps it would be appropriate for all of us who enjoy fine Tulips, Hyacinths, and other garden bulbs to give thanks for the indomitable courage and resourcefulness of that dean of masterly horticulture, the Dutch nation with its lands below the level of the sea.

Unlike Tulips, the Veronicas, or Speedwells, are native in various parts of the Eastern and Western worlds. There are more than a hundred species of them in the general area of New Zealand, and at least as many more in temperate Europe and North America. The kinds we grow in our own gardens in this country are almost invariably European.

324

325

In at least three respects—blossoms, fruits and autumn foliage—the European **CRANBERRY-BUSH** (324) is one of the most colorful of the important Viburnum tribe. Its closest rival is the American Cranberry-bush, a New World species so similar in appearance that it is difficult to tell which is which . . . Another view of the **VERONICA** (325) opposite.

The alluring blossoms of these often woolly-leaved favorites are the complete antithesis of Tulips. Individually they are very small, but collectively they form compact, beautifully tapered heads as much as eighteen inches long in certain cases. White, blue, purple, pink, or lavender, these eye-catching spires above the often-silvered leaves are welcome exclamation points on the flower pages of June, July, and perhaps even August.

The daintiest of the whole Veronica group, bar none, is a Corsican mite whose shining green leaves are less than a half-inch long. It hugs the ground as closely as a plant can, and gradually spreads into a solid mat that may be a foot or more across yet only a quarter inch thick. Just above it, in June or July, wee pale blue flower steeples point boldly skyward.

In May another European creeper hides the ground in shady places with many yards of shining evergreen leaves sprinkled with wide-eyed blue or sometimes white blossoms a full inch across. Whether you elect to call it Common Periwinkle, Trailing Myrtle, or Vinca Minor is just a matter of choice, since all are correct. It sailed from the old country with the colonists when they set out for America long ago, and apparently it took to the new land as gladly as they did. For generations it has been a favorite country ground cover, for it rarely hesitates to spread extensively. Even today you often find it growing wild in secluded spots from which all trace of human habitation has vanished.

Besides its primary role of eight-inch blanket where such a covering is needed, Trailing Myrtle is a generous provider of special-effect indoor decorations. Short stems of it, each with a couple of leaves and a flower or

326

This type of **TUFTED PANSY** (326) may have been one of the varieties from which the more or less single-color Violas were developed. It is a native of Spain and the Pyreness Mountains . . . Today there are many color forms of **VIOLAS** (327, 328), with more appearing every year. Each bloom has a small yellow spot in the center.

327 ↓

328 ↓

two, are perfect for a variety of nosegay containers. Also, when floated in a shallow, clear glass bowl they are as delightful as anyone could wish.

During the latter days of May, or perhaps in the early part of June, the broad, flat flower heads of the European Cranberry-bush come into their own. They are among the finest produced by the shrub tribe known as Viburnums, a sizable group that is native in the New World as well as the Old. "Cranberry," in this instance, has no botanical significance. It implies merely a resemblance in the size and color of the autumn fruits which, unfortunately, are usually much too tart for edible use.

This upstanding, twelve-foot shrub actually bears two types of flowers in the same head. The large ones around the edges are sterile and serve primarily to attract insects which will aid in the pollination of the numerous much smaller blooms nearer the center of the circle. These, of course, are the ones responsible for the subsequent crop of fruit.

When autumn comes the Cranberry-bush's vigorous, maplelike leaves turn red too, and for a week or so the whole plant glows with unforgettable color in the waning sunshine.

During comparatively recent years a new type of flowering plant called Viola, or Tufted-pansy, has gained marked popularity in American gardening circles. It is a neat, rather dense little thing which provides a steady succession of fair-sized blossoms from May to August, especially in regions where the summers are fairly cool and the soil rich and deep. Its over-all effect is quite different from that of regular Pansies, partly due to an absence of longish, sprawling stems but, more noticeably, to the single-color character of each flower. Violet blue, apricot, white, purple, deep yellow, ruby red, orange, and light blue are all available in the market nowadays. Usually these colors are somewhat lighter in the center of the blossoms. This range is likely to be considerably broadened within the next few years.

Technically the Violas are perennial plants, but some of them will bloom in their first year if the seeds are sown very early in the spring. They average only about six inches in height—just right for small garden beds, the front edges of flower borders, and many rock gardens. Unlike numerous other spring and summer flowers they do especially well in locations which are partly shady. If all the uncut flowers are snipped off as soon as they fade, the plants may continue bearing new ones until early autumn.

Plant Names Are often Puzzlers

Every now and then the popular names of plants lead to baffling puzzles. A case in point is these delightful Violas and their Pansy cousins. It does not help much to explain merely that all Pansies are Violas but not all Violas are Pansies. So let's look at the record for a moment.

In Queen Elizabeth's day a little English wildflower called Pansy was so beloved by all Britishers that, as Shakespeare's Ophelia said sadly, "Pansies, that's for thoughts." Everyone knew and many grew this wildling in his

329

PANSY (329, 330, 331) flowers have numerous colors and combinations which often lead to amazingly human expressions. There are also single-color forms of strikingly rich, velvety appearance. Plants of the finest varieties have only one flowering season.

330 ↓ 331

332

Super-size **PANSY** (332, 333) blossoms are difficult to grow in a garden. Those huge ones sold in good florist shops are greenhouse-raised.

333

garden, and in time there came to be two fairly well-defined types. It is thought that one of these, with three different colors in its petals, became the basis of our gorgeous modern Pansies. The other type, whose blooms were primarily yellow throughout, was the primary ancestor of the Violas we know today.

Both of these groups belong to a huge, virtually world-wide tribe collectively known as the Violets. Nearly all its members are noted for their astonishingly promiscuous habit of interbreeding endlessly among themselves. Even the best botanists have plenty of trouble deciding what father and what mother are responsible for which child. To cap all this, a great many Violets shoot their seeds several feet through the air as soon as they are fully ripe. This gives them a better chance to grow without being crowded.

Regular Pansies got their start in England when, soon after the fall of Napoleon, plants with blossoms of various colors began drifting in from continental Europe and even Russia. With these and other selections from among their own varieties the British Pansy fans really hit their stride during the first half of the Victorian era. Great Pansy shows became the order of the day and competition for the largest and showiest blooms was fast and all but furious. There were special classes for glossy blacks, blues, and pinks, and sections reserved for whites, yellows, and other varied blossoms whose colors were symmetrically displayed on the lower petals.

Then, in 1860 or so, came the revolution. It was touched off by the arrival of an entirely new brand called Belgian or Fancy Pansies. Their petals had no prim edgings, and the colors were anything but symmetrical. Many different colors and shades were arranged in striking fashions. Conservatism of every sort seemed to have been banned by these newcomers.

And the staid British people took them enthusiastically to their hearts. The popularity of these foreigners grew so rapidly that the show managers

334

had to open a special place for them in the exhibition halls—a place which, wonder of wonders, was called Fancy Pansies and permitted the wildest of color combinations and markings. As the enthusiasm increased, the size and variety of the blossoms grew with it until, if we were to see some of those old winners today, we would hardly believe our eyes.

Many of the modern Pansies are the most human-looking of all the world's flowers. The blooms of some of the specially grown exhibition types are as much as four inches in diameter and are carried on stalks as thick as lead pencils. Such proportions can be attained only under greenhouse culture, although skilled gardeners occasionally approach them by using very high-priced strains of seeds and giving the young plants special soil and winter protection. Not even these experts, however, expect their plants to yield more than one flowering season, for the typical Pansy is only a biennial with a maximum life span of two years at best. Most of the truly handsome ones you buy in full bloom during early spring and plant in the garden came from selected seeds sown in the preceding August.

The Common Calla from South Africa has been a favorite winter-flowering house plant in the Northern states for many years. In California and the South gardeners often include it in their outdoor plantings as well.

35

336

The major oddity of this exotic plant is that all its extremely small true flowers are packed on that rodlike central stalk. The queer, flaring trumpet surrounding it is actually a sort of distorted leaf protection for the unsuspected blossoms and their seeds-to-be.

Some six thousand-odd miles northeast of the Calla's home port lies the land of the Wisteria, China's largest and most spectacular vine. Although it apparently was not introduced to the West until the early eighteenth century, it has prospered mightily under our auspices. Some of our oldest veterans have trunks a foot thick at the base, and only drastic pruning has kept them from spreading far beyond the generous spaces originally allotted to them. Even so they are a wonderland of beauty every spring when myriads of clustered, fragrant blue and whitish blossoms festoon them.

Finally, at the end of this gallery of the temperate Old World's floral gifts to the West, pause a moment before the Asian Weigelas. Hardy, well-mannered, and bright with white, pink, or red tubular flowers in spring or early summer, they stand firmly in the front rank or ornamental shrubs.

337 ↓

In warm climates the believe-it-or-not **CALLAS** (334) can be used effectively in mixed outdoor plantings . . . The old reliable **WEIGELA** (335) has an intriguing habit of bearing differently colored flowers on the same bush. It reached American gardens many years ago and is still a popular favorite because of decorative quality ability to grow almost anywhere . . . **YELLOW CALLAS** (336) are smaller plants than their white-flowered cousins and often favored for indoor use . . . May brings the unmatched beauty and fragrance of **WISTERIA** (337) that magnificent Chinese vine which may live for a hundred years.

Flowers of the Old World

TROPICAL ZONE

The flowers of the tropics are as varied as those in temperate parts of the world. Some of them are as exotic in appearance as the steamy jungles from which they come, and some have all the frank realism of a New England summer day. But one and all, large or small, are living evidence of Nature's infinite resourcefulness.

Water-lilies are perfect examples of breath-taking beauty coupled with adaptation to the practical needs of plant life. Many of the highly colorful ones are native in tropical Africa and other equatorial regions of the Old World, while the temperate members of their far-flung family are inclined toward quieter whites and yellows. Yet the entire group exists, often for many years, by the following general methods.

The mainspring of Water-lily life, as it were, is a stout tuber, or rootstock, firmly anchored in the mud beneath three to six feet of water. Many of the chemical elements necessary for plant growth are available in that mucky underwater world, but their cycle of constructive service can be completed only when certain parts of the plant have access to abundant fresh air and unobstructed light from the sky. So out of that sunken rootstock many astonishingly strong, rubbery stems emerge and head for the surface. At the tips of most of them are the leaf buds, which, when they approach the surface, expand and become those rounded, floating Lily pads with which everyone is familiar. These function through the growing season in the same fashion as do the leaves of all other, more orthodox plants.

The remaining, usually thicker stems originating in the rootstock bear the flower buds. When these ultimately open above the surface and are

All the true **WATER-LILIES** (338) have two types of stems: flower producers and leaf producers. The floating "pads" on the latter help protect the blossoms from rough water. All the stems are several feet long.

339

340↓

ALOES (339) are so accustomed to life in dry regions of the tropics and subtropics that they are harmed by watering except during their active growing season. The sap of some species has medicinal value . . . The blooms and foliage of **SHELLFLOWERS** (340) are equally ornamental . . . A **BUTEA'S BLOSSOM** (341) may be either orange or scarlet.

34

342

343

One peculiar trait of the **BOTTLE-BRUSHES** (342, 343) is the way their flower clusters encircle the twigs which continue growing and producing leaves beyond them. Their popular name is well justified by the appearance of this strange blossom and twig combination. The second of these photographs is a very close-up view . . . **BOMBAX** (344) is sometimes called Silk-cotton Tree because the bark of some members of its tribe yields commercial fibers such as Kapok. The individual blossoms, which are about six inches long, are either red or white, depending on the particular species. Its common name comes from the silky or cottony appearance of the capsule which contains the seeds.

344

ready for pollination and ultimate seed production, they are safeguarded against water damage by their own floating ability plus the wave-calming action of the colony of pads which closely surrounds them.

In Florida and other parts of the Deep South the stiff, spiny leaves and red or yellow blossoms of the Aloes are often featured around public buildings and in parks. Frequently they grow in large pots rather than the open ground, so that they can be more easily moved to safety if a severe cold wave heads their way. Most of them are guests from Africa, where some of the fifty or more species have grown wild for countless centuries. At one time they were highly popular greenhouse oddities.

Shell-flowers, from India, Malaya, and thereabouts, are considerably more gracious in habit. The largest kind attains a height of a dozen feet and its comparatively narrow leaves are almost two feet long. The whole plant sets a fitting stage on which to display those strange streamers of crinkled, many-colored flowers.

Of far larger stature is the Bombax, a native of about the same Old World region. It has been planted here and there in southern Florida, where

345

its large red blossoms, as much as four inches long, are clustered near the ends of the branches, where they put on a spectacular display. In its homeland Bombax ultimately becomes a tree seventy-odd feet tall. One of its best-known although distant cousins is the New World Balsa, or Corkwood, from whose light, buoyant wood the Indians of the high Andes construct curious rafts and our own small boys build model airplanes and other toys.

In Florida also, as well as in the warmer parts of California, various species of the Australian Bottle-brushes, or Callistemons, are frequently grown out of doors. They comprise a dozen or so shrubs and trees of various heights and outlines with long, slender leaves and myriads of small cream-white to red flowers in cylindrical masses at the tips of the twigs. The stamens of each blossom project well beyond the petals with the result that the whole cluster strongly suggests a domestic Bottle-brush.

346

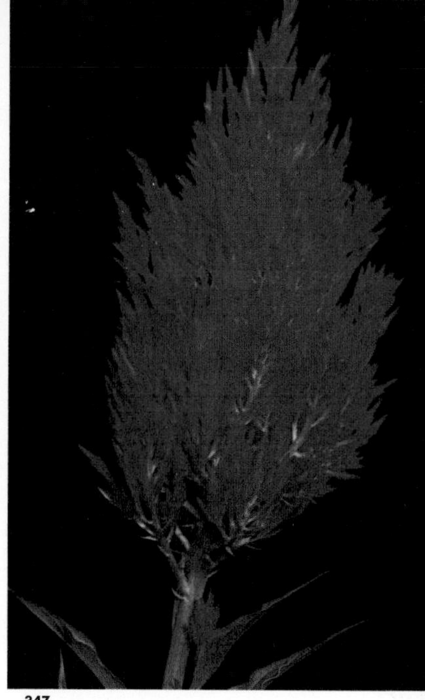

347

COCKSCOMBS (345) are grown in gardens almost everywhere in both hemispheres. This is a view of them in Hong Kong where the climate is definitely tropical . . . Close-up views of **COCKSCOMB** (346, 347) flower heads disclose a wide variety of curious textures.

When the flowers have gone, the core of this "brush" is covered with little decorative seed cases which cling there long after they have opened and scattered their ripe contents. And, for still another surprise, the twig they encircle keeps right on growing beyond them as if it were the twisted wire handle of a real brush protruding in the wrong direction.

Out of India and Burma comes a small group of trees and hard-stemmed vines as odd as any plants the tropics can show. These are the Buteas, whose brilliant crimson blossoms grow in startling groups and, when dried, are capable of yielding a yellow or orange dye. With us, however, their chief value is the part they play in helping to make our Deep South a floral fantasy land.

Red in leaf as well as flower, the five-foot Love-lies-bleeding, or Tassel-flower, seems to symbolize a short and gaudy life such as only the tropics can provide. Yet this astonishing plant has done equally well for years in the sunniest parts of temperate gardens provided its seeds are sown in the spring. The first sharp autumn frost puts an end to its show, and indeed to the entire plant. One marvels that so much can be achieved in so brief a time.

A comparable display is staged with the same speed by the Cockscomb tribe, although most of its members are somewhat shorter at maturity. They too are old-fashioned favorites, with some of their most impressive forms being due in large part to the efforts of plant hybridizers. A few of the thirty-odd true species are found wild in the American tropics, but the bulk of the modern types are traceable primarily to India.

There are two main natural classes of these exotic flowers. The first one, whose individually small blossoms are massed in curiously formal, distorted patterns suggestive of a cock's comb or crest, is the reason for the

348

349 ↓

350 ↓

351

LOVE-LIES-BLEEDING (348), in the Garden of Gethsemane, makes an incredible display for an annual plant . . . The Cockscombs, also, are one-season annuals and long-time garden favorites. This is an example of the **PLUMED COCKSCOMB** (349) . . . **CRESTED COCKSCOMBS** (350, 351, 352, 353) lend themselves to a wide variety of garden settings.

352 ↓

353 ↓

354

357

The true blossoms of a **BANANA TREE** (354) are hidden inside what might be called a master bud. This is located at the end of a heavy hanging stem which grows longer as the flowering season progresses. As it does so the huge terminal bud produces more and more groups of blossoms and thereby increases the number of fruits above it . . . **GOLDEN SHOWER** (355), or Candle Bush, is so dramatically handsome when it comes into blossom that it stands in the front rank of the Cassia clan. Under favorable conditions it becomes a strikingly beautiful tree with straight trunk and slender spreading branches . . . The **CYCADS** (356) are not true flowering plants in the modern sense, yet they are extremely decorative by reason of their glossy, palm-like foliage. In the case of a male plant such as this one the peculiar cone-like mass of scales produces only pollen . . . **RADERMACHERIA** (357), from southeastern Asia, reaches a height of twenty feet or so and blossoms gorgeously . . . The opening flower buds of a **MANGO** (358) seem much too small for the production of those big, luscious fruits which succeed them. It rates as one of the most important food-producing trees in the tropical and subtropical regions of both hemispheres.

355

356 ↓

358

whole group's popular name. In true garden parlance these fowl-like fellows are referred to as the Crested Cockscombs.

The second section is quite different in appearance. It is characterized by feathery or plumy flower masses, some of which are decidedly informal in their effect. Despite the suggestion of similarity between Cockscombs and Love-lies-bleeding the latter scorns good, rich soil while the former demand it!

In this country, as well as abroad, Cockscomb flowers are often dried for winter use as indoor decorations. This sounds simple enough, yet only by taking specific steps can the best results be obtained. The first one is to cut the stalks when the blossoms are covered with dew. Then set them upright in an empty jar and leave them in an airy, dry, shady room for three days. Next, hang them upside down until they are completely dry and ready for use.

Do you wonder if gardeners actually go to all this trouble? Yes, many of them do. For truly successful gardening, you see, is often the outdoor hobby of naturally meticulous people.

Any way you choose to take them, the tropical and subtropical Cycads are peculiar. Some people call them Sago-palms, but they are not even distantly related to Palms despite the appearance of their curving, stiff-leaved fronds. Only the male plants produce anything that might be called flowers. Even these are infinitely small and form a mass somewhat like a glorified Pine cone.

Two Ancient and Honorable Guests

Historically these extremely primitive plants were going strong before any true flowers came into existence. That dates them back about 200,000,000 years, when even dinosaurs were still no more than a gleam in Evolution's eye. Seeds, as we think of them, lay somewhere in the future. Plant multiplication was accomplished chiefly by microscopic spores. And, as though to prove their confidence in ancient ways, the Cycad we grow in our modern greenhouses and Deep South gardens still follows a slight modification of that routine which prevailed so long, long ago.

It has been well said that the Mango is of greater importance to the people of tropical lands than the Apple is to those who live in the temperate parts of North America. This is particularly the case in southern Asia where this handsome fruit has been known and grown since the beginning of recorded time. During the past couple of centuries it has also become a leading product of the New World tropics. Many new varieties have been developed which are larger and far more pleasing to the taste than any of their early ancestors.

The most important Mango species appears to have originated in India, Burma and perhaps Malaya. It is an erect or sometimes spreading tree capable of reaching a height of eighty feet, and its leaves may be more than a foot long. Sometimes the fruits reach a length of six inches.

359

361

All Orchids are odd and often as utterly fantastic in form as is this tropical **SLIPPER ORCHID** (359). Members of its group grow on the ground instead of on tree branches like many other Orchid types. They are often called Green Orchids and their blooms last a long time after being cut . . . The **ROYAL POINCIANA** (360, 362) is one of the world's most famous flowering trees in Florida as well as other suitably warm regions. It thoroughly deserves its other popular name of Flamboyant. Its great blossoms are unique in the obvious contrasts present in their structure . . . The well named **CROWN OF THORNS** (361) belongs to the tropical division of the great plant genus known as the Euphorbias. One of its famous cousins is the Poinsettia. The whole group contains about one thousand distinct species. Nearly all these grow naturally in dry, sunny places and some are found only in regular deserts. Crown of Thorns is one of the few kinds whose brilliant color makes it worthwhile in the Deep South.

360 ↓

362

Greenhouses in the North and gardens in southern Florida are the best locations in the United States to see the cute little **PENTAS** (363), introduced from its native African home. It seldom exceeds a height of two feet, yet its tubular pink or sometimes purplish flowers are as much as an inch long. This is about the only one of its genus that is cultivated.

363

We can leave that cheery subject and come to two kinds of Cassia trees that are often seen flowering out of doors in middle and lower Florida as well as California. One of them is the Golden Shower, or Pudding-pipe Tree, whose yellow blossom sprays are followed by seed pods a foot or more long. It is this species, a native of India, that yields the Cassia pods used in medicine. The other one, called Pink Shower, is quite similar in appearance except for the color of its flowers and its much shorter pods.

Occasionally, too, different species of Cassias are imported by individuals in search of new flower sensations. In many instances it is impossible to pin-point their country of origin, since Cassias inhabit virtually all of the world's tropics and there are close to four hundred species of them.

From regions farther south, largely the Malay Archipelago and the Philippines, comes a group of fifty-odd species and numerous varieties often called Slipper Orchids because of the peculiar form of their lower central portions. Almost invariably the "slippers" are set off by a pair of long, lateral sepals topped with a single shorter one that stands upright as though it were keeping an eye on the whole design.

These strangely exotic flowers have long been familiar to botanists, but only in comparatively recent years have they attracted much public attention. Nowadays they are a notable potted-plant feature in large flower shows and a considerable number of private greenhouses. It is a curious fact that they are rather easy to manage under suitable conditions and are almost continuously in active growth.

Another greenhouse and warm-climate garden oddity, this time from Madagascar, is the so-called Crown-of-Thorns. Its stiff, four-foot stems are heavily armed with inch-long spines which naturally suggested its popular name. The showy red bracts (the true flower parts occupy only the central portion) are its chief attraction. They are almost always in evidence but put on their biggest show during the winter months.

Madagascar has come through with a far more spectacular triumph in the person of the Royal Poinciana, or Flamboyant. This magnificent tree, which is wide-spreading and may reach a height of forty to sixty feet, is one of the priceless features of frost-free regions such as Bermuda, the West

364 365 366 367

Indies, southern Florida, and Southern California. Its individual scarlet and yellow blooms measure three or four inches across. They are followed by dangling, beanlike pods as much as two feet long.

Out of tropical and southern Africa comes a pretty little shrub called Pentas whose long-tubed blossoms form an irregular head about three inches broad. Their color varies from lilac to pink and even rosy purple. It is a charming midget only a foot or two high, justly favored for outdoor planting in the Deep South. Once in a while, too, it shows up in a northern greenhouse.

It is a toss-up whether the flowers we know as Globe Amaranths should be considered as belonging to the East or the West, in as much as they are found in the wild state in numerous tropical regions of both hemispheres. This clearly indicates their hot-country heritage and its implications of choosiness with respect to environment. Yet these showy plants are grown successfully in many northern gardens where, throughout the summer

The stiff-stemmed **GLOBE AMARANTH** (364) flowers serve three worthy purposes, since they are equally good for garden display, cutting, and drying for winter decoration indoors . . . There are several general similarities between **STRAWFLOWERS** (365, 366, 367), and Globe Amaranths, such as strong stems, blossom colors, short lives and suitability for cutting and drying . . . These dramatic, summer-flowering **GLORIOSAS** (368) are grown in pots.

368

months, their white, purple, rose, or orange blossom heads put on a memorable display. Most of the varieties reach a height of about a foot and a half, but one less ambitious kind stops at only half that size.

Such non-tropical success results from the fact that the Globe Amaranth, like Love-lies-bleeding and Cockscomb, grows quickly from spring-planted seeds and reaches flowering age within two or three months. For this brief period the plants find enough warmth in northern summers to satisfy them. They would not live more than one season anywhere, since they are annuals in the strictest sense of that term.

The Helichryssum, or Strawflower, out of Africa and Australia, fits into the same category of garden performance. It grows twice as tall as the Globe Amaranth and, like the latter, its blooms are often dried for winter indoor decorations. In case you are interested in this desiccated and admittedly dust-collective purpose, it is *not* necessary to wait until the flowers are covered with dew before you cut them!

A few years ago American amateur gardening circles went harmlessly demented over a strange, exotic beauty that was glamorously billed as the Glory-lily. It was quite tall and slim-stemmed, and as it approached the flowering stage it helped support itself by tendril-like extensions of its own graceful leaves, which twined around anything they touched. No true Lily has any such bizarre habits, but that was beside the point. What really mattered was the airy, delicate beauty of the huge, varicolored blooms when they finally opened. Their general conformation certainly suggested Lily flowers, but no Lily could match their flutings, curves, and smoothly flowing lines.

Now that the early name Glory-lily has been largely discarded in favor of the more accurate Gloriosa, this floral masterpiece from Africa and Southern Asia has made a firm place for itself in our horticultural affections. In the North it is best grown in greenhouses or—by experienced folk —in well-ventilated dwelling houses. For these purposes the tuberous roots are planted in pots from January to March for summer and autumn bloom. But in the warmer parts of California and the Deep South Gloriosas can

369

CHINESE HIBISCUS (369) flowers and all their relatives have a peculiar method of assuring the formation of an ample number of seeds to provide future generations. From deep in the center of the blossom, just above its point of attachment to the stem, a long, tapering column rises. The center of this is partly occupied by the flower's ovary which is furnished at its tip with five minute stigmas that appear in the close-up photograph as round spots at the ends of short stems. Below these are numerous stamens, each of which produces pollen. Fertilization occurs within the ovary after grains of pollen have come into contact with the stigmas. The resultant long, oval seed capsule is divided into five segments, coinciding with the five stigmas.

be grown permanently in outdoor gardens. An intriguing part of their nature is that their most brightly colored blossoms are produced only where there is an abundance of sunshine. Wherever and whenever they are obtainable the blooms and foliage are a good flower arranger's delight.

The name Chinese Hibiscus automatically calls to mind one of the most fabulous displays of flower beauty to be found in Southern California and southern Florida. This fast-growing shrub, generously furnished with glossy leaves and a wide range of showy flowers, was introduced to the Western world from Southern Asia more than a century ago. As we mentioned on an earlier page, its single or double blossoms, sometimes almost six inches wide, come in an amazing variety of pinks, reds, and whites, with new colors and combinations appearing almost every year. Where these innovations will eventually lead is anyone's guess, for Hibiscuses seem to be endlessly resourceful when supplemented by man's ingenuity.

The Hibiscus group as a whole, together with its complexity of relatives, might well be described as citizens of the world. Few temperate and tropical lands are without its representatives. A full breakdown of its membership would show that some are trees, others shrubs, and a large number are garden-type flowers that may last from two to many years. Yet through them all runs the family trademark of that curious columnlike group of central stamens, so immediately obvious and at the same time fascinating under the closest of detailed study.

The warmer regions of the Orient have furnished us Westerners with many fantastic flowers, great and small. Yet it is doubtful if any of them are stranger than the Chinese Hat Plant, whose combined blossom and fruiting parts actually show some resemblance to a miniature old-time Chinese hat. Botanically it bears the jawbreaking title of *Holmskioldia sanguinea,* the first half of which commemorates one Theodor Holmskiold, a Danish nobleman and scientist who died in 1794. The second half, of course, refers to the somewhat blood-red color of its flowers.

370

372

When the **HIBISCUS** (370, 371, 372, 373, 374) seeds are ripe the segments separate, spread outward and, as they dry, split open and release the seeds which fall separately to the ground and, if they are lucky, develop into new plants. This characteristic of stamen and stigma relationship in the Hibiscus group can be seen in all of the photographs on these pages except the double blossom (373) and the partially double (371) . . . In the case of (374) the pistil-stamen image at the right is merely a shadow cast by the actual column at the bottom of the flower. Expert hybridizers have worked on the Hibiscus for a long time, which is the chief reason for its large number of varieties. Some years ago thirty-odd new hybrid forms were sent into Florida from Honolulu alone, and still their number continues to increase.

373

371 ↓

374 ↓

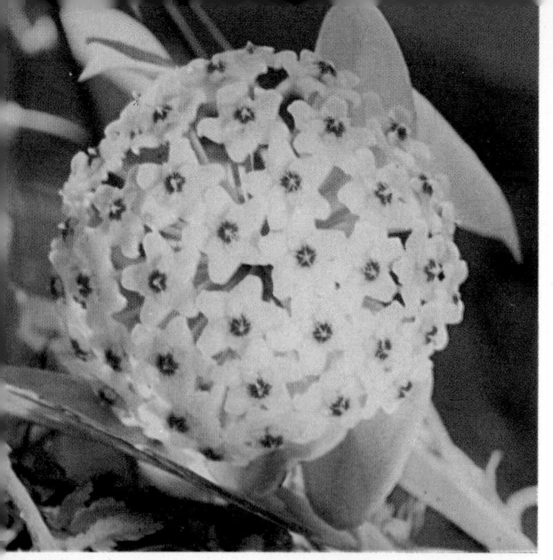

375

378

376

The **WAX-PLANTS** (375, 376), whether grown indoors in the North or outdoors in the Deep South, are particularly notable for their thick, shining leaves and heads of handsome, wax-like blossoms. In the case of this kind the many individual flowers are also very fragrant. It does well as a house plant if provided with a large slab of bark to which its stems can fasten themselves . . . When a **CHINESE HAT PLANT** (378) comes into bloom it is easy to believe that something has happened to its flowers. Each one projects an inch or so beyond the center of a solid cone which actually does have some resemblance to the hats Chinese farmers wear when working in the rice fields . . . This is one of the several forms of **GARDEN BALSAM** (377) that can be grown today in a considerable number of colors and forms, thanks to the hybridizers . . . **PATIENCE PLANT** (379) belongs to the same clan as the Garden Balsam, although its blossoms are somewhat different in appearance. Both of them have the family habit of firing their ripe seeds through the air.

377 ↓

379

There are believed to be only three kinds of Hat Plants, divided between Africa and Southern Asia. This one comes from the subtropical parts of the Himalayan region where, on its home grounds, it grows as a straggling bush from ten to thirty feet in height. Its three-inch leaves are evergreen and help a little to modify its ungainliness.

Probably the best chance in America of seeing a Chinese Hat Plant in the flesh is in southern Florida or perhaps California, where it is sometimes grown outdoors by specialists in exotic flowers. Greenhouse owners abroad rely on keeping it under glass in order to provide the sort of climate it demands. In neither case is it likely to attain its full potential height.

There Are about 100 Wild Wax-plants

The much better known Wax-plant, or Hoya, is another Oriental whose official name does honor to a horticulturist: Thomas Hoy, who once was the Duke of Northumberland's gardener. It is native in Southern China and southward and has been a favorite house plant for many years in this country as well as abroad. Folk who have greenhouses sometimes train it to grow on lattice supports attached to the inside of the glass walls. In the Deep South it is often grown as an outdoor oddity which may become a dozen feet or more high. In that region it is almost continuously in flower.

The chief attraction of Wax-plants lies in their waxlike, extremely fragrant white blossoms with pink centers. In northern houses these are produced only during the summer months. One variety has thick, white-edged leaves which improve its year-round appearance considerably.

A Wax-plant ranks as a climbing or trailing evergreen shrub. Unlike most shrubs it produces short, aerial rootlets along its stems which habitually attach themselves to tree bark or any other surface which offers a supporting grip. When gardeners grow it in a pot or tub, they usually set a long slab of bark-covered wood in the soil to furnish this grasping opportunity and at the same time provide an appropriate background.

There are probably about a hundred kinds of Wax-plants growing wild in the vast stretch of tropics from Asia to Australia. Many of them are known only as dried specimens collected by roaming botanists. Such samples often make precise identification very difficult, so it may be a long time before we learn the full story of this curious plant group.

With us the Garden Balsam or Lady's-Slipper, out of India, Malaya, and Southern China, is a genuinely old-fashioned favorite whose face has been considerably lifted through the years. Originally there were some half-dozen wild species of it, offering excellent opportunities for improvements of which the plant hybridizers were well aware. As a result there are now varieties whose showy single or double blossoms embody such colors as rose, blush, white, salmon, and rosy purple. Some of them are delightfully camellia-like in form, and all are freely produced during the single summer season, to which the life of this appealing plant is unfortunately limited.

A close cousin from Zanzibar, customarily called Patience-plant, has po-

380

383

MELALEUCAS (380), which belong to the general Bottle-brush group, have the family habit of bearing flower clusters encircling twigs that continue growing beyond them . . . There are times when one is tempted to think that the **KALANCHOE** genus (381, 382, 384) is a sort of botanical nightmare. All the hundred-odd species which comprise it are complete individualists and do unheard-of things. Some of them produce many baby plants along the edges of their leaves. As these infants grow they send roots out into the air and finally drop to the ground and promptly begin to lead normal lives. As for the blooms, they are fairly reliable about growing in clusters, but some of them face the sky while others droop downward as wearily as if they had lost their last friends. About the only really consistent thing about the group is that practically all its members have rather thick, succulent leaves. As a general rule, the flowers remain in good condition for quite a long time . . . The **IXORA** genus (383) has its puzzles, too, for the unusual reason that many of the garden varieties have been given scientific names by people who were not botanists and had little knowledge of botanical accuracy requirements. But they are beautiful shrubs, for all that.

381

382 ↓

384

tentially longer life but is valued as an indoor rather than an outdoor treasure. Its large flat blossoms, each furnished with an odd, long, upward-curving spur, are always single and vary from white to salmon, pink, rose, and brick-red. Few other stocky, well-branched plants are so consistently generous with their flower displays.

Kalanchoës, too, are justifiably popular house plants. Indeed, some of their hundred-odd species are so appealing they are often on sale in what we called five-and-dime stores during the good old days before those incredible emporiums upped their prices to banker levels. One of the Kalanchoë offerings there is likely to be labeled Life-plant, Miracle-leaf, or Good-luck-leaf and accompanied by a printed sales talk that would make Madison Avenue turn green with envy. Unless the thing is too dried out, it will actually produce new plantlets along its sides or tip—a time-honored habit with many members of this astonishing flowering group.

The cream of the Kalanchoë crop, from the standpoint of color and general attractiveness, has no prevailing popular name. A botanist would identify it as *Kalanchoë blossfeldiana,* admittedly a far less attractive asset than its thick, glossy leaves and spreading heads of enduring red or orange blossoms. Vast numbers of this and somewhat similar forms of the tribe are sold every winter in the North. They rarely fail to brighten the dreariest day if kept near a window where, whenever the sunlight does appear, they will be able to bask contentedly in it.

Far south, of course, these natives of the Old World tropics may be grown out of doors. Many of them are capable of reaching heights of one to three or four feet. Yellow, purple, and red are their principal colors, according to which species you have.

Ixoras Come in Nearly All Colors

Out of India, Java, and other tropical sections of the Far East comes another complex group of very different plants called Ixoras. Among them are small trees as well as shrubs, all with evergreen foliage above which stand striking flower clusters of white, rose, or scarlet. There are more than one hundred and fifty species of them all told, and their home territory is unbelievably vast. Outside of the warmest parts of the States they are strictly greenhouse subjects. Under experienced care they can be made to bloom in flowerpots while still small by comparison with their mature size.

The outstanding features of these exotics are the dimensions and colors of their massed flower heads together with the handsome evergreen leaves below them. Gardeners in lower Florida who know them intimately may show you immense specimen bushes practically covered with flowers during most of the year. Orange-scarlet, white, rose, and salmon—these are just a few of their colors. One variety, a pink, is delightfully fragrant.

Ixoras as a group are remarkably fast growers where conditions are to their liking. Some varieties have been known to reach a height and breadth of more than ten feet in only three years.

385

388

The central mound of a **WATER-LILY** (385, 388) blossom is astonishingly intricate in form, but even its smallest parts play an essential role in the all-important project of seed production. After pollination occurs the flower sinks under water until its seeds ripen and float to the surface. There are innumerable varieties of these worldwide aquatic beauties . . . About eighty kinds of **SCAEVOLAS** (386) are found in the Old World tropics, but most people have never seen even one of them. In our part of the world they are primarily greenhouse plants. Some of them are small shrubs, and the whole family has a habit of producing glistening, round fruits of surprisingly large size . . . The **CRAPE-MYRTLE** (387) is among the finest of the Deep South's flowering shrubs. In spite of its tropical Old World origin it sometimes survives our Middle States' winters if special protection is provided over its root area . . . **POMEGRANATES** (389) start life surrounded by petals, more or less as Apples do. The flowers of some varieties are double and much less starry.

386

387 ↓

38

There are many variations of the Old World tropical Melaleucas, one of which is a white-flowered species which Floridians often call Cajeput, or Punk Tree. It has curiously spongy bark which flakes off in papery pieces and gives the trunk and larger branches a strange attractiveness. Some old specimens of it in the southern part of Florida are thirty feet high. And in one section this same species has spread into the Cypress swamps and made itself perfectly at home there. Perhaps, as far as Melaleucas are concerned, Florida and Australia are not too different in their requirements after all.

History of the Water-lily

More than two thousand two hundred years ago, according to the records of those times, the royal forces of Egypt launched one of their many forays against the equally warlike Assyrians. This one was an unqualified success, for in addition to capturing great treasure in gold, precious stones, ebony, and ivory the raiders brought back a Water-lily plant and a Pomegranate. No doubt both of these were added to the already superb gardens of one of the elite, for even then Egypt was well started on its horticultural career. For all we know to the contrary those two plants were identical with the ones we have today.

It would be impossible to trace the origins of many of the Water-lily varieties of modern times. For scores of years the hybridizers have been busy crossing and recrossing to produce new colors, sizes, petal shapes, fragrances, degrees of hardiness, seasons of bloom, and just about every other quality you could think of. Their basic stock for the development of this work has been drawn freely from the temperate and tropical regions of both East and West.

Much of this notable creative effort has been made here in the United States by private individuals and certain nurserymen, as well as by public institutions, of which the Missouri Botanical Garden is perhaps the leader. It involves far more than mere enthusiasm and a knowledge of plant genetics. There must be special aquatic greenhouses with complete control of temperature where the tender tropical kinds will be perfectly at home. Outdoor pool installations are also essential, since several North Temperate species have been frequently used in hybridizing and would be thrown off balance by too much warmth at the wrong time. And finally, in temperate regions where so much of this work is done, there must be provision for safe winter root storage of those out-and-out tropical sorts to which a touch of freezing could be fatal.

Has all this been worth while? Emphatically yes. Today the Water-lily display pools in scores of public parks and gardens across the country draw crowds of admirers all through the spring and summer. From mid-spring until autumn frost the show continues with scarcely a day of slowdown. It even varies noticeably from hour to hour, for each type of Water-lily has its special times for opening and closing its great blossoms. Nowhere else in the plant world is there such a fast-changing kaleidoscope of living color.

390 391

Gardeners who like soft colors in their flower plantings often choose one or two kinds of **LEADWORTS** (390) even though the subtropical ones may be injured by winter cold . . . **AFRICAN-VIOLETS** (391, 392, 393), are temperamental away from their homeland, but well worth trying.

The recorded history of the Pomegranate may not go back as far as the Water-lily's, but this smallish, bushy tree is no newcomer to the field of cultivated plants. It is a native of Southern Asia and is thought to have been introduced to Southern Europe by the Carthaginians. Theophrastus described it with considerable accuracy some three hundred years before the birth of Christ, and the great Roman naturalist Pliny did likewise early in the Christian era. In both instances the Pomegranates in question may have been almost like those which are so well known in our own South.

Down there, as well as in other regions where Pomegranates are grown in cultivation, they are valued for their foliage and showy, one-inch orange-red blossoms as well as the large, many-seeded edible fruits which develop from them. Many of us have eaten these with enjoyment. But not everyone knows the peculiar uses to which these Apples of Carthage, as they were once called, have been put. The bark of their roots, for example, is the source of a well known astringent medicine. The fruit's rind, for many generations, was boiled to produce a remedy for tapeworms. Oddest of all, the pulp around the seeds themselves is the father of that pink liquid which countless mixed-drink addicts know as grenadine.

A little below the northern limits of the Pomegranate's North American range you enter the realm of the famous Crape-myrtle. It too is a tropical Asian—a marvel of beauty that may become as much as twenty feet high.

It can be truthfully said that the Crape-myrtle's flowers are its fortune. They come by the thousands in late spring and through the summer—great trusses of pink, blush, red, bluish, lavender, or white crinkly blossoms an inch or more across. No wonder that Southerners can never have too many of them, even after all these years.

The origin of the Leadworts is a bit confused in as much as some of them come from temperate China and others from definitely tropical India

392 393

and southern Egypt. One, which is a stand-by blue-blossomed perennial in many of our northern gardens, can stand cold weather with no apparent ill effects except that it is awfully slow about waking up in the spring. Their background is still further confused by the fact that the tribe includes small bushes as well as soft-stemmed kinds that die down to the ground every autumn.

Even the reason for their peculiar family name is uncertain. There is a popular theory that it refers to the lead-colored flowers of some of the tropical species. Some of those who have studied the matter attribute it to a long-lost tradition. In any event, the blossoms are shaped much like those of the Phloxes. Most of them are predominantly blue, while certain tropical kinds are white or red.

In contrast with this, African-violets have just one native country to worry about—tropical Africa. Their only confusion is that they are not true Violets but relatives of the aristocratic Gloxinias. Botanists say that their correct name is Saintpaulia in honor of their discoverer's German family. It was in 1890 or thereabouts that a son who was an imperial district governor in East Africa sent home some seeds or plants to his father, Baron Walter von St. Paul-Illaire. Thereupon the baron introduced them to the director of the Royal Botanic Gardens at Herrenhausen. Few Americans even heard of them until nearly forty years after that event. Yet today they are one of our most-talked-about house plants.

Once the plant hybridizers really got to work on these shade-loving exotics, astonishing things began to happen. The original blue blossom color was broken up. Pink, white, mauve, and purple varieties poured out in ever-increasing numbers. Singles and doubles multiplied incredibly. So

394

397

MADAGASCAR PERIWINKLES (394, 396, 397) are bushy eighteen-inch fellows which have glossy leaves somewhat like those of Laurel. Their perfectly designed blossoms open in a steady procession of whites or shades of rose all summer and until autumn frost finally puts an end to them. Each flower measures more than an inch across. In the Deep South they are dependable perennials, but in colder climates they have to be grown fresh from seed every year. In all cases they are perfect for sunny places which need colorful blankets . . . The one and only **BLUE LACE-FLOWER** (395) reflects great credit on its native Australia with four-inch heads of astonishingly slender blossoms. Whether in the garden or cut and placed in water in the house they are unmatched by any other cultivated plant. Furthermore, these delightful upright growers are easy to manage in almost any sunny garden where the soil is well-drained and reasonably productive. They make themselves at home in temperate as well as hot countries, for they are annuals and so never have to worry about winter cold . . . The **AFRICAN TULIPTREE** (398), or Flame of the Forest, is one of Florida's really stunning showpieces.

395

396 ↓

39

did such novelties as curly, large, little, dark, light, erect, pinkish, bicolored and droopy leaves. But always there remained in the center of each flower that touch of yellow which is the family hallmark.

There are many hundreds of African-violet varieties available today. Growing them to maximum size and beauty is an absorbing hobby in countless homes across the country. There is a thriving African-violet Society, which lays down strict rules for the judging of entries in the numerous important shows. Some of the individual plants competing in such affairs cover a two-foot circle with their thick, downy leaves and dozens of glorious blossoms.

Many authorities assert with complete sincerity that African-violets are easy to grow. This is true—sometimes and for some people. But an impartial investigator touring the innumerable homes where these plants are found would probably find as many failures or near-failures as he would real successes. Should he become curious enough to delve into the causes for such discrepancies, he would reach the conclusion that "easiness" actually connotes incessant fussing and watchfulness. There are temperatures to check and cold drafts to thwart. Bugs and diseases must be combatted and strong sunlight moderated. Too much and too little water are equally harmful, and all applied water must be at least as warm as the air in the room. The soil in the pots where the plants live has to be mixed in accordance with some special formula. And so on and on almost *ad infinitum.*

All hail to the dedicated African-violetists, for their rewards and pleasures are indeed great. And for the rest of us—well, here's hoping!

Three Beauties from Faraway Places

The best known Vinca, or Periwinkle, is an evergreen spreader and its present relative, the Madagascar Periwinkle, is far less self-sufficient. In its tropical fatherland this plant is a dependable perennial, but in northern New World gardens we must grow it fresh from seeds every year. No effort could be more worth while, however, for the large rose or white flowers stand out splendidly against the shining leaves below them. Sunny garden spots in need of mass covering are perfectly served by these erect, eighteen-inch plants from down under.

Australia is the island-continent to which we owe the matchless Blue Lace-flower, a triumph of pale blue daintiness. It is another of those hereditary annuals which are indispensable among gardeners who like to have a good supply of flowers which last well when cut and placed in water indoors. There is no record of this clean, upstanding two-footer ever letting them down. Its form and general effect suggest a refined blue version of that handsome field "weed" which is known widely as Queen Anne's Lace.

There are about twenty-five members of the group to which the Blue Lace-flower belongs. Most of them are Australians, with the rest credited to Borneo, New Caledonia, and the Celebes.

How very different are the glowing orange-red or scarlet blossom sprays of that tropical African Spathodea! Some of the individual blooms com-

399

posing them are four inches long and so oddly formed that one's wonder increases the more closely they are examined.

Indeed, the whole plant is one of Nature's outstanding creations. It is a true tree which, in one of the two or three known species, may reach a height of seventy feet. The evergreen leaf clusters are close to two feet long and bear leaflets a little smaller. In the young stage their undersides are covered with unbelievably delicate down which subsequently vanishes.

The warmest parts of the United States, and also the West Indies, are about the only places on this side of the Atlantic where Spathodeas are to be

400↓

BIRD-OF-PARADISE FLOWER (399), despite its outlandish looks, is not too difficult to grow. It is from Africa . . . **OLEANDER** (400), a Southern choice . . . That **FRIED EGG TREE'S** (401) flowers are prettier than their name.

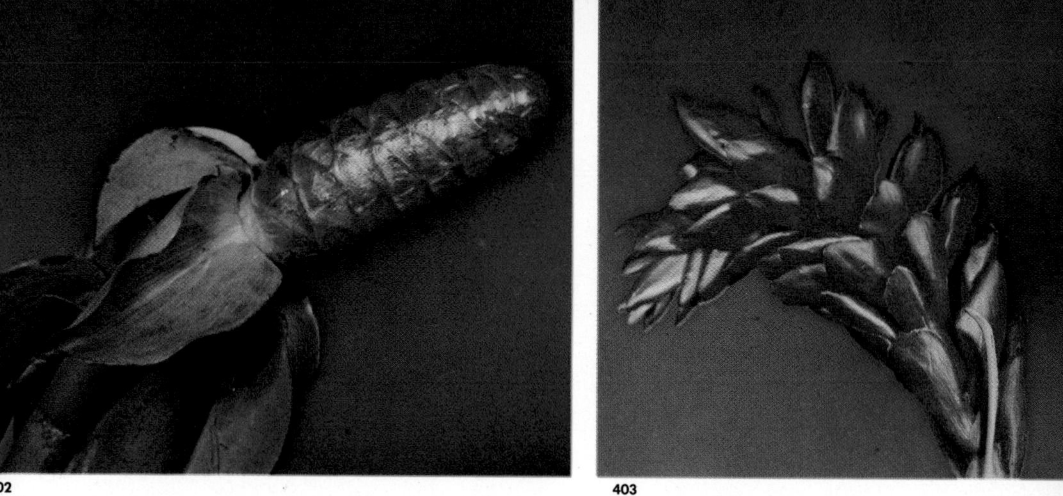

402 403

No one is certain about the exact origin of the tropical **GINGER** (402, 403) group, but several of its members do well in southern Florida. There are about a half-dozen kinds of them, all with aromatic leaves, "gingery" roots and sprays of peculiar little flowers.

seen. They definitely rate as collectors' items in any tree grower's estimation.

The incredible blossoms of the African Bird-of-Paradise Flower defy adequate description. Their lower part is somewhat boat-shaped, while the rest suggests a cross between the mythical flying phoenix and a collection of unruly feathers. The whole assemblage may be almost ten inches long and half as high. The plant has no true central stem—merely a number of stiff, foot-long leaves growing on a few stalks and topped with the blooms.

Oleanders, with their slender evergreen leaves, are immensely popular throughout the Deep South and other comparatively warm sections of the country. Even Northerners value them as summer ornamentals which have to be wintered in greenhouses because of their Mediterranean objections to cold weather. In the South these twenty-foot bushes are magnificent for many weeks after their countless blossoms begin opening in April. The Egyptians knew and prized them in their gardens thousands of years ago.

Northern Africa has given us a very different shrub or small tree whose formal name is Oncoba. Southerners, however, call it Fried Egg Tree because, twice a year, it is covered with white-and-gold flowers suggestive of tasty fresh eggs fried "sunny side up." This peculiar outlander forms a dense, bushy mass of thorny branches and twigs which is impenetrable from the ground upward. It may cover a thirty-foot circle and measure twenty feet in height. In Florida the lower part of this pile is often pruned to make the upper section into a sort of canopy under which you can walk and examine the blossoms closely without fear of being scratched by the spines.

The Common Ginger plant, which probably originated somewhere in tropical Asia, is now cultivated in southern Florida as an ornamental as well as to provide excellent homemade ginger in various forms. It is a rather reedlike fellow three or more feet tall whose oddly shaped blooms are spotted with yellow and purple. The ginger you eat comes from its thick, fleshy roots.

404

405

Outdoors in our southern states, and in greenhouses and large conservatories far to the north, the grace and myriad yellow blossom sprays of **ACACIAS** (404, 405), or Wattles, are as famous as they are unforgettable. There are hundreds of different kinds, hailing from the warm regions of both hemispheres, but Australia is probably their main headquarters. South Africa is alive with them, too, as Kipling knew when he wrote of ". . . the smell of the wattle by Lichtenberg, riding in, in the rain."

Among the flowering trees in California and the Deep South it would be hard to find a group more spectacular than the Acacias, or one more tangled from the standpoint of botanical background. There are at least five hundred true species of them and heaven knows how many varieties scattered through the world's tropics and subtropics. Australia, Southern Europe, Queensland, the East Indies, Chile, the Philippines, Mexico, Tasmania, California, Florida, Missouri, New Mexico, and Texas are all on their list of homelands. Where and when their tribe actually originated are anybody's guess. But there is no question that they have proved useful for many purposes besides ornamentation. Medicines, gums, cattle fodder, soap, and fibers have been made from them. One Mexican species, the Bull-Horn Acacia, even provides snug homes for vicious ants which valiantly defend it against browsing steers and other possible enemies such as overinquisitive people! The Acacia's name is derived from the Greek word for a point or thorn.

All Acacias are alike in having thorny trunks and branches, finely divided leaflets, and yellow to white pea-like blossoms. Often the latter grow in pendent sprays whose grace and beauty are beyond comparison.

Acacias, on the whole, are also notable for their fast rate of growth and short lives. Several kinds have been known to grow ten feet in four months and reach a height of twenty-five feet in six years. They are fully mature at the age of thirty, and begin to deteriorate soon afterward. This is indeed a short life compared with numerous other tree species in various parts of the world which live for a hundred years or more.

406

407

The blossoms of **SCHOTIA** (406) are gorgeously showy from start to finish. There are only a half-dozen species of these shrubs or small trees, ranging from ten to twenty-odd feet in maximum height. The one portrayed here is grown outdoors in southern Florida and occasionally in large northern greenhouses . . . One of the most popular **CLOCK-VINES** (407) in the Deep South is this big-flowered fellow from Bengal in India. It is a very tall, strong climber with individual blossoms a good three inches wide. Normally they are blue with white centers as shown in the photograph, but there is also an all-white variety which is seldom seen . . . **FIG-MARIGOLDS** (408) are among the oddest plants that ever came out of the hot, half-desert regions of South Africa. Their thick, narrow leaves and stems store up the water of infrequent rains, and the whole plant hugs the ground to conserve its energy.

408

The Schotia presented on this page is a native of South Africa and is seen fairly often as an outdoor ornamental in lower Florida and the southern part of California. It may develop into either a shrub or a small tree depending partly on its location.

The Thunbergias, or Clock-vines, are also free-flowering beauties that climb around cheerfully on arbors, porch trellises, small trees, or what have you. There are blues, whites, buffs, and oranges among them, with or without additional colors for good measure. As a rule the blossoms are from an inch and a half to two inches wide with petals of different shapes which may give them a curiously lopsided look.

Fig-marigolds are a god-send to gardeners who have dryish, sun-baked spots where most other worthwhile flowers would fail. There are more than 300 of these tough Old-worlders, most of them South Africans. We even have two species which are natives of California although they are seldom grown under cultivation. Many Northerners grow certain Fig-marigolds as house plants in winter and summer.

Flowers of the New World

TEMPERATE ZONE

A FINE flower garden in full bloom is a cross-section of the world's choicest ornamental plants. North, South, East, and West have contributed to its beauty, often at the cost of infinite human time and effort through many centuries. Here, within prescribed limits of space, Man's artistry and Nature's wonders meet on equal terms.

Yet behind the aesthetic charm of such a scene lie many basic realities. Plant existence is completely dependent on certain intricate chemical elements and their effect on numerous microscopic organisms. Light, air, moisture, and food are as vital to plant lives as to ours. No involved laboratory tests are more sensitive and complex than those which a Phlox or Rose or Iris passes every day of its existence.

Mingled with these and other scientific essentials are semi-human factors which are not always recognized. Plants, like ourselves, have varying "personalities," although they cannot speak, hear, or see as we understand those faculties. Some of them are so vigorous and dominating that, without our equally forthright counteractions, they would soon crowd their weaker and less assertive neighbors to death.

There are finicky ones, too, which sulk or succumb unless they receive the right amounts of water, heat, sunlight, or shade to which they have become accustomed. Even hereditary mortality rates vary enormously among plants. Every good gardener knows that he must be constantly prepared to replace this or that favorite which has reached the end of its allotted road.

And then there are the bugs and blights which a garden's keeper must be alert to foil the minute they appear. Their name is legion and their power of destruction great, despite the fact that they are merely playing their

The most satisfying New World gardens are stocked with choice plants from both hemispheres (409). **LILIES, HOLLYHOCKS, PANSIES, YEWS** and others from the East thrive beside Westerners like **PHLOX** and **PETUNIA.**

410

411 ↓

412 ↓

North American ancestry predominates among the **GARDEN COLUMBINES** of today (410, 411, 412, 413, 414, 415). Some of the countless hybrids have a bit of European blood in their veins, but the most graceful and vari-colored forms are based chiefly on species from our West. It is entirely possible that the structural and color range covered by these hardy, long-lived hybrids will be further extended in the years to come as a result of bringing in western wild species which have not yet been used in the crossings made by plant breeders.

413

proper parts in Nature's vast web of life. When plants are growing in their normal wild environments, these conflicts usually remain in acceptable balance. But the massed conditions in a pleasing man-made garden create complications which, in effect, are abnormal.

So beneath the loveliness and universal appeal of a flower garden there is much more than meets the eyes of the uninitiated. Perhaps, after all, a true gardener is born rather than made.

In electing the Columbine clan to open the New World portion of this book we have been influenced by the fact that no other flowers are such dainty garden features when spring merges into summer. This is surely their major contribution, yet not the only one. Even before the buds appear a delightful mat of soft fluted leaves takes form over the plant's base and, growing taller and wider, often persists until autumn days arrive.

Columbines in their wild state range through much of the temperate world, but the exquisitely elongated "spurs" of our leading modern hybrids are predominantly the contribution of Western American species. In some instances these fascinating appendages attain a length of three or four inches. Always they are the essence of slender grace.

Every Columbine's spurs are functional as well as appealing to the eye. In the tip of each one there is a drop of clear, sweet nectar which is eagerly sought by the long, hollow tongues of hummingbirds and the equally mar-

414↓ 415↓

416

419

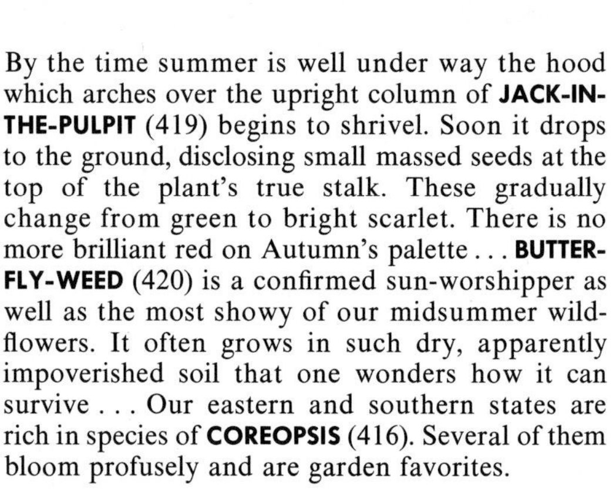

By the time summer is well under way the hood which arches over the upright column of **JACK-IN-THE-PULPIT** (419) begins to shrivel. Soon it drops to the ground, disclosing small massed seeds at the top of the plant's true stalk. These gradually change from green to bright scarlet. There is no more brilliant red on Autumn's palette . . . **BUTTER-FLY-WEED** (420) is a confirmed sun-worshipper as well as the most showy of our midsummer wild-flowers. It often grows in such dry, apparently impoverished soil that one wonders how it can survive . . . Our eastern and southern states are rich in species of **COREOPSIS** (416). Several of them bloom profusely and are garden favorites.

417

418 ↓

420

velous watch-spring proboscises of many butterflies. All of these creatures, in the course of sipping the sweetness from flower after flower, inadvertently transport pollen grains which help swell the crop of small glistening seeds which are the Columbine's sole means of perpetuating its kind.

Two Unique North American Natives

No woodland wildflower is more cheerfully welcomed in the eastern half of the United States and Canada than Jack-in-the-pulpit. It bears little resemblance to a true flower, but fancifully suggests a thin, ascetic preacher by the name of Jack standing erect in the shelter of a curiously striped and hooded pulpit. Although he does not look it, he is covered with the only actual blossoms the plant possesses. The rest of the display serves merely to attract insects and afford a measure of protection from rain.

In open fields fully exposed to sunlight the hot days of July bring out the startlingly brilliant blossom heads of the Orange Milkweed or Butterfly-weed. Sometimes they are held a good three feet above the ground—a perfect height for the parade of butterflies which visits them day after day. The plant's numerous stiff, hard stalks carry a sticky white sap suggestive of diluted canned milk. In September hundreds of seeds escape from their opened pods and sail far away, each equipped with a parachute of silvery threads lighter than any gossamer. This rugged, long-lived native American occupies the same geographical region as the Jack, although its preferred environment differs.

The Catalpas are among our showiest New World trees and consequently are widely planted in northern as well as southern regions. Most of them are capable of growing at least fifty feet tall and bearing scores of eight-inch spires of bloom at their branch tips. The petals of these clutter the ground briefly when they fall.

Through our eastern and midland regions as far west as Texas the broadly branching Wild Indigos, or Baptisias, open their spires of pea-like blossoms at various times during the summer months. Several of them which reach a height of two or three feet are often grown in gardens. The showiest of these, and the most popular, is a blue-flowered species from Pennsylvania and westward. Most of the clan sport blossoms of either white or yellow.

Widely separated regions of the South are the original sources of some of our showiest and most dependable annual garden flowers. They are grouped under the general name of Coreopsis and grow to a height of one

Two dozen or so kinds of **BAPTISIA** (417) grow wild in the eastern half of the United States. Their blossoms vary somewhat in color but are always succeeded by regular pods filled with seeds. Soon after these ripen the entire above-ground part of the plant turns black. But the roots remain alive and send up strong new shoots the following spring . . . The **CATALPAS** (418) produce seed pods, too, sometimes as much as eighteen inches long. These look so much like gigantic String Bean pods that their parents are often called Bean Trees.

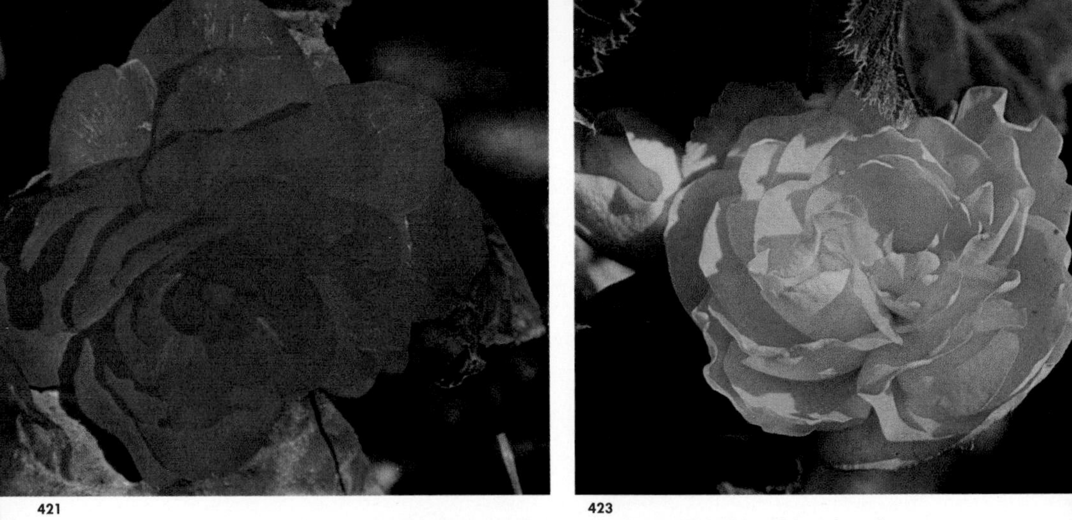

421 423

The glamorous **TUBEROUS BEGONIAS** (421, 422, 423, 424) of today are essentially cultivated hybrids derived from numerous species and natural varieties of which the great majority are native to the temperate mountainous regions of South America. The examples shown on these pages are only a small fraction of the available kinds.

to three feet. All summer they are gay with single or double blossoms an inch or more wide—yellows, oranges, crimsons, and mahogany browns in endless combinations.

The little South American republic of Bolivia, home port of the astounding Tuberous branch of the mighty Begonia family, reaches so close to the equator you would expect it to have a tropical climate. However, its location high in the Andes Mountains puts much of it in the temperate class. It is a perfect demonstration of how altitude can conquer latitude.

These spectacular plants have surged into the front ranks of America's ornamentals only in rather recent years. England and Europe, on the other hand, have known and prized them for nearly a century. Our tardiness in doing the same probably resulted from rumors that they are extremely difficult to grow. The plain truth is that they come well within the capabilities and equipment of anyone who takes the trouble to ascertain their basic needs and then treats them intelligently.

422↓ 42

425

426

Single as well as double blossoms are to be found among the present-day **TUBEROUS BEGONIAS** (425, 426, 427, 428). All of them depart from the habit of Begonias as a whole by growing from roots which look almost like irregular bulbs. They remain in bloom for an amazingly long time, especially during the summer months.

No other plants that grow from bulbs or bulblike tuberous roots can surpass the blooms of these Begonias in variety of form and color coupled with an exceptionally long flowering period. Their individual blossoms range from a gratifying three-inch diameter to an incredible one of eight inches. The variety of petal types and arrangements is all but endless, and so are the hues they represent. Blue and its closely associated tones are the only colors that Tuberous Begonias cannot achieve.

From July until frost the Tuberous Begonia is at its flowering best in shady outdoor places. For such locations many people start the roots in flowerpots indoors during early spring and move them outside, pots and all, when the weather has become warm. It is equally feasible to keep them in a sunless place indoors and enjoy their beauty for many weeks.

Flowering Dogwood, which grows naturally in woodlands from Maine to Florida and westward as far as Minnesota and Texas, is often hailed as America's finest flowering tree. Its countless blooms are usually three to

427 ↓ 428 ↓

430

431

432 ↓

The enormously popular American **FLOWERING DOGWOOD** (429, 430, 432) is only one of a large tribe composed of shrubs as well as trees and containing members scattered through much of the northern hemisphere on both sides of the Atlantic. The smallest of all is a lovely five-inch midget native to our northern tier of states . . . One of the Asiatic tree kinds is the **KOUSA DOGWOOD** (431), which flowers later than our own beloved species and produces its seeds in compact clusters which remind one of ripe but rather undersized Strawberries. This hardy Oriental deserves greater use in this country than has yet been accorded it, for it prolongs the Dogwood season considerably in addition to being thoroughly attractive on its own account.

four inches wide and vary from pure white to magenta pink. In deep woods it may reach a height of forty feet, almost twice its usual stature.

The popularity of this wholly American tree is richly deserved. Every month in the year brings out at least one of its stellar attractions. The first great display comes in May, when the four little lavender-gray bracts which have protected its true flower buds all winter separate at the top and then expand laterally into the famous "petals." Before they fade and fall they will have served their second purpose of attracting insects that will insure pollination of the collection of tiny true flowers in the center of their circle.

By late August the stage is set for a major return performance. The bunches of true flowers have been replaced by oblong green fruits which already show traces of the brilliant coral red which will be theirs in another month or six weeks. By that time, too, the lustrous five-inch leaves will be a dull crimson against which the fruits flame unforgettably. And finally, all winter long, the bark of twigs and small branches is a soft gray lavender.

As you examine the close-up photograph of the Dogwood blossom, you will notice that the tips of all the bracts are twisted and discolored. These

433

434

are the areas where they were somewhat intertwined during the winter. To their last day they will carry this emblem of the protective service they performed.

The Dogwood race is a large one and widely distributed over the Northern Hemisphere. Most of its members are rather shrubby in character, and some have brightly colored bark. One, a delightful midget of the north country in the Old as well as the New World, is only a few inches high. By way of comparison with our own Flowering species we are introducing a photograph of its worthy Japanese and Chinese counterpart, the Kousa Dogwood. You will notice the marked difference between the shape and carriage of the bracts belonging to these two kinds. Besides this, Kousa's fruits quite closely resemble small, roundish strawberries.

Many of the Dogwood group have served strange but useful purposes through the years. Their family name comes from the fact that a decoction made from the bark of one species was used in England to wash dogs suffering from mange. The fruits of another are an old-time food of the Eskimos. The dried bark of our own Flowering Dogwood has furnished an efficient tooth powder, and the broken ends of its twigs served many Southerners as toothbrushes during the War Between the States and the trying "reconstruction days" which followed it.

To partly shaded places from Maine to Georgia and Missouri the drowsy months of July and August often bring the pale, stately flower spires of the native Black Snakeroot, or Cohosh. Many American gardeners who love it as a cool accent in their flower border plantings are unaware of the fact that its heavy underground crown and roots have been utilized in the med-

435

436

BLACK SNAKEROOT (433) is perhaps the tallest of our eastern wildflowers, apart from vines, shrubs and trees. It is also very long-lived and completely hardy . . . From its native Pennsylvania the bright little **GOLD STAR** (434) is sometimes transplanted into gardens . . . Rocky woodlands are the home of the beloved old **DUTCHMAN'S-BREECHES** (435), one of the first native flowers to come into spring bloom . . . This **COREOPSIS** (436) has never lost its place among America's most favored perennial flowers.

icinal field for generations. It is potentially one of the tallest hardy perennials of its general type, since it occasionally reaches a height of eight feet.

During the same part of the season the gorgeously golden Coreopsis continues the floral display it began in June and may prolong into September. This is a hardy, dependable relative of the shorter-lived Calliopsis. Both are wildflowers in the Southern states and have a tendency to increase their blossom size somewhat under the less competitive conditions of a well-managed garden. Perhaps its unfettered ancestry is one reason why Coreopsis so often pops up in all manner of unexpected places to which its seeds have somehow managed to escape.

Coreopsis is a sun lover and would be definitely miscast in the rocky, well-shaded woodlands where the Dutchmans-breeches is at its best from Nova Scotia to North Carolina and west as far as Kansas. This dainty little wildling is a prime favorite of those who know their woodlands in April and early May, although it seldom survives in cultivated gardens. Only in the general character of its foliage and amusingly inverted "breeches" blossoms does it suggest its kinship with the larger old-fashioned Bleeding-heart, which so many generations of gardeners have cherished.

Gold Star, a well-named perennial wildflower from the southeastern states, is only one of many which gardeners have largely overlooked. Even its admirers admit that it is far less showy than Peonies or Irises, for instance, but it has fully as much "personality" as dozens of popular cultivated favorites. It often blooms when only a few inches high, and at close range the design of its five little petals and their connection with the heart of the flower are captivating.

Dahlias Have a Long History

When Hernando Cortez invaded Mexico in 1519 and founded the colony of New Spain, he discovered that the Dahlia was a long-established favorite in the gardens of the Aztecs. Whether those ancient plants were identical with the wild types which grew among the Mexican mountains at that time is problematical. But drawings made of them sixty years later by one Francisco Hernández, another Spaniard and something of a naturalist to boot, prove that they resembled our modern Duplex and Peony-flowered forms. Hernández recorded, too, that there were many more kinds whose colors varied from white to shades of yellow, red, and purple.

Seeds of those old-time Mexican flowers reached Spain in 1789 and became the first known ancestors of the Dahlias of today. And at about that time the name "Dahlia" was given to them in honor of Andreas Dahl, the famous Swedish botanist who did so much to bring plant order out of chaos.

The history of Dahlias since those bygone days is a strange story of ups and downs. By the year 1810 they had gained widespread popularity in Europe and England. Interest in them soared until, in the 1840s, it reached heights comparable to the great Tulip mania which had swept Western Europe two centuries earlier. Then came a long, slow slide down hill, followed by the upturn which these gorgeous flowers presently enjoy. It is an odd fact that this Old World fluctuation was closely paralleled in America.

There are those who hold that modern cultivated Dahlias outrank all other flowers in the variety of their sizes, forms, colors, effects, and uses. Among them there are huge "cabbages" more than a foot wide and correspondingly thick and heavy; the plants which produce them may be six feet tall and must be tied to strong posts for support. At the opposite end of the scale you find little "bushes" whose trim, elfin blooms suggest miniature, many-colored golf balls. In between these extremes there are broad petals, narrow petals, petals that curl, and petals so tightly rolled that they resemble thin pencils. Throughout the whole size range are tousled blooms and coiffured ones, uprights and floppies, geometricals and fancifuls. A walk through any good professional Dahlia grower's fields at the height of the late summer flowering season is like fantasy land come true.

This immense diversity is a tribute to the genius of plant hybridizers and, perhaps more basically, to the Dahlia's inherent character. No nurseryman can stay in business unless he sells his products to paying customers. Many of the latter prefer big dahlias and gaudy colors, just as others like small, paler-colored ones. It is the latter type of these plants which seems to be gaining fastest at the present time. But who knows what the trend may be a few years hence?

Small and medium-size **DAHLIAS** (437) are so immensely varied in form and color that a mass planting of them can be breath-taking. Gladiolus is one of the few other flowers that will succeed among them by thrusting upward through the Dahlias' strong growth.

438

441

439

440 ↓

442

443

444

446

The **DAHLIA** (438 through 447) is one of those flowering plants which become a virtual cult among gardeners because of their prodigal variety of sizes, colors and forms. In this case the wild plants found in Mexico several centuries ago apparently took a number of different forms, a tendency which, in later years, gave the professional growers a perfect opportunity to expand their variety by hybridizing and re-hybridizing. A second factor in their fantastic success is the ease with which the numbers of most varieties can be increased. The commonest method is to "divide" or separate the peculiar thick roots after the close of each growing season. This often results in two to five or six new plants for every one which was originally planted. Another technique is to cut off young stems and induce them to form roots of their own. These two methods produce new plants exactly like their parents. Finally, the hybridizers achieve all their new varieties by sowing seeds.

445 ↓

447 ↓

448

449

The southern shrub which is known to many as **CAROLINA ALLSPICE** (448) and to others as Sweet Shrub deserves both of these names. It has two delightful fragrances built into it, one in its leaves and the other in its oddly formed and colored flowers . . . Most cultivated **GAILLARDIAS** (449) are based on one far western species. They bloom for many weeks, even from May until autumn frost.

Many of the eighty-odd species of Fuchsia are tropical American wildflowers, but those we grow as house plants in the North and out of doors in milder climates are traceable to only one or two types from Bolivia, Chile, and Peru. Like Dahlias, they were tremendously popular during the middle of the last century and are still valued as somewhat mid-Victorian ornamentals. So many Californians grow them year-round in their gardens that in some sections they are one of the star floral features. Their name stems from Leonhard Fuchs, a German professor of medicine and botanist of the sixteenth century.

Nearly all of the Fuchsias are either shrubs or small trees and inclined to be long-lived. They are fast growers, too, and some are capable of reaching a height of twenty feet or more under favorable conditions. In suitable outdoor climates they are often trained to cover walls and fences where, in full summer bloom, they make stunning masses of greens, reds, and purples.

Another very different New World shrub is the intriguing Carolina Allspice, at home in the higher parts of the Carolinas and southward where the soil is rich on the hillsides and stream banks. When its curious brownish maroon blossoms are warm they are strongly reminiscent of the scent of ripe strawberries. An equally delightful fragrance comes from its leaves when you crush them in your hand. Generations of discriminating folk have planted this fine shrub successfully on their home properties as far north as New York City and even into New England.

Almost every state from the Mississippi westward to the high mountains has its native wild Gaillardias and quite properly boasts about them. Some are annuals and some perennials. All twelve species are worthwhile and

450

451

There are some two thousand cultivated varieties of **FUCHSIA** (450), each with a personal name bestowed on it by the hybridizer who introduced it to the gardening trade . . . **BEE-BALM'S** (451) curious flower heads vary from red to lavender depending on species and variety. The red ones especially attract hungry hummingbirds.

most of them, together with several hybrid forms, are treasured in countless gardens in this country and abroad.

Gaillardias are natural-born showmen. They are graceful, upstanding, and display their red, yellow, orange, and mahogany-brown blossoms steadily from early summer to late autumn. Certain varieties have double flowers as much as two inches across; others are single and a little smaller. The slender stems, which usually raise them a couple of feet above the ground, are clean and springy. All in all, Gaillardias are as useful in the house as in the garden, for they last beautifully when cut and placed in water.

The red-flowered Bee-balm of the Appalachians and nearby regions is far less reticent in its ways. Shade and sunlight suit it equally well, provided the soil is reasonably moist. Its straggly yet showy blossoms, borne at the tops of three-foot stalks, are famous for their attractiveness to hummingbirds and butterflies, which spend many summer hours probing them for the nectar they contain. There is an even more abundant Bee-balm species of similar appearance except that its flowers are pale blue or lavender.

The Sunflower tribe has many merits and some demerits. Most of its members are of North American origin, including the familiar giant which is the state flower of Kansas and is capable of growing from one seed to full maturity in the space of a single season—a matter of perhaps twelve feet. This is the Sunflower which is now grown commercially in many countries for its myriads of large, oval gray seeds. Each of them is loaded with nourishment. Large industries have been developed for extracting their valuable oil in addition to growing them for unprocessed human and poul-

452

453

It is in the center of a **SUNFLOWER** (452) that the highly nutritious seeds are formed. Those of some species are so large that they are widely used for human food and also processed commercially for the oil which they contain . . . **VIRGINIA SPIDERWORT** (453) grows a foot or more high and often escapes from gardens to the sort of woodland surroundings from which it originally came.

try food. Even the plant's leaves, sometimes a foot long and very broad, are harvested for cattle fodder. It would be hard to find a plant with greater versatility in its values. The greatest of these, of course, is the seed crop which can be ruined by inexperienced growers who cut the plants down too soon. They should be left until the seed heads are fully ripe. Then the heads should be cut off and hung upside down in a dry, airy place to dry thoroughly.

The very small true blossoms of a Sunflower, regardless of its size, are massed together so that they form a solid disc surrounded by a single or double ring of petal-like rays. The latter are traditionally yellow—or were until something new and wholly unexpected occurred in 1910. That was the year when Mrs. Cockerell found one strange Sunflower plant growing wild near her home in Boulder, Colorado. It proved to be a freak form of the common yellow Sunflower of the Plains. The remarkable thing about it was that its rays, instead of being the normal yellow, were strongly suffused with red.

The seeds collected from that out-of-order plant marked the beginning of a series of highly scientific breeding experiments which, continuing through the years, resulted in a whole series of garden Sunflowers in chestnut red, bright red, crimson, old rose, lemon, and almost black. Many of these modern types are now available abroad as well as in America. But probably they would never have come to pass if that one roadside plant in Boulder had not happened to catch Mrs. Cockerell's discerning eye.

All the Spiderworts, on the other hand, are Americans. The one most often seen is Virginia Spiderwort from the mid-South. Its violet, purple, pink, or white spring blossoms have made it a popular garden flower across the Atlantic as well as here at home.

54 455

The majority of our garden **GEUMS** (454), with the exception of the small kinds grown in rock gardens, come from a single species introduced from Chile. They reach a height of two feet and bloom freely all summer . . . That long-time favorite, the fragrant **HELIOTROPE** (455) is another worthy ambassador from the mountain regions of western South America. Not all specimens have equal perfume.

The Geums, for which many rock gardeners have great praise, are remarkably widespread in the temperate and cold regions of the world. Chile, Switzerland, Greece, North Carolina, arctic America, and the Rocky Mountains are only samples of the places where they grow wild.

There are marked variations in the general character of these cosmopolitan plants. Trailers, tuft makers, and strong uprights are all represented in the family circle. The one noticeable trait which runs through nearly all of them is the blossom color: shades of either red or yellow. A few species have long, plumy seeds that are delightfully decorative.

For many generations in this country and overseas the Heliotrope has been a stand-by among house-plant enthusiasts and greenhouse owners. The most popular ones are vanilla- or narcissus-scented, a trait which is most frequent among specimens with purplish rather than white blossoms.

Botanists believe that there are more than two hundred and fifty Heliotrope species. The kinds we grow so frequently indoors and sometimes in gardens, however, are thought to be descended from only two Peruvian wild species. Both of these are inclined to be rather shrublike in character, as though they could not escape a trace of the true bush habit which marks some of their cousins.

The mountains of Peru, with an assist from neighboring Bolivia, have also furnished the dramatic Ismene, Basket-flower, Spider-lily, or Peruvian-daffodil. This is one of our finest summer-flowering bulbs. The tubular parts of its fragrant blossoms are about four inches long and their flaring rims narrow into gracefully curved extensions which often remind one of spider legs. The normal color is white, but there is one yellow hybrid variety and another whose petals are exceptionally "spidery." Both of these have blossoms somewhat larger than those of the original species.

456

457

458 ↓

459

The **ISMENES** (456) are among the best bulbs that have come to us from South America. There are several types of them, normally reaching heights up to two feet. Early summer is their flowering season in the garden. Like many of the other bulbs, they can also be made to bloom indoors during the winter . . . Almost any sunny, well drained garden spot satisfies the delightful little **CRESTED IRIS** (457). Give it half a chance and it will thrive for years without any attention except occasional summer watering. By way of contrast, compare its blossoms with one of the **JAPANESE IRIS** hybrids (458) . . . September brings great masses of delicate **JEWEL-WEED** (459) into bloom where the ground is damp or even boggy. The blossoms are so delicately balanced at the stem tips that the least disturbance makes them tremble . . . Our native **CORAL-BELLS** (460) are the delight of gardeners in search of airy effects.

460 ↓

Jewel-weed, an abundant wildflower in moist ground throughout the eastern half of North America, is strikingly fragile-looking in comparison with Ismene. Its orange, brown-spotted blossoms are suspended from such slender stems that the slightest disturbance starts them trembling. The entire branchy plant is so soft and sappy that its ability to reach the normal height of three to four feet seems doubtful indeed. Such an achievement is due partly to the fact that Jewel-weed often grows in such large, dense masses that all the plants in them help to hold each other up.

The name Jewel-weed arose from the silvery bubbles of air which cling to its leaf surfaces when they are held under water. Another of its odd titles, Touch-me-not, is an outgrowth of the startling way its ripe seed pods burst into curly twists when you touch them. The real purpose of this peculiar trait, of course, is to scatter the seeds over an area of several feet instead of dropping all of them in one spot. Many a back-country boy knows the fun of gingerly placing a ripe pod on his tongue so that it quite literally blows up in his face. And he knows, too, that rubbing a handful of crushed Touch-me-not leaves on bee stings eases the pain considerably.

A Nationwide Host of Coral-bells

An even larger territory is claimed by another appealing wildflower group, the Coral-bells, or Heucheras. Their range is from coast to coast and from Mexico to the arctic. Several kinds of them are long-time garden favorites because of their dainty, airy blossoms held well above ground-hugging leaf mats. The tribe as a whole supplies heights running from three inches to two or even as much as three feet.

Coral-bells are as good-tempered as they are pretty. They will grow almost anywhere provided the soil is halfway decent. Full sun and full shade are taken in stride. The months of June and July are the best time for their graceful sprays of flowers in a variety of reds, pinks, and white. Small wonder that flower cutters as well as flower growers never tire of them.

While it is true that most of our Garden Iris types are of Old World origin, temperate North America is by no means lacking in fine kinds of its own. Perhaps the showiest of these are the immensely varied Louisiana Irises, which are still in the experimental stage as far as suitability to northern conditions is concerned.

No such questions bother the self-reliant Crested Iris, which grows wild in upland regions of the southern and midland states. Although only six inches tall, it readily makes itself at home in practically all sunny spots, even those which are subject to bad summer droughts. A strong young clump of it spreads surprisingly fast into a mat which may eventually cover several square yards. In mid-spring its numerous and exquisitely neat blue blossoms touched with gold are a memorable sight. When they have gone the shortish leaves make a creditable showing through the rest of the season.

The mountains of the Northwest, too, are rich in entrancing Dwarf Irises of many kinds and colors. And the lower half of the Mississippi River country comes through with the unique Copper Iris, whose bronzy-red

blooms, a couple of feet above the ground and some three inches broad, bring a fresh color note to the late spring days.

Everyone who enjoys flowers likes to see them growing outdoors, for then they are at their best. It is a less fortunate fact that too many flower gardens are planned and executed along such regimented lines that the plants themselves are little more than masses of impressive color. In the old days of grandiose living these purely formal plantings were striking through their sheer size and magnificence. For most of us that era has rather unfortunately vanished. So what about the present with its unavoidable space limitations in so many instances?

The general answer is that no area is too small to have its thoroughly enjoyable flower display. A thoughtfully planned and maintained border such as the one on the opposite page is the ideal, of course. But may there not be as much true pleasure latent in a single Poppy, Iris, or Lupine plant as there is in a dozen or a hundred of them?

Close Examination Is Rewarding

Every flower whose portrait appears in this book has its own special appeal to those who follow a skilled photographer's advice to "move in very close on it if you are looking for a real surprise." Choose a quiet, sunny day for this experiment and take along a high-power pocket magnifier; there are endless new beauties in textures, lines, and color distributions waiting to be discovered through its lens. As a few examples:

Faint smudges of pollen dust will turn into fields of golden pebbles. The tip of a single pistil becomes a symmetrical design whose perfection would challenge the pen of a master draftsman. Leaf veins are transformed into rivers fed by well-spaced connecting brooks which divide and redivide as they become smaller; these are the streams of life through which the leaf is fed. Colors which seemed dull to the unaided eye take on a haunting translucence impossible to analyze.

There will be undreamed-of animate life, too. Comical little green or blackish bugs, completely harmless, come popping out of blossom centers and twiddle their feelers as they stare briefly with alert red or yellow eyes. Aphids clinging to a stem become herds of impossibly bloated elephants. A wee gray beetle turns into a prehistoric monster. All this and much more are part of the daily world of flowers.

In early June the Drooping Leucothoë of our southern Appalachians opens its sprays of little flowers shaped much like those of Blueberries. In the setting of lustrous, deep green leaves and arching branches their waxy whiteness is perfectly displayed. The tinge of pink which sometimes marks them comes as the last word in daintiness.

Many strong-growing perennial flowers such as **ORIENTAL POPPIES, LUPINES, COLUMBINES** and **BEARDED IRISES** (461) combine well in late spring regardless of their homelands.

462

464

463

465

46

This woodland evergreen shrub is distinctive in its foliage as well as blossom characters. In autumn the graceful, six-inch leaves become a warm bronzy red which lasts throughout the winter. Then, with the coming of spring, they slowly return to green. No human being could be more meticulous about changing costume colors to match the seasons.

Mountain-laurel Is a Sharpshooter

The famed Mountain-laurel is even more enduringly evergreen, although its leaves lack the Leucothoë's change-of-color trait. It is also larger and more rugged and grows wild through a much more extensive wooded area: New Brunswick to Ontario, then southward to Florida and west to Arkansas and Louisiana. Ordinarily its height is anywhere from four to a dozen feet, but in parts of the southern Appalachians it becomes a forty-foot tree.

As the Mountain-laurel's fluted, pink-and-white buds start to open, they disclose a wonderfully ingenious device. Every blossom's central pistil is surrounded by a circle of springy stamens, each of them bent outward to where its tip is held in a special petal notch. When the flower opens wider and approaches maturity, these captive stamens are released and every one snaps up and fires a tiny puff of pollen straight at the waiting pistil. So accurate is their aim that fertilization is practically certain.

Chile furnishes another triumph in the person of Prettyface, or Leucocoryne, a small bulb whose groups of fragrant blossoms on eighteen-inch stems are delightful every spring. In our northern climate it is usually grown as a winter-flowering house plant, but the lower part of the South is warm enough for it to be planted permanently in the garden.

Gay Feather, native in many places from Maine to Florida and Texas, is more accurately known as Liatris. It can take practically any kind of temperate climate and like it. In some places people call it Blazing Star, but that is beside the point. What really counts is that strong, six-foot flower stalk with its head of small purplish or sometimes white blossoms.

The gorgeous Tahoka Daisy, or Purple Aster, is a notable showpiece of the Western mountains from Colorado to Arizona. Its plentiful blossoms often measure more than two inches in diameter. In the clear mountain sunshine their rings of purple to pale violet rays surrounding the golden true flowers massed in the blooms' centers are beautiful beyond words.

Most of the several hundred species of wild Lupines are natives of Western North America. In especially favored parts of that general region

LEUCOCORYNE'S flower heads (462) are exceptionally graceful as each stem bends under the weight of its blossom . . . **LIATRIS** (463) raises its vertical flower stalk higher than the average person's head. It is one of our toughest native Americans . . . Shaded places come naturally to **DROOPING LEUCOTHOE** (464) whose five-inch evergreen leaves turn to rich bronzy red for the winter . . . **TAHOKA DAISIES** (465), pride of our western mountains . . . **MOUNTAIN-LAUREL** (466) is superb throughout the year. Its greatest glory comes when it blooms in June.

467 468 ↓ 4

In their wild state **LUPINES** (467, 468, 469, 470) are enduring plants, but most of the hybrid varieties which are grown in gardens today have sacrificed some of their ruggedness on the altar of exceptional beauty. The finest of all are the Russell Lupines, living proof of one of the greatest plant hybridizing stories ever told. Some of their stalks are five feet tall, with the whole upper half a mass of blossoms. Where the climate and other conditions suit them these hybrids are true garden treasures. Our numerous native Lupines are less spectacular but decidedly worthwhile. One of them, widely known as Blue Bonnet, has been chosen by Texas as its State Flower. Most of the 330-odd known species are North American in origin. A few of these grow as regular shrubs. Taken as a group, their colors cover a very wide range.

470

they sometimes grow so thickly that the ground for mile after mile is bright with the prevailing blue and white of their blossoms. Only a few kinds are found in our Eastern states, Mexico, Central and South America, Africa, and in places around the Mediterranean Sea.

In view of this predominantly New World background it seems odd that much of the outstanding hybridizing work that has been done on these highly popular plants was accomplished in Britain by a modest, soft-spoken English gardener named George Russell. When he started his experiments in 1911, he had only the natural blue and white-flowered kinds to work with. Yet by 1937 there were scores of breath-taking Russell Lupines in pink, orange-yellow, red, royal purple and gold, apricot, sky-blue, amethyst, and many intermediate tones and shades. Even the size of the flower spires had been more than doubled through the genius of just one quiet little old man.

George Russell's achievements have had a powerful impact wherever Lupines are grown under cultivation. Those who have known only the native wild kinds can scarcely believe their eyes when they see some of the modern varieties in gardens. Yet it must be admitted that not all sections of the United States are climatically suited to their needs. Hot, dry summers are likely to discourage the better Lupine hybrids, notwithstanding the fact that countless generations of their ancestors have met such problems successfully. It may be, too, that those old-timers had the advantage of just the right amount of natural lime in their soil.

Apparently atmospheric conditions are also involved in this gardening difficulty. Today's hybrids, like their forebears, require ample sunshine. But they must also have plenty of artificial watering whenever the soil approaches dryness. Perhaps, after all, their vastly heightened beauty has been won at the cost of some weakening in their inherited toughness.

Magnolias, as a group, are interhemisphere flowering trees or large shrubs of widely varying sizes and types. Our Southeastern states have contributed three of the largest kinds, the most impressive of which bears the somewhat irreverent popular name of Cucumber Tree, presumably because of its

471

It is a curious fact that, although the most impressive and largest flowered Magnolias are native to the southern portions of the United States, the kind which we know best is the hybrid **SAUCER MAGNOLIA** (471) presented here. It appears to have originated in France more than a hundred years ago as a cross between an Oriental tree-like form and another which is more of a bush. This mixed ancestry accounts for its characteristic half-tree, half-bush appearance and its height of only about twenty-five feet. There are about a dozen varieties of it with individual blossoms ranging from five to nearly ten inches in diameter when fully expanded. In the northern States it usually starts to come into bloom in early May. As the colorful seeds ripen they will dangle briefly on slender threads.

peculiar Cucumber-shaped seed heads. In its native range from New Jersey to Georgia and as far west as Illinois and Arkansas it sometimes reaches a height of ninety feet or even more.

Not far behind it in stature is the eighty-foot Southern Magnolia, whose fragrant, pure white blossoms with purple stamens measure anywhere from eight to fourteen inches in width depending on the particular variety involved and the state of its age and health. And the third-place winner in the American group, also with big white, fragrant flowers, is the Bigleaf Magnolia, about fifty feet tall, wide-spreading and equipped with leaves nearly three feet long and one third as broad.

Magnolias, an Expression of Friendship

A number of these large New World Magnolias were introduced into France during the days of the Empress Josephine when interest in America and its affairs was at a high point. One of Her Majesty's particular favorites was a fine old specimen of the Southern Magnolia whose towering size, huge blossoms, and evergreen foliage especially delighted her. It was in France, also, that Magnolias received their family name as a mark of honor to a certain Pierre Magnol, one-time professor at the Montpellier Botanic Garden.

Most of the American Magnolias have pale gray bark and white or whitish blossoms, several kinds of which are deliciously fragrant. For real flower color in this attractive tree group one must turn to the Saucer Magnolia, a Japanese hybrid introduced to the Western world more than a hundred years ago. It is a smallish, shrubby sort of tree with wide-flung branches and scentless flowers that come in a variety of pinks, purples, and rose shades mingled with white. As indicated in the photograph on the opposite page they open early in the spring, even before the leaves appear. It has been highly popular with us for many years and is extremely showy.

All of the Magnolias, regardless of origin and flower color, bloom in the spring. Most of them also have a second brief period of distinction in late summer or early fall, when their peculiar pyramidal clusters of brown or scarlet seeds ripen on the twig tips. Each seed separates from its companions and dangles by a threadlike filament for a time before dropping to the ground. At this stage the trees are often a-flutter all day with robins, thrushes, vireos, and other fruit-eating native birds to whom soft, pulpy, ripe Magnolia seeds are a special treat.

A great botanist has rated the Pentstemons, or Beard-tongues, as a typical North American group. One kind comes from Asia and many grow wild in the cooler parts of Mexico, but that is about the extent of their internationalism. They are lusty, colorful plants and deserve the attěntion of every gardener. The Western states and Canada are their main headquarters.

All Pentstemon blossoms are tubular and carried on straight, spiry stalks from two to three feet tall. Their many-colored petals flare outward prettily, somewhat in the manner of Gloxinias. Such hybridizing as has been done on them clearly indicates that their possibilities in the direction of further garden value are very great indeed.

472 473

The bright yellow, pink, or white Evening Primroses, often better known as Sundrops and Golden Eggs, are more effective in their natural homes than in gardens. This is not because of any inferiority in the size, color, or form of their individual blooms. The trouble is that they open so erratically and last for such a short time that massed effects are difficult to attain. They have a way of coming out in the late afternoon or around sunset, which accounts for part of their name. The synonyms of Sundrops and Golden Eggs are used chiefly in the West and refer to the petal colors of some species as well as a family fondness for sunny places. One Western kind, with a long, abundant succession of big, fragrant pink or white blossoms, forms extensive masses in numerous exposed places among the sandy, apparently sunbaked dunes which flank parts of the Columbia River in the far Northwest.

474 ↓ 475

76 477

PENTSTEMONS (472, 473), if well selected from among the more than 100 native North American kinds, are excellent and dependable garden flowers . . . Although this **EVENING PRIMROSE** (474) is only two feet high it has four-inch flowers . . . The **VIRGINIA BLUEBELL** (475), a woodland American wildflower that is unforgettable when its oddly tinted blossoms open . . . In May the **GREAT SOLOMON'S-SEAL** (476) curves upward in the woods for a yard or more. The slender bell flowers which festoon its stalk seem especially appropriate . . . Raggedy bunches of queer little blossoms top the stout stalks of the low-growing **PACHYSANDRA** (477) as spring gets under way.

Our Western mountains are also rich in Mertensias, delicately blue-flowered and with a tinge of that hue even in their leaves. The majority of them are living examples of pastel coloring at its best. Often they grow in vast colonies of unimagined beauty.

In the East we have only one native Mertensia species, the matchless spring-flowering Virginia Bluebell. It grows wild here and there from lower New York State to South Carolina and Tennessee. Usually its local colonies are in damp woods where the pinkish buds appear before the tree leaves come out. Soon after flowering all the plants die down to the ground and give no further sign of their presence until the following season.

The very small subshrubs known as Pachysandras are also divided between the East and the West. One is a native of Japan. Another grows wild from West Virginia to Florida, and a third kind hails from Western North America. All are used as ground covers in shady places because of their habit of spreading thickly into larger and larger patches. The foreign one and our own Westerner have evergreen foliage, while the species from the Southeast loses its leaves in autumn, as do so many other shrubs.

The oddity of plant names has no limits. For example, it would take some actual earth digging to see the origin of the title Solomon's-seal. It lies a couple of inches underground where the plant's hard, creeping rootstock is marked at intervals with seal-shaped scars each representing the spot where one of the tall annual stems has died. Perhaps the original King Solomon used a seal of similar design.

478

There are at least sixty species of these graceful, arching woodlanders that grow wild in temperate parts of the Northern Hemisphere. The most important American kind reaches a height of three to five feet in its home territory from New Brunswick to Michigan and southward to Florida. Its pendent, greenish-white blossoms open in late spring and are followed by bluish berries.

The Moss, or Creeping, Phlox has come a long way since it was just a simple little country wildflower born among the Appalachian uplands or northward into Michigan and Ontario. Through the years it has won international fame by reason of its needlelike evergreen foliage, profuse spring flowers, and ability to spread its dense blanket over almost any sunny, well-drained place. In the beginning its wide-eyed blossoms were limited to tones ranging from strong magenta down to white, but nowadays delightful

479

MOSS PHLOX (478) and **WOODLAND PHLOX** (479) are two outstanding eastern members of this typically American flower tribe. The former is now available in a number of intriguing pastel shades. Woodland Phlox grows upright for one to two feet. Both species are spring bloomers.

salmons, pinks, and lilacs have been added to the original list. Rock gardeners and all others who seek pleasant plant coverings for cultivated sunny spots of any size welcome this hardy little fellow with delight.

Indeed, the Phloxes as a group are indispensable in ornamental gardening everywhere. There are about fifty true species of them. All are native Americans save for one lone Siberian.

The taller perennial Phloxes which are such stand-bys in almost every summer flower garden have been developed chiefly from a second woodland species native in Pennsylvania and thence westward and southward. Its original flowers were pinkish purple grading down to white. They varied a great deal between these limits, a tendency which has helped tremendously in the development of the large number of colors and combinations present in our modern cultivated plants. If seeds of the latter are given an opportunity to sprout and grow up, the majority of their flowers will revert toward those of the wild forms—an obvious though unwelcome tribute to the vigor of the ancestral stock. After several such generations they will be back where it all started.

An Artist's Palette in Phloxes

A third group of fine Phloxes is the annuals, now available in dwarfs of six to eight inches as well as mediums of about twice that height. These have been developed by careful selection and breeding from a native species of the Southwest known locally as Texas Pride. They are easy to grow, flower profusely, and show an amazing variety of pastel shades as well as the stronger colors. The individual blooms produced by some of these outstanding modern varieties are four times the size of their early antecedents.

Not all wild Phloxes have this erratic color nature. There is one invariable true lilac-blue kind that grows wild in rocky woods from New England southward. It is a delightful spring bloomer about fifteen inches tall and an ornament to any garden where the soil is fairly rich. There is no danger that its descendants will grow up to be color backsliders!

The Evergreen Rhododendrons which are usually seen in the United States and Canada fall into two categories. One of these is partly Asiatic and the other wholly American. Both are magnificent when in flower and are widely used in ornamental plantings large and small.

Probably the showiest ones with the greatest variety of color are known as Catawbiense Hybrids. Their original ancestor came from the southern Appalachian Mountains and was taken to England in 1809. There it was crossed with several other kinds from the Himalayas, including a blood-red species. The resulting plants were subsequently back-crossed to break up their flower colors still further. And finally the Catawbiense Hybrids came back to us with such rainbowlike blossoms as their old grandsire never dreamed of producing.

The pure-blooded Catawba Rhododendron still thrives in uncounted millions among the Great Smokies and in other parts of the mountains from

480

483

481

484

482 ↓

485

486

488

ANNUAL PHLOXES (480–490) are a major section of this All-American plant family. An astonishing variety of types and sizes has been developed by hybridizers in comparatively recent years, utilizing only a single true species growing wild in the Southwest. In several instances even the shape of the petals has been radically altered. More conventional shapes are shown in the blossoms on this page. A few species in the Perennial Phlox group furnish the mainstay of many summer gardens. There are hundreds of hybrids today, most of them reaching a height of two to four feet and flowering through most of the summer and early autumn. Their colors run from pure white to blazing red, thus offering abundant opportunity for selecting hues which will harmonize with other kinds of plants even in the largest flower border. However, the best color scheme may be sadly wrecked if Phloxes are permitted to ripen and drop their seeds, for when the latter grow up their flowers may not match those of their parents.

489

487 ↓

490 ↓

491

American evergreen **RHODODENDRONS** (491, 493) have been widely used in breeding new hybrids . . . **PINXTER-FLOWER** (492), a lovely non-evergreen Rhododendron.

492 ↓

493

Virginia southward. In late May or June vast tracts are unforgettably bright with its big lilac-purple blossom heads.

In the same general region, and much more sparingly as far north as the Canadian border, there is another all-American species with rose-colored and sometimes white flower trusses. This is the so-called Rose Bay, a giant that may become a veritable tree thirty-odd feet tall.

The king of full-blooded American Evergreen Rhododendrons, in the judgment of many experts, is the comparatively small Carolina Rhododendron. This is another of the several species found in the North Carolina hill country, but the only one with pale all-pink blossoms. Its flower heads open in May, well ahead of its cousins, and the purity of their color against the thick masses of neat, dark green and almost glossy leaves is a high spot in any flower lover's year, even though the whole plant is no taller than a man.

Oddities of Rhododendron Life

All of these Hardy Rhododendrons have a curious way of rolling their leaves into cigar-shaped cylinders and pointing them toward the ground whenever the temperature falls below the freezing point. This is a cold-weather protective measure to avoid undue loss by evaporation of that stored internal moisture which is essential to life and cannot be replaced while the roots are in a virtually dormant state. Without such a precaution the whole bush might be so weakened it would be dead by spring.

The smallest of all Rhododendrons is the Lapland Rose Bay, a ground-hugging mite with quarter-inch leaves and purplish blossoms of scarcely larger size. Often its over-all height is only two inches, yet it can withstand weather that would kill many of its larger relatives in a matter of days. With us it grows wild near the top of Mount Washington and a few of the other highest peaks in New England's Presidential Range. Far Northern Europe and Asia know it too, for long winters and short summers are a normal part of its way of life.

Mexico's mountains are the source of many fine flowering plants. One is the Blue Salvia, or Blue Sage, which is a particular favorite of discriminating gardeners. Its close relative, the Scarlet Sage, is too flagrantly blazing for many who prefer delicacy to sheer power. So the violet-blue, Wedgewood blue, or white of the present form are a welcome relief.

Blue Sage is not too tall—about two feet. It is also quite shrubby in growth and provides a good background with its mass of pointed, gray-green foliage. Against and above this its eight-inch blossom sprays are delightfully displayed in late summer.

Technically the Blue Sage is a perennial and so will live for years in a warmish climate. In the North, however, the winter cold is often too much for it. So there, as in the case of many other frost-tender plants, its seeds should be sown indoors during February or March and the young plants transferred to the garden as soon as danger of spring frost has passed. Such a head start enables them to flower freely before autumn days arrive.

Early every spring, in countless country places through the eastern half of the United States and nearby Canada, the Bloodroot blossoms spread like dainty white saucers above their young, half-closed leaves. Most of them are more than an inch across, and for a few days they close late in the afternoon and reopen early the following morning. Their show is a rather brief one, but while it lasts there is nothing among our Eastern wildflowers which matches its universal appeal.

The Bloodroot's favorite home is in deciduous woods where its flowering and seed setting can be completed before the tree leaves are large enough to exclude the sunlight. By June the glossy, chestnut-brown seeds are ripe and tumble comfortably to the ground a few inches below. But the leaves, on their separate stalks, keep on growing until they are nearly a foot across. Meanwhile the plant's thick, hard rootstocks have sent out new branches, the seeds have found spots to sprout, and as the years pass the colony sometimes spreads over an acre or more.

The curious common name of this old favorite is well deserved. The whole plant is filled with a bitter, reddish-orange juice. The Indians, whose name for the Bloodroot was Puccoon, extracted this liquid from the roots and used it to paint their bodies and color their woven-grass baskets.

About midsummer, when the shade-loving Bloodroot leaves have stopped growing, the adjacent sunny fields are often flecked with the gold and rich brown blooms of Black-eyed Susan. This, too, has been a favorite American wildflower for many generations and is often grown in naturalistic gardens. Some of its largest blooms are four inches across, seemingly too big for the slender, down-covered stems to support. They are excellent for cut-flower use, since they last for a week or more after being placed in water.

Theoretically, Black-eyed Susan's natural range is from Ontario to Florida and Texas. In practice, however, the plant has spread far to the northeast of this line. One is likely to find it growing wild in suitable surroundings almost anywhere south of the St. Lawrence and east of the Mississippi.

The familiar Scarlet Sage has an excellent and much less eye-searing cousin whose name is **BLUE SALVIA** (494) . . . The exquisite snowy blossoms of **BLOODROOT** (495) thrusting up through a mass of Scillas into the early spring air. They will close their petals every night.

494 ↓

495

496 497

BLACK-EYED SUSAN (496) is one of America's most adaptable wildflowers. It will blossom and persist in almost any soil provided there is abundant sunlight . . . **PINK SILENE** (497) is a sort of Cinderella plant, for it is far prettier than its hundreds of relatives.

The Silenes, or Catchflies, are a motley group of some four hundred species widely scattered over the world. Most of them have little ornamental value and some are merely pest weeds. But at least two of the North American kinds are decidedly worth seeing and examining.

One of these is the Pink Catchfly, a low, tufted plant of the Northeastern states with one-inch blossoms of pale to deep pink. The other has considerably longer stems and larger scarlet blossoms. In both species the slender, tubular bases of the flowers are covered with fine sticky hairs, a family peculiarity which accounts for their common name.

The story of the Marigolds reminds one of the origin of Catawba Rhododendrons. It began in the days of Mexico's conquest by the Spaniards. The seeds of two wildflowers from that luckless country were smuggled into Europe aboard galleons and soon acquired the title of Rose of the Indies. The larger one made itself much at home along the north coast of Africa and is believed to have been taken to England by some of the corsairs who helped liberate Tangier from the Moors. That occasion won for it the name of African Marigold. The smaller kind was taken to England by the French Huguenots about 1573 and has been called French Marigold ever since.

In recent years these two Marigold types have been interbred so successfully that an amazing number of sizes and effects are now an accomplished fact. There are chunky six-inch plants with four-foot cousins. Carnation-flowered, round balls, Chrysanthemum-flowered, singles and ruffles are standard practice today in blooms that sometimes are as broad as six inches. Pale yellow, cream, primrose, deep orange, garnet, and red, alone or in combinations, are some of the modern available colors. Even the characteristic strong odor of the foliage has been largely eliminated.

Two innovations have thus far eluded all the hybridists: blue blossoms and pure white ones. The first of these will probably never be achieved, for

498

499 ↓

500 ↓

501

502

The probabilities are that **MARIGOLDS** (498 to 502), which botanically are not really Marigolds at all, were popular flowers among the Aztecs centuries before white men reached North America. There must have been various types of them even in those far-off days, judging by the number of blossom colors and styles now in existence.

even a suggestion of blue is foreign to Marigold nature. But there is a possibility of pure white appearing someday. One prominent breeder believes this so strongly he offers a reward of $10,000 to the first person who sends him Marigold seeds which will produce pure white flowers at least three inches across!

Another of man's achievements with Marigolds has been to breed out most of the strong-smelling oil glands which originally existed on their leaves. At the same time the size of the blossoms has been greatly increased. Practically all of them live for only one season, but during that short time their flower production is prodigious.

There are many other types of native American flowers, in tropical as well as temperate regions, which are undoubtedly susceptible to great diversification by skillful hybridizing. This does not necessarily imply that they can be changed as fantastically as the Marigolds, for that is a situation which can be determined only by thorough trials. Material for this sort of experimentation appears to be especially abundant west of the Great Plains. That part of the country has not been botanized as thoroughly as the East and Midwest, largely because of the physical difficulties of combing the rugged mountain regions which it includes.

Some of the dozen or more far western Trout-lily species are so lovely and distinctly varied in size and colors that they may well prove to be some venturesome hybridizer's delight. There are numerous members of the Composite Family, too, which have enticing possibilities—perhaps as great as those of the Columbines of which we have already written. The native Asters also might be a good place to start, for two of our fine eastern kinds of this strong-growing group have already yielded a number of delightful hybrid varieties.

503

505

Temperate North America has practically a monopoly of the spring-flowering Trilliums. Only four of the thirty-odd species are attributed to the Old World. The name Trillium, from the latin *triplum,* means "triple." All of the plants' aboveground parts, except the stems, come in threes or multiples of three—three leaves, three petals, six stamens, and so on.

Trilliums are confirmed woodlanders. Their greatest concentration is in the southern Appalachians with outposts far northward and westward. One of the most widely distributed is the Great White, whose big, showy blossoms turn pink with age. Another is the Wake-robin, with purplish-red, yellow, or white blooms.

Wake-robin is one of the really early spring wildflowers, often opening its strong-smelling blossoms even before the leaves of the trees are large enough to cast shadows. It grows naturally in damp open woods from northern New England southward through the Appalachians as far as the western part of the Carolinas.

Altogether there are almost 100 species of Thalictrums, varying greatly in height and growing naturally in dampish ground which may be shaded by trees or out in the full sun according to the preference of the particular kind. The majority can withstand cold winters, and all of them are capable of living for a number of years in acceptable surroundings and paying annual decorative dividends which no other plants can exactly match.

504 ↓

The **WAKE-ROBIN TRILLIUM** (503) earned its intriguing first name by opening its softly colored blossoms in early spring . . . **GREAT WHITE TRILLIUMS** (505) flower a couple of weeks later. Both species grow in woodland places . . . All of the **MEADOW-RUES** (504) have delicate foliage and fantastically fuzzy flower heads. They grow best in rich soil.

506 507

MONKEY FLOWERS (506) in one form or another grow wild from Alaska to Chile. Some of their deep yellow, blotched blossoms are startlingly unique. Petal irregularity is one of their dominant characteristics . . . **STOKES-ASTER** (507) is not actually an Aster, despite its general appearance. It is a native of the Deep South but often survives the winter in gardens as far north as Boston.

The Thalictrums, or Meadow-rues, are Old as well as New Worlders. Some garden forms, like the one in the photograph, have foreign blood in their veins. Their general character, however, echoes the tallest of all, our own eight-foot beauty that grows wild from Maine to Florida.

The blue, pink, cream, or white Stokes-aster, or Stokesia, is a much less complex native of our Southern states. Few summer-long garden flowers surpass the beauty of color and form of its blossoms, held a foot or more above the ground by strong, enduring stems. Some of them are a good five inches in diameter.

The reputation of this thoroughly worthy plant has suffered somewhat from misinformation originating years ago. For example, several of the older and apparently authoritative books on gardening advised readers that in the North Stokes-asters can be grown only in greenhouses, a theory which later experience has discredited. There was also an erroneous belief that they are wonderful drought-resisters. The result of this was that hundreds of gardeners never watered them at all, with fatal consequences whenever a dry summer came along.

Monkey Flowers have escaped handicaps such as these. They are astonishingly cosmopolitan in their climatic needs. In some regions they live for a number of years, and in others their outdoor life is restricted to a single season for reasons which are not too clear. There are several different forms of them, the largest attaining a height of two or three feet. The petals are irregular in shape and size, sometimes producing effects suggestive of Snapdragons. In some forms the showy blooms are spotted with darker color which give them resemblance to grotesque faces. This, of course, is the reason for the singular name of Monkey Flower which has been the popular alias for many years.

Flowers of the New World

TROPICAL ZONE

FLORIDA, Southern California, and parts of the Gulf Coast have much to be grateful for in the abundance of their tropical and subtropical outdoor flowers. These regions are gathering places for a wealth of equatorial beauties from far and near as well as many from cooler sections. There is not a month of the year without its memorable outdoor flower show. Included in it are numerous hot-country blossoms which Northerners can enjoy in their summer gardens only because they grow very rapidly from spring-planted seeds and complete their seasons in a few months.

A famous showpiece of the Deep South is the fabulous Bougainvillea from Brazil. It is a climbing shrub so vigorous that frequent pruning is needed to keep it within reasonable bounds. Walls, trees, strong trellises, and archways are incredibly gay with its purple blossoms. Sometimes these are so numerous they virtually hide the leaves. Actually this display is provided by the big flaring bracts rather than by the small true flowers they enclose. There is also a taller rose-colored type. Still a third kind is brick red, but this form is so devotedly tropical it can be safely grown only in the southernmost parts of Florida. More photographs on pages 236, 237.

The Bougainvilleas apparently gained their popular name soon after Louis de Bougainville, the first Frenchman to cross the Pacific Ocean, returned from an expedition to the South Seas in 1768 in search of possible new colonies for France. While his ship was taking on supplies in Rio de Janeiro his young botanist protégé went plant-hunting on shore and eventually returned with specimens of the Bougainvillea.

BOUGAINVILLEAS (508) vary somewhat in their flower color and vigor of growth, but all of them are marvelously showy when in full bloom. They grow fast and willingly when planted in full sunlight.

509

510

ALLAMANDAS (510) are highly ranked among the climbing shrubs from the New World tropics and adapted to outdoor growing in our warmest regions. They specialize in enormous numbers of flaring blossoms many of which are followed by large, prickly seed capsules.

Some of the almost 200 kinds of **ARISTOLOCHIAS** (509, 511) are likely to be seen outdoors in the Deep South or else in a northern greenhouse. Their family is distributed widely through the world's warm and temperate regions, including our eastern states where it is represented by a vine commonly known as Dutchman's Pipe. All of them have an odd habit of making their small true flowers very hard to find.

Aristolochias are among the world's most fantastic plants. Many of them are climbing shrubs and some are regular vines. The blossoms of all are shaped like long-stemmed meerschaum pipes; hence their Dutchman's-pipe title.

The seed-producing part of the blossom is located where the mouthpiece of a real pipe would join the bowl. Below it is a large hollow, U-shaped section which flares outward at its far end. In one variety this incredible outspread area is nearly two feet wide and has a hanging "tail" of even greater length. Practically all the tropical species are grotesquely colored in the general fashion of the photographs on these pages.

There are close to two hundred different kinds of Aristolochias, mostly native in tropical parts of the Old World and the New. The majority of them have a distinctly disagreeable odor which appeals to flies and some other insects. When these creatures eventually manage to crawl down and then up through the bowl to the source of the smell, they may never find their way out again. In such cases it does not need a lively imagination to think of the flower as a sort of insect trap, complete with alluring bait.

Allamandas are another group of mostly climbing shrubs from Brazil, the Guianas, and, to a lesser degree, from Central America. One of the most frequent varieties bears innumerable large yellow-orange blossoms whose throats are dotted with a few light spots. It is very free-blooming and so vigorous it will take over a house roof if given the opportunity. A thin-

512 514 513 515

ner and more wiry kind that is frequently seen is lemon yellow in bloom and generally grows less rampantly.

These Allamandas, and a few of their close relatives, are often handled in heated greenhouses and conservatories in the North. Their inborn tendency to cover space is satisfied by training them along the walls and rafters.

The traditional mystery and strange beauty of the tropics find tangible expression in the Anthuriums, natives of the central and warmer parts of South America. There are some six hundred species and many additional varieties of them, hardly more than a handful of which are cultivated in this country. Their need for a warm, moist atmosphere limits their permanent use to greenhouses, conservatories, and other well-heated places in the North and careful outdoor treatment in the very deep South. Some of them grow only a foot or so tall while others creep or climb.

These fantastic plants, ornamentally speaking, fall into two general categories: those valued chiefly for their decorative leaves, and those whose

The hundreds of **ANTHURIUMS** (512, 514) produce their true flowers on a long central column which, in some instances, is brilliantly colored . . . In the warm southern surroundings which it needs the **CORAL-VINE** (516) blossoms almost half of every year . . . The name of the **SHRIMP PLANT** (513, 515) comes from the color and formation of the peculiar bracts which overlap the actual flowers. The latter project beyond these coverings. The photographs show different species.

516

primary attraction is the blossoms. The very small true flowers are massed on the central spike, which protrudes from a broad, flattened bract that is often incredibly colorful. In the occasional species where this feature is on the dull, smallish side the burden of display is carried by the huge velvety leaves in a variety of astonishing shapes. Individual blooms have been known to last three months before fading, even under artificial growing conditions.

To those who have seen Anthuriums in their dim jungle homes it is rather incongruous to find them confined to pots and displayed in sophisticated city shops, hotel lobbies, and the like. At least one such person, viewing them there, was seen to turn away a little sadly, shaking his head and muttering, "Strange are the uses of publicity."

Coral-vine, Mountain Rose, Love's Chain—just pick your favorite name for the handsome, pink-flowered vine which botanists call *Antigonon leptopus*. It is as ambitious as it is graceful, an odd combination which was demonstrated by a single Florida specimen which once grew along a wire from the Rosalind Club House in Orlando to the middle of Orange Avenue.

This Coral-vine can actually climb almost anywhere it wants to go. Tree branches are especially favored places, much better than the limited opportunities offered by trellises. During the process the plant takes time to bloom brilliantly for four or five months every summer. And all through this pleasant period its dark foliage contributes a fitting accompaniment to the memorable color notes.

Among tropical American plants there is probably only one whose flowers merit naming it after a popular sea-food. This individual is a little evergreen shrub, extremely sensitive to cold, which is becoming widely known as Shrimp Plant. It grows about eighteen inches high and when flowering time comes it produces long, flattened, reddish-brown sprays in a curiously overlapping pattern which strongly suggests the flexible plates of a big shrimp's tail. These remarkable structures consist of bracts, not true flowers. The latter are underneath and could easily pass unnoticed by a human observer. The arrangement is just another version of the old principle that

517

518

519

Florida's **BLOOD FLOWER** (517) is a cousin of the northern Butterfly-weed . . . **BAUHINIA** blossoms (518) are queer enough to justify the common name of Orchid-tree. Another distinctive oddity is the way the leaves always grow in perfectly matched pairs . . . The big, irregular leaves of this **BEGONIA** (519) are speckled with white on top. Underneath they are red.

it pays to advertise (to insects), as practiced by the Dogwood, Poinsettia, and many other showy plants whose actual flowers are small and insignificant.

Subtropical Florida need look no farther than its own sunny wastelands to find that brightest of the Milkweeds whose everyday name is Blood-flower. Its little blossoms are massed into showy, flattish heads whose color varies from scarlet to strong orange and sometimes purplish. The only other Milkweed which can challenge their display is an occasional Butterfly-weed, its cousin from the more northerly states.

Every Milkweed plant has a curious device which helps ensure pollination of its own as well as its neighbors' flowers. Between the sides and the stamens of each tiny blossom there is a ring of five minute, cornucopia-like receptacles in which lie masses of the gummy pollen. As a visiting bee or other insect scrambles around on the flower head, scraps of this fertilizing material stick to his feet or mouth parts and are thus transferred bodily to another blossom where they may prove useful. Most Milkweed stems are almost as stiff as twigs. They are filled with thick white sap.

521

This **COMBRETUM** (520, 521) is a New World tropical species not often seen in cultivation; it is fairly representative of the tribe as whole. The first photograph is a very closeup view. In the other, the peculiar flower buds are just beginning to open.

The Begonia pictured on the opposite page is representative of the fancy-leaved section of an ornamental flowering plant group that is widely distributed through the tropical and subtropical parts of the world. Estimates of the total number of Begonia species run from 500 to 1,300, and no authority is willing to guess how many more thousand natural variations and downright hybrids there are. New ones keep showing up every year, for Begonia growing has become a virtual cult among numerous house-plant and greenhouse addicts in both hemispheres.

It is easy to understand why these immensely varied plants appeal so strongly to so many. For one thing, large numbers of them are as colorful in their leaves as in their oddly formed blossoms. Their range of size and growing habits is wide, too, and their lives are long.

Combretums, on the other hand, are considerably more conventional. Their clan numbers about two hundred and fifty tropical shrubs, trees, and climbing vines, chiefly natives of Southern Asia and Africa. The one you are most likely to see in American greenhouses and outdoors in Florida and Southern California is a Madagascan with evergreen leaves and showy masses of red flowers. It has at least two odd relatives, one of which yields a butterlike substance eagerly eaten by the Kaffir tribes of Africa. The other one, in quite recent years, has gained something of a reputation as a remedy for opium addiction.

Many plants have been named after people, but as far as we know only one commemorates two human beings. Its scientific name of Bauhinia honors John and Caspar Bauhin, brothers who ranked high as herbalists back in the sixteenth century. And the reason is that all its leaflets come in inseparable pairs.

In non-scientific circles some Bauhinias are known as Orchid-trees because of their colorful, fantastically shaped blossoms. There are around

one hundred and fifty species hailing from the tropics of both hemispheres and comprising trees, shrubs, and climbing vines. Most of them are definitely in the believe-it-or-not class, and yet they are not difficult to "tame" provided the climate is acceptable to their tropical nature.

When a Brazilian Flame Vine blooms in the deep Deep South, no one can doubt the appropriateness of its name. It practically blazes in countless places—high in the trees, on roofs, along walls and fences. It belongs to a group of warm-country New Worlders which includes the rather similar but hardier Trumpet Vine, or Trumpet Flower, which sometimes survives even southern New England winters without suffering too much from the cold.

Just What Does "Jungle" Mean?

Tropical jungles are of many types, depending upon their locations and the natural factors which govern the lives of plants. Rainfall, winds, altitude, available light, and geological formations all play parts in the final result. The two characteristics common to all jungles are the density of the plant inhabitants and the fantastic adaptations by which they survive.

In most jungles where trees of any size are present there are two life levels which might be called the understory and the canopy. The former is an incredible tangle of low, leafy plants often intermixed with mosses, while the latter represents the wholly different life of the treetops. Bridging the gap between them is a third plant world, many of its members so constituted that they can thrive without contact with any soil at all. These are the so-called Air-plants, such as many Orchids, tree-clinging Ferns, and some of the Pineapple clan, whose roots are anchored in the tree bark as firmly as if they were in the earth. Air and ample moisture, with all they imply in the way of essential nutrients, enable these strange forms to produce their leaves and often gorgeous blossoms for years on end. They are not parasites, for they inflict no damage whatsoever on their hosts. Yet without their airy perches they would vanish from the scene.

This plant world far above the soil is still more incredible in the great tropical rain forests, where the sun never penetrates the leafy treetop canopy. The struggle to reach the life-giving light is unending. The big trees themselves have no lower branches, for they would be useless in the semigloom. Strong vines clamber to their tops, produce leaves and blossoms, and drop ropelike stems back to earth where they can take root and eventually send new generations climbing skyward.

The understory of these rain forests is a strange land of dampness and green gloom. Primitive mosses and lichens of countless sizes are everywhere. Ghostly butterflies with transparent wings flit here and there. Ant-birds call weirdly in their endless hunt for food. Teeming life is on all sides, but there is little flower color. That is reserved for the treetops far above.

Not all tropical **JUNGLES** (522) follow the pattern of gloom and crowded growth often associated with them. Along the big forest edges there is often a variety of strange plants, some of them very beautiful.

523

524 ↓

The **BOUGAINVILLEAS** (523, 525, 527) from Brazil have been introduced into many other tropical lands, including the Far East. Yes, that is the Taj Mahal at the left . . . Tropical America gives us the peculiar **PARROT FLOWER** (524) which is related to the Bananas. Those bright colors are in the bracts, not in the pale flowers under them . . . The infinite multitude of the primitive plants which botanists call **BROMELIADS** (526, 528) is represented here by two tropical Americans as unlike each other as black and white. Outdoors they are restricted to warm climates, but Northerners are now making successful as well as spectacular house plants out of them. Basically they live on air and water.

525

527

PARROT FLOWERS seldom grow more than four feet high, yet they have leaves which are sometimes eighteen inches long. These, among other characteristics, are signs of their kinship with the Banana tribe. Each of the orange-red bracts measures almost three inches from end to end. In the warmer parts of Florida these plants are sometimes grown outdoors in rich, well watered soil where their foliage effects are stunning.

One type of Bromeliad, often seen growing on tree limbs in Florida, is the Tillandsia group. Its members are perhaps the most brilliant of southern Florida's native Air-plants, and they are abundant on the branches of Cypress trees. In spring their brilliant, usually red flower heads are visible for long distances as they rise above clumps of stiff green leaves.

The deserts of our Southwest may not lie within the geographical tropics, but their location with respect to mountains and wind currents certainly gives them a subtropical if not fully tropical climate. The result is that many of their flowers are different from any other natives on our continent.

526 ↓ 528 ↓

529

530 ↓

The **GIANT CACTUS** (529) of our southwest deserts is the largest of an astounding plant group with more than twelve hundred members. It reaches a height of fifty-odd feet and a total weight of six tons. Scores of different **CACTI** (530) in numerous shapes and sizes grow wild in the extreme Southwest. Others are found in dry, barren regions as far north as the Colorado Rockies. One species thrives along our eastern seaboard as far north as Cape Cod. Many of the Cactus subdivision known as **ORCHID CACTI** (531, 532) are widely grown as house plants. Today there are dozens of varieties, all of them characterized by stems consisting of a series of broad, flat sections almost suggestive of leaves. These portions produce the showy blossoms. (532) is often called Prickly-pear Cactus.

531

532

Prominent among these oddities is the Giant Cactus, or Saguaro, a huge treelike plant which reaches fifty feet in height, weighs as much as six tons, and may live for several hundred years. Its bulky trunk and limbs are living reservoirs for storage of the rain water which occasionally spills across the desert sands. Many months pass without a drop falling, but the Saguaro never falters when the time comes to send out its abundance of satiny blooms, each of which is close to four inches long and half as wide.

From the same dry regions come many of the smaller Cacti which are often grown in warm-country gardens as well as northern greenhouses and homes. The numerous forms of so-called Orchid Cactus are among the showiest of these, for their four- to ten-inch blooms come in various reds, whites, and yellows. The plants themselves are usually ungainly, but this trait is forgotten as soon as their glowing blossoms begin to appear in spring or early summer.

All members of the immense Cactus family have thorns. In many, many cases these are capable of inflicting painful injuries on any person foolish enough to touch them firmly. Their purpose is purely defensive, however, and they rarely fail in their assignment of protecting the plants' vital parts. Without their guardianship many of the various desert creatures, eagerly seeking water, would feed on the moist, pulpy parts in which the plants' own supply is stored to tide them through the dry months ahead.

Large numbers of Cacti are equally remarkable in the variety of their formations. Every detail is as perfect in its lines and geometrical balance as if it had been worked out meticulously on the drafting board of a mechanical designer. Exactly the right number of spines are arranged just so in every cluster. Certain depressed areas are separated by equally uniform ridges. Deviations from the prescribed patterns of each species are virtually unknown. It is no wonder that Cacti as a whole have been called the Fantastic Clan.

533

534

Yellow-elder is a warm-country bush or regular tree of perhaps twenty-odd feet whose sprays of bright yellow flowers pick up the southern sunlight so superbly that they are popular from our own Deep South far into the true tropics. These blooms are followed by slim pods filled with winged seeds which skim merrily away as soon as they are released. They have already escaped from the brown, twisted pods in the lower left corner of the photograph.

The Cleomes, or Spider-plants, on the other hand, are quite the garden rage nowadays. They grow rapidly to a height of three or four feet while forming upright flower clusters which add another six inches to the stature of their main stalks and side branches. The lowest buds in each of these heads open first and their spidery, usually rose-and-white blossoms remain in good condition for several days. By the time their petals fade and fall, their companion buds farther up have taken over the display duties. New clusters keep forming through most of the summer.

Cleomes are annuals and come from tropical America, yet they know very well how to get along in northern gardens. Give them one season to produce and drop their numerous seeds and the future will generally take excellent care of itself. The following spring twenty new plants are likely to pop up by themselves for every one you originally set in the ground. And after another year—well, the law of arithmetical progression keeps right on working.

The time may well come when Cleomes are so widespread that people will think of them as regular North American wildflowers instead of immigrants from beyond our borders. Indeed, they have already taken to numerous uncultivated places in their constant effort to get ahead in the world.

One's first impression of a Calceolaria's blossom is that most of it looks like the toe of one of those puffy slippers worn by medieval gentlemen when they were loafing around the palace rooms. Most of them are yellow spotted with brown, and they grow profusely at the tips of stems that are seldom less than a foot or so long.

These peculiar plants originated principally in South America and northward through Central America into Mexico. They have been known and

35

536

Gardeners from Florida to southern California delight in planting **YELLOW-ELDER** (533) on their home grounds. Its natural range goes into South America . . . Tropical native though it is, the self-reliant **CLEOME** (534, 535) produces countless cold-enduring seeds. They form inside the slender, hanging pods shown in the photograph on this page . . . Believe it or not, these are **CALCEOLARIA** blooms (536).

grown in northern greenhouses for a long time but have never gained as much popularity on this side of the Atlantic as they have enjoyed in England. Today it is unusual to see them outside of large flower shows except in parts of the Deep South where they are used to some extent in gardens.

Tropical America has also sent us the cordially welcome Pink Shower, a flowering shade tree of rare loveliness. Its long, drooping sprays of blossoms are so graceful they do actually suggest a softly falling shower of pink.

There was a time not too many years ago when the only Cannas grown in gardens were bold, big-leaved affairs topped by small, garish blossoms that were generally red and occasionally yellow. Today these plants have many more greatly diversified and far larger blooms in soft pastels and numerous other pleasing colors. Yet, perhaps because they are even more dominating than their redoubtable ancestors, they have only begun to regain the old Cannas' onetime popularity. Their principal use is to form large, stunning masses in parks and around public buildings where the maintenance of less rugged plants is something of a problem.

The Canna, whether improved or unimproved, is essentially tropical in effect. It is native in the tropics of both hemispheres, with the majority of its original species credited to the tropical and subtropical Americas.

Cannas grow rapidly from seeds, but modern hybrid varieties produced in this way would revert in the direction of their distant forebears. The only way gardeners can be sure of getting young hybrid plants of any kind that will be in the exact image of their parents is by what is called vegetative

537

The probabilities are that **CANNAS** (537, 538, 539, 540, 541) have been grown as cultivated plants for thousands of years, although dependable evidence of this is hard to come by. They are so tropical in appearance as well as origin that their huge leaves and spectacular blooms seem out of place in northern gardens. Some of them reach a height of eight feet, even in these days when hybridists have made available many varieties with more compact growth and softer, less garish flower colors. They make their best impression in tropical or at least subtropical surroundings.

538 ↓

539

propagation. This means obtaining some part of the physical structure of the old plant, such as a stem or a root section, but never a seed, and inducing it to make independent growth of its own.

In the case of Cannas this is accomplished by cutting apart their thick, fleshy roots and planting each piece separately. Hybrid Dahlias, Peonies, Day-lilies, and many other choice flowers are multiplied in similar fashion. The reasons behind these "chip off the old block" methods of building up a stock of hybrid plants involve certain natural laws of heredity which are full of genes, chromosomes, dominants, recessives, and a lot of other technical words. Even the present very sketchy outline of the factors involved may suggest the thought that expert hybridizers are born and not made.

Such men, indeed, must have vision as well as persistence and technical know-how. The best ones can look at a handsome plant in full flower and decide that this or that detail of color, leaf, petal form, stem strength, branch formation, and so on can stand some improvement of a definite sort. Then comes the task of locating some other member of the same race which, even though it may have other shortcomings of its own, may possibly supply the desired influence. Once this goal has been reached, the problem becomes one of crossbreeding the flowers of both, sowing the resultant seeds—and hoping. Clearly the lot of a hybridizer is not always a happy one.

The Cannonball Tree is one of Guiana's strangest native plants. It is large, sturdy, and when cultivated and well cared for spreads broadly enough to provide welcome shade with its big evergreen leaves. South Florida is probably the best place to see it unless you are in a position to travel to the truly tropical regions where it grows wild.

Several of the Cannonball's habits are unorthodox in the realm of trees. One of its peculiarities is to send out quantities of blossoms directly from its main trunk and along the large branches in defiance of the usual branch-tip practice of other trees. These flowers are pink, red, or yellowish, extremely fragrant, and hang in dense, showy sprays two or three feet long. The grayish brown fruits which often appear among them are hard enough on the outside to be regular old-fashioned cannon balls six or eight inches in diameter. The fruit shells are sometimes scooped out and used as crude

542

543

The **CANNONBALL TREE'S** blossoms (542) are not responsible for its odd name. That honor goes to the brownish, hard-shelled fruits which succeed them . . . **ANGEL TRUMPETS** (543, 544) are a motley crew, big-leaved and inclined to be strongly scented. But their blooms are stunning.

utensils. When fully ripe the whole thing has a most disagreeable odor. Yet the inside pulp is said to be eaten and even made into beverages by some of the native tribes. It is astonishing to see these great "balls" hanging side by side with the two- or three-inch blossoms.

There are about nine known species of these exotic trees, only one of which is cultivated to any extent. There is (or used to be) an unusually fine one growing on the grounds of the Royal Palm Hotel in Fort Myers. If it is no longer there, an inquiry or two among tree-minded residents will probably disclose the whereabouts of another good one.

The Daturas, often called Angel-trumpets, are wholly different in habits and appearance. Some of them are shrublike and grow wild in Mexico, Peru, and Chile. India has another kind, and Texas is also represented. One of them, a tropical American which has run wild in various parts of the United States, is rather scornfully called Jimson-weed.

All Angel-trumpets have big, coarse leaves and trumpet-shaped flowers of surprising size. In several cases the blooms are six or seven inches long and half as wide at the open end. There is also a family tendency for these flowers to be triple-lined, like one big cornucopia with two smaller ones fitted loosely inside it. Most species are strong-smelling, which may or may not be an asset as far as people are concerned.

The large seeds of these puzzling foreigners are contained inside fat, spiny pods which suggest a cross between a pincushion and a diminutive porcupine. They certainly do not disclose the fact that they belong to the same family as the White Potato, which was originally a fellow-countryman of theirs in the Andes Mountains of South America.

The contrast between Angel-trumpets and Cosmos is almost startling. Whichever way you compare them, one is everything the other is not. The Cosmos, for example, is one of the world's daintiest and most refined

544

545

Even though a **COSMOS** plant (545) may stand six feet high it never loses its grace or the clean loveliness of its pink, red, white or yellow blossoms, some of which are five or six inches broad. Few people suspect that it is allied to the coarse-growing Dahlia.

flowering plants, in growth and structure as well as actual blossoms. We can thank Mexico for it, as we do for so many other fine flowers.

It might be said that Cosmos is all things to all flower gardeners who are seeking an abundant supply of summer and autumn blossoms that are equally good for cutting and outdoor display. Years ago the only available variety bloomed so late that in the North it was often cut down by frost before it reached its full prime. But that handicap has been overcome by the development of forms which not only start flowering earlier but also cover a broader color range. White, yellow, orange, and several shades and combinations of pink are now readily available in varieties whose mature height ranges from three to six feet. Some of their blooms are five or more inches in diameter and all are airily poised on slender, graceful stems.

There are said to be about twenty full species of wild Cosmos, all of them North Americans and the majority native in Mexico. The same dainty, almost fernlike foliage characterizes all of them. The kinds that are commonly grown in our gardens are annuals and complete their amazing lives in the course of a single growing season. There are few better examples of how much latent beauty and power of growth can be packed within the casing of one slender, plain-looking little seed.

To flower gardeners the world over, as well as many other folk who have never sown a seed or planted a plant, the name Nasturtium is a household word. Some think of it as an amazingly beautiful flower, and to others it connotes the chief ingredients for tasty "cress" salads and sandwiches.

Nasturtiums grow wild in the cooler parts of Chile, Peru, and perhaps Mexico. There are tall ones and short ones; single flowers and double flowers, scented and unscented; reds and yellows and oranges and mahoganies alone or combined. Records indicate that in the sixteenth century they were introduced into Europe from Peru. Apparently they soon won

546

547 ↓

548 ↓

The **NASTURTIUM** tribe (546, 547, 548, 549) rates as one of the most adaptable New World plant groups. Its members range from one-foot mounds to six-foot trailers and climbers. Some modern varieties are sweet-scented, and the round, cool green leaves of all have a pleasantly spicy flavor. They prefer a fairly cool climate because of their mountain origin but will grow almost anywhere except in marshy places. This is one of the reasons why they are so popular the world over. It seems strange that even in its chief homeland among the Andes Mountains no Nasturtium lives longer than one year after it sprouts from a seed.

549

acclaim there for their ornamental as well as edible qualities. It may be that they first reached the United States by way of the early colonists.

These onetime wildflowers have provided an excellent example of the prodigious demand for novelty which sometimes develops among flower gardeners. The story runs thus:

In the 1920s Mr. J. C. Bodger, a prominent seedsman in California, noticed some exceptionally brilliant golden Nasturtiums growing in a small garden. The owner agreed to let him have a supply of seeds when they ripened sufficiently. After Mr. Bodger had built these up to a good stock of his own, he sent small test packets of them to other leading seedsmen. The resultant blossoms had their first public showing in 1931 under the variety name of Golden Gleam. And the following year even the ten tons of seeds Mr. Bodger had on hand were not enough to meet the world-wide demand.

Petunias are even easier to grow than Nasturtiums, once they get started. Also they have a considerably longer season of bloom. Their ancestors came primarily from the southern regions of South America and consequently even their descendants with the most fantastically face-lifted blossoms have a considerable ability to take chilly weather as well as hot, and like it. Gardeners know that they will grow in almost any kind of soil and can stand shade as well as sunshine. The last of their season's blossoms may not give up the ghost until there have been several sharp autumn frosts.

It must be admitted that growing ones own Petunias from seeds is not always easy, for the seeds are very small and often slow to sprout in comparison with those of other annual flowers. But nowadays many neighborhood garden stores sell strong young Petunia plants every spring, all ready to be placed where you want them. These are especially useful to customers who are somewhat in the inexperienced gardening category.

Most modern Petunias produce seed quite freely. If the blossoms which produced them were superior it is natural for an owner to plan for more of the same by saving the seeds. Disappointment often follows such a plan merely because the parent plants were hybrid varieties and therefore incapable of producing descendants exactly like themselves. It is much better to buy new seeds annually from reliable professional seedsmen.

550

553

551

552 ↓

554

The decorative uses of **PETUNIAS** (550, 551, 552, 553, 554, 555, 556) are unusually varied. Mass plantings of them in the garden are superbly effective, and so are the compact and trailing types when combined in outdoor windowboxes. Individual plants can be trimmed and grown in pots for strategic spots on outdoor terraces. It is also possible to enjoy them indoors all winter. Add to all this the immense variety of modern Petunia blossoms, and their world popularity is obvious.

555 ↓

556 ↓

POINSETTIAS (557, opposite) become sizable shrubs in warm regions where they grow outdoors through the year. They are doubly effective when backed by tall, slender Cacti. Moist soil helps to keep them healthy, for there is ample moisture in their original jungle home . . . Tropical America is also the source of the **FLAME VINE** (558), or Pyrostegia, a strong climber with evergreen leaves and brilliantly showy when in bloom. In this view the club-shaped buds are just beginning to open. They will be followed by seeds equipped with "wings" which will help them to scatter widely.

558

Poinsettias, those eye-stopping green and scarlet plants which are so closely associated with the Christmas season, came out of the moist, shady parts of tropical Mexico and Central America and took the holiday gift-plant world by storm. In their home territory they reach a height of ten feet, but we rarely see one even half that size in cultivation. One reason for this is that they have a tendency to become straggly with advancing years. Only specialized greenhouse management will assure their greatest effectiveness.

Of course Poinsettias have flowers, but they are relatively insignificent. The flaming red display is brought about by the upper leaves, which are quite narrow in comparison with their greenish companions lower down. Few if any other plants show such astonishing contrasts in their mature foliage, apparently based entirely on mere position. It can be assumed that here again is an example of how to attract insect pollinators by giving them something bright to arouse their curiosity.

It is perfectly natural for recipients of gift Poinsettias to try and prolong their beauty for another season. Unfortunately such an objective cannot be attained without very special facilities and attentions. It is so difficult that even professional growers, with all their greenhouse experience, raise a new crop every year and plan to bring the plants to their greatest peak during the winter months.

The same tropical part of Brazil which contributes many other bright plants is responsible for another striking group of clambering shrubs called Pyrostegias. There are only three or four kinds of them, but their reddish-orange flower show is unforgettable. The plants are great climbers on fences, roofs, and many other places where their curling, hold-fast tendrils can get a good grip. One of their assets is the handsome, three-group evergreen foliage through which the interesting form of the main stems shows here and there and demonstrates how the climbing trick is done.

It is the crimson-orange blossoms, however, which are the greatest attraction. They appear in great drooping clusters at the branch tips.

There is only one California Poppy, but what a one it is! Its big papery blossoms are such a brilliant canary yellow they seem almost dazzling as they sit poised on their two-foot stems. Their customary spread is two

559

561

inches, but now and then there is a three-incher. This is California's State Flower. It has a close relative called Mexican Tulip-poppy, and the two plants are quite similar in many respects.

Tulip-poppies, like many other Mexican flowers, are perennial in their native land but cannot survive the winter in colder regions. Northern gardeners easily circumvent this sensitiveness by sowing fresh seeds every spring. This enables the young plants to get such a fast start they often begin flowering in early July and keep it up until hard frost. Californians and many Southerners, on the other hand, know that their plants often persist for several years before replacements are in order.

Thousands of years ago and long before the first white men reached America, the Aztec Indians of Mexico used the flowers of the Frangipani as offerings in their religious rites. So highly were these gorgeous blossoms valued that anyone touching them or even smelling their fragrance after they had been dedicated was subject to the death penalty. We do not know just what species of this outstanding shrub and tree group was so greatly honored by the Aztecs, but it is reasonable to assume that it was one of the two native kinds that divide the area from Mexico to Peru.

All of the several dozen Frangipani species known today are natives of the American tropics. Their fame has spread throughout the world, for they

560↓

The superlative **CALIFORNIA POPPY** (559) comes in charming colors beginning with pale yellow and deepening to orange . . . **FRANGIPANIS** (560, 561) are also variable colorwise. Their fragrant blossoms, borne on bushy trees as much as twenty feet tall, have won world-wide fame through the centuries. The tree is a native of Mexico, where it attained great religious significance under the Aztecs. It is a favorite in all warm regions.

562

Most of the **JACOBINIAS** (562, 563) are perfect examples of small shrubs with large flower clusters. There are probably forty kinds of them, hailing from Mexico and as far south as Bolivia and Brazil.

563

are among the most fragrant of all flowering plants known to mankind.

The jungle country of Brazil has provided us with another fine old plant, the Jacobinia. It is completely different from Frangipani in appearance but just as distinctive in its own peculiar fashion. By the time it is halfway to its full height of a few feet, its fantastic blossom clusters begin to appear above the heavily veined leaves. Each narrow flower is curiously curved outward at the top as though it were glad to get away at last from its closely crowding companions.

Just for a change, the popular name Lantana is identical with the one scientists have assigned to a little flowering shrub which grows wild from Texas and lower Georgia southward into truly tropical America. We usually see it as a potted house plant whose height of a foot or so is somewhat less than its size in the wide-open spaces from which it comes.

Many tropical and subtropical plants show their dislike for confinement by failing to bloom well. Not so Lantana. It is one of the easiest worth-while plants adapted to window-gardening. Given half a chance, it will continue flowering well for weeks on end. Its tight, bright blossom heads, two or more inches in diameter, are variously colored but always pleasing.

There are just two things Lantanas cannot endure: freezing temperature and naphthalene flakes. The reason for the first of these dislikes is easy to understand in view of the plants' warm-country background. But the naphthalene-flakes danger is still an unsolved mystery.

Oddities of leaves and flowers are the chief reasons for the ornamental use of Jatrophas in Northern greenhouses and out of doors in the Deep South. Apart from such purposes they have a number of other unexpected values. The oil contained in one species supplies a helpful ingredient for soap-making. Some Mexicans eat the seeds as if they were peanuts. Another

564

565 ↓

56

To most American garden folk the **LANTANAS** (564, 565, 566) are merely smallish house plants whose bright blossom heads go far to lessen the gloom of winter days. In tropical parts of the world, however, where these popular fellows can stay outdoors at all times, they reach greater size. This is not too surprising in view of the fact that they are shrubs with a potential life span of years . . . The **JATROPHA** (567) species shown here is often called Tartogo. Its tribe is locally credited with medicinal virtues. Yet botanists describe Tartogo's trunk as "swollen and gouty."

567

kind is utilized for hedge-making in Central America. And a large percentage of the one hundred and fifty species has local reputations for medicinal uses. This probably explains why one tropical American is occasionally called Bellyache Bush.

The connection of religion with certain flowers has existed in one form or another throughout the ages of recorded time. One living example of it is found in the name Passion-flower, which is borne by a strong-growing vine native in Brazil and often grown in the South as well as in greenhouses and some private homes in the Northern states. Many devout people have felt that its four-inch blossoms are symbolic of the Crucifixion.

According to this belief, the ten petals represent the apostles who saw the Crucifixion. The darker circle inside them stands for either the halo or the crown of thorns. Some liken the five central stamens to the five wounds, although others assert that they are emblems of the hammers which were used to drive the nails. Lastly, the coiling tendrils with which the vine grasps its supports could be the scourges, and the fingerlike leaves the many hands of the persecutors.

The "Shaving-brush-trees" are considerably less imaginative in their symbolism, which is quite without religious implications. All thirty-odd kinds of them are native in the West Indies region or on the mainland, and each has blossoms strongly suggestive of the brushes on which all whiskery men relied before the advent of brushless creams, lather tubes, and similar shaving gadgets of the present automatic age.

Some of these fantastic blossoms are thirteen inches long before they open and disclose the threadlike mass of pistils. Pinks, whites, yellows, and an occasional red are the dominating colors, according to the particular species. The majority of the trees themselves are rather small, but one, a native of Panama, has been known to reach a height of ninety feet in its crowded home jungles, where all trees must reach upward for light.

The Oxalis family is an enormous one found chiefly in the warm parts of the world but containing a few species that succeed only in cold temperate climates. Most of them are grown primarily as winter-flowering house or greenhouse plants. The one in the present photograph, however, is well adapted to reversing this trend. By keeping its thick roots dormant during

568

570

569

571

Whatever may be thought about the symbolism of **PASSION FLOWER** (568), it is undeniably weird in its structure and coloring . . . Several members of the **OXALIS** clan (569) are grown as winter-flowering house plants . . . **SHAVING-BRUSH-TREE** (570) lives up to its name . . . One of the several forms of **NICOTIANA** (571).

the winter it can be induced to do practically all its flowering in the summer. If this seems like a mean trick, remember that gardeners will do anything to get results.

Among the night-flowering garden plants the Nicotianas reign supreme because of the delicious scent of their blossoms. The kind that is most widely grown in our middle and northern gardens is a perennial in its native South America but cannot be trusted to pull through colder winters. So countless gardeners merely plant fresh seeds each spring, confident in the knowledge that the desired results will follow during the latter part of the coming summer.

Nobody really knows how many kinds of Orchids there are. A number of years ago the figure stood at fifteen thousand plus an unguessable number of hybrids. Additional species are being discovered every year, and thus far there seems to be no limit to the number still to come. It is entirely possible, if not probable, that ten years from now the grand total will have passed the twenty-five-thousand mark.

One important reason for this uncertainty as to the number of forms in existence is that the jungles of tropical and subtropical regions around the world are the major home of these astounding plants. Such areas are extremely difficult to penetrate and equally trying to see through. A further obstacle is the fact that the majority of the species are Air-plants and grow only on tree limbs and in crotches. When those sites happen to be a hundred feet or so above the ground, the physical effort of climbing up to them is staggering. Even a telescope would be of little help, since authentic determination of a new orchid is a matter requiring the physical presence of the plant itself and working on it in a well-equipped laboratory.

The Plant World's Most Spectacular Story

Not all Orchids are tree dwellers, of course. Certain groups of them grow on the ground much as other plants do. These are far easier to collect and consequently have a lower percentage of unknowns. But the problem of thoroughly combing their vast, tangled homelands still remains.

It is not generally realized that a considerable variety of Orchid types live on the ground in temperate and even cold temperate parts of both hemispheres. Some of them appear so different from the customary Orchid forms, colors, and habits of growth that only an expert botanist can recognize their affiliation with the clan. One of the commonest species in our Northern and Central states looks for all the world like an elongated, very thin greenish-white corkscrew. This Northern group, like the other terrestrial ones, has been quite thoroughly worked out.

A vast number of the fine tropical Orchids such as are seen in botanical-garden collections, commercial and private greenhouses, and the better florist shops can be traced back to the New World tropics, where their forebears have lived for thousands of years. Some of them have a degree of Old World ancestry, too, for a great deal of man-controlled hybridizing has been under way for many years in the world's leading botanical centers and even by some amateurs.

Out of all this has come greater experience with the exacting requirements of Orchid life and increasing knowledge of how their needs can be met under controlled conditions of light, temperature, and moisture. It has also been learned that some of the really fine types are reasonably good-natured and tolerant of human inexperience. The time has already come for a certain amount of successful Orchid-growing in ordinary homes to be really feasible. Thus far the types recommended as most likely to succeed are the Cattleyas, Laelias, tropical Cypripediums (Lady's-Slippers), and perhaps Dendrobiums. A few good books on this intriguing project have appeared and more will doubtless follow as experience expands.

Anyone contemplating the growing of tropical Orchids at home should realize that success with them can never be won without meticulous attention to such details as the growing material for their roots, its degree of moisture, and the amount and character of the light which the plants receive. Ordinary house plant care will not suffice. And forgetfulness is one of the quickest short-cuts to failure.

A greenhouse—even though it is a little one—is ideal because of the year-round facilities for light, humidity and temperature control which it provides. Many of the smaller-flowered kinds of Orchids probably require greenhouse conditions for continued success in the North. In the warmest parts of the South, of course, a considerable variety of Orchid types can be maintained successfully outdoors where the climate and character of the plants' native homes can be closely matched.

For those who may wish to grow Orchids in the house, here are some basic principles to keep in mind:

Broadly speaking, the plants need an average temperature ranging between sixty and eighty degrees. Greater heat than this may not harm them unless it continues for some weeks. But temperatures of fifty or less, even for a short time, are decidedly risky.

Stuffy, stale air is harmful, so some provision for avoiding it at all times is essential. And watch the humidity! In an average house during the winter heating season the humidity may be as low as fifteen percent. For Orchids this percentage should be at least tripled. This usually calls for the use of humidifying trays or some other system whose air-moistening output can be suitably regulated.

In the North, where the intensity of the winter sunshine is comparatively low, Orchids should be kept in a south window where they will be in as much direct sun as possible. In summer, when sun intensity is high, light shade such as can be provided by light gauze curtains is advisable during the middle hours of the day. From June to early September it is often helpful to hang the plants outdoors in the shade of trees where they will not be subjected to strong winds. Of course they should remain in their regular containers during this period.

All of the tree-dwelling Orchids should be planted in Osmunda fiber—actually the dead roots of certain large Ferns. This should not be constantly watered. Instead, giving it a very heavy soaking and then no more until it is fully dried out. This alternate drenching and drying is at least a simulation of what happens to the plants in their wild tropical homes except during the height of the rainy season.

Ground-dwelling Orchids, such as the Ladyslippers, can be grown in pots of regular garden soil. In general their requirements of moisture, sun, temperature and air follow those of their tree-living cousins.

A greenhouse for **ORCHIDS** (572) need not be large provided it is well regulated with respect to its light, temperature and air moisture. As a rule each plant has its own individual pot or other container.

573

576

574

577

Most groups of plants have certain underlying flower characteristics running through all their respective members. But the **ORCHIDS** (573, 574, 575, 576, 577, 578, 579, 580, 581, 582, 583, 584) are incredibly variable. Some of their blossoms are huge and fantastic, others small and almost prim in their dainty simplicity. Yet, at least among the tropical kinds, the majority have an immediate distinction that is all their own.

575 ↓

578 ↓

579

582

580

583

The Orchid Family is extraordinarily complex in its botanical organization, largely because of the vast number of true species and the frequency with which they hybridize on their own account as well as under man's guidance. The twelve examples presented on these pages are only a tiny fraction of the total number of kinds in existence throughout the tropical and temperate parts of the world on both sides of the Atlantic.

581 ↓

584 ↓

585

586

None of the several **PERESKIAS** (585) looks much like the rest of the Cactus Family to which it really belongs . . . Among the succulent, or water-storing plants, the jolly little **PORTULACA** (586, 587) is a universal favorite. It thrives in the driest, most sun-baked places . . . **REDBIRD-CACTUS** (588) is not a Cactus, despite its name. It belongs to a large group which includes Poinsettia as well as the astonishing Crown-of-Thorns. Like them, it is so exotic in appearance that it seems to border on the impossible.

For gorgeous and varied color masses close to the ground in dry, sunny places the Portulaca or Sun-rose, is in a class by itself. The numerous white, yellow, pink, salmon, or rose-red blossoms are surprisingly large for the size of the plants. Sometimes they are striped with contrasting hues. There are singles as well as doubles; the latter are really suggestive of little Roses. Every one of them shows to maximum advantage, too, for the foliage is so sparse and slender it never gets in the way.

Portulacas have been known and grown in gardens for many years in the North as well as the South. Away back in 1829 an article in the *Botanical Magazine* gave this description of them as they appear in their native Brazilian home " . . . in light, sandy soil . . . between the Rio Saladillo, or western boundary of the Pampas, and the foot of the mountains near Mendoza. On the western side of the Rio Desaguardero plants were in great profusion, giving to the ground over which they were spread a rich purple hue, here and there marked with spots of an orange color, from the orange-colored variety which grew intermixed with the rest." It seems incredible that these brilliant little beauties should be close kin to that garden weed, the despised Pusley!

The mighty Cactus family includes a small Mexican, South American, and West Indian division called Pereskias. Their flowers are different from those of other Cacti for the curious reason that each one has a stem of its own. These blooms vary in color from white to rose on plants which are either spiny shrubs or climbing vines. One of the latter type is often called Lemon Vine because of the way it grows and the shape of its leaves. Another common name is Barbados Gooseberry, which originated as a result of its fruits' appearance.

587

588

Redbird Cactus, or Slipper Plant, is another oddity with a jumbled name. Botanists call it *Pedilanthus tithymaloides,* a tongue twister derived from Greek words signifying "shoe flower." A glance at the shape of one of its blossoms shows that the Greeks were right again.

This Redbird character is a six-foot bush with milky juice and thick, fleshy stems. It came originally from the West Indies, Central America and northern South America, and has a couple of dozen cousins.

There is little doubt that the most brilliantly red garden flower widely planted all over the United States is the Scarlet Sage, or Salvia. In its native Brazil it becomes an eight-foot shrub, but its tropical nature is such that in temperate regions its outdoor life is limited to a single season during which it may reach three feet from early-planted seeds. In late summer, and even more profusely in autumn until a sharp frost cuts it down, its blossom spires outblaze all the rest. There is also a white variety, and some of its blue-flowered cousins have gained considerable favor among gardeners who are a little tired of forthright red. In its proper settings, however, such as public parks where it can be massed in formal beds located in large-scale surroundings, the Scarlet Sage is superb.

The Abutilons, or Flowering-maples, are far less inclined to take over the whole neighborhood. They are well-mannered shrubs or occasionally trees not even distantly related to Maples despite the Maple-like shape of their leaves. The original home of most of them is the tropical Americas; only a small portion of their sizable group came from the Old World tropics. Those we see on this side of the water are largely hybrids or derivatives of true species whose identity cannot be accurately determined.

The fame of Flowering-maples is based on the spectacular beauty of their blossoms rather than their foliage. These flowers are surprisingly large and curiously formed, particularly as to the central column, which is formed by the numerous stamens. The color range is bewildering, for it includes such combinations as white heavily marked with rich purple and red; pale bluish; orange and brown; red and lemon; pink and yellow; and lavender and white. One kind from Chile has all-blue flowers a full three inches across.

589

590 ↓

591 ↓

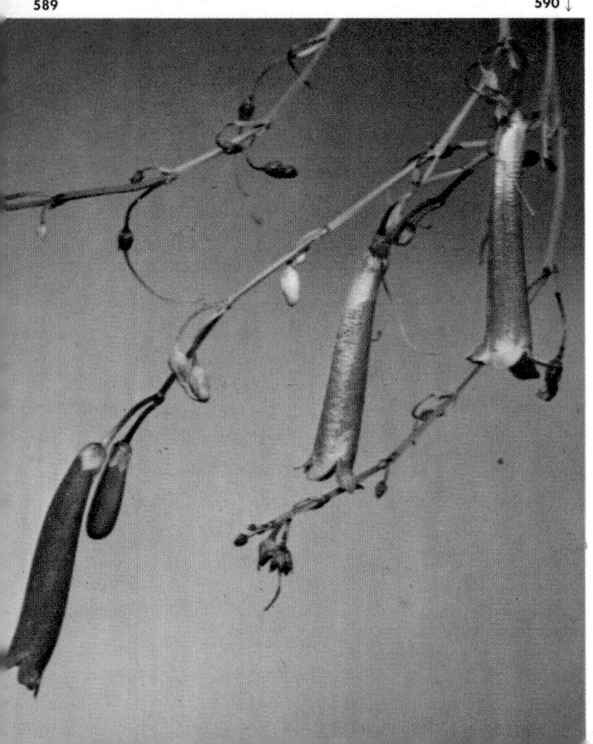

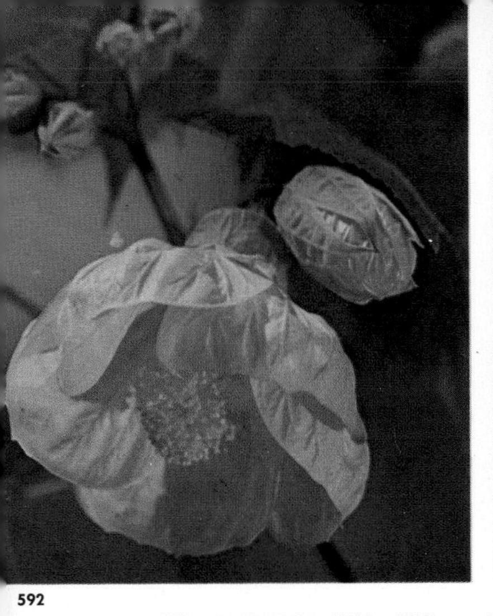

592

593

The **RUSSELIA** (589, 590), or Fountain-plant, is a branchy, droopy shrub about four feet high with almost no leaves but many slender flowers . . . **SCARLET SAGE** (591), out of Brazil . . . A typical example of **FLOWERING-MAPLE** (592) . . . One of the **AGERATUMS** (593), or Floss Flowers.

Many types of Flowering-maples flourish outdoors in the Deep South. In the North, however, their warm-country ancestry limits their use to winter-heated quarters such as greenhouses and dwellings, perhaps with a summer vacation outdoors. On the whole their papery petals and general appearance suggest the Mallows and Hollyhocks, to which they actually are related.

Tropical America is again responsible for some fifty-odd species of out-and-out twining vines among which are several of great merit. Since none of them appears to have any popular name, we shall have to go along with the botanists and call them Stigmaphilons, which admittedly does not look especially alluring or even easily pronounceable.

It is perhaps indicative of the inconceivable millions of different flowering plants that only a few of these last striking vines have been brought under cultivation. Even this treatment, eliminating as it does at least a few natural obstacles, is limited to their own homelands and the warmest parts of the United States. Rarely if ever do they survive for any length of time in northern greenhouses, for reasons which are obscure in the present state of our ornamental-plant knowledge.

Among the tropical flowering upright shrubs or small trees the several kinds of Tabebuias are exceptionally decorative. They grow wild in tropical and subtropical Central and South America, whence they have been introduced into comparable climates in the United States and elsewhere around the world. Their dark evergreen leaves, each with a pale rib up the middle, are as much as seven inches long and notably handsome when the sunlight touches them at different angles. Against their background the tubular, trumpetlike blossoms are dramatically displayed.

There seems to be no end to the number of stunning flowers Brazil has contributed to the decoration of the grounds around our southern homes.

594

596

There is a good chance that this Brazilian **GLOXINIA** (594) is the chief ancestor of our fine modern varieties . . . Here is one of those **STIGMAPHYL-LONS** (596) whose cultivation is such a problem . . . **GLORY-BUSH** (595), another notable Brazilian . . . **A TABEBUIA** (597), master of display . . . No other plant equals a **CHRISTMAS-CACTUS** (598).

The Glory-bush, or Princess Flower, is still another to be added to that long list. It is only a medium-sized shrub, but its strikingly colored blossoms often measure five inches at their widest part. Unfortunately each one lasts for only a day or so, but the procession of new ones continues for several weeks as if to compensate for this peculiar handicap.

Brazil makes still another addition to her list with one of the original Gloxinias, a form whose large flowers vary from violet to red and even white. This particular species is believed to be the principal ancestor of our modern florists' Gloxinias, perhaps with the co-operation of some undetermined natural hybrid varieties from the wild.

The Christmas-cactuses are a confusing crew even to botanists, but there is no argument over their having come from—yes, it's Brazil again! Down there they are regular Air-plants and grow on trees along with many kinds of Orchids. With us, however, they are almost always grown in pots and kept in the house or a greenhouse during the winter, with perhaps an outdoor summer vacation. If all goes well, they start flowering about Christmas

595 ↓

597 ↓

598

time, thereby justifying their popular name. Some people call them Crab-cactuses because of the oddly jointed sections of their stems.

All but one of the hundred or so Verbenas are natives of the New World. The important garden forms appear to have come originally from Peru and other temperate parts of South America. Hybridizing has complicated their full lineage, but not their habit of flowering freely and in wide variety from end to end of the summer months.

It seems strange that a single plant group such as the Verbenas should vary from completely delightful ornamentals to homely weeds whose only surprise is that they have any flowers at all. Yet this is the situation which the hundred or so members of this noteworthy tribe present.

The Verbenas which are grown in gardens come chiefly from tropical and subtropical America. In the wild state they are naturally showy, with their

599

601

Modern **VERBENAS** (599, 600, 601, 602, 604) are a glorious blend of many naturally showy species of which the majority came from tropical or temperate parts of South America . . . The so-called **MEXICAN SUNFLOWER** (603) is really a sort of shrub whose blossoms suggest those of single Dahlias . . . Among the flowering bulbs native to tropical America there is much to be said for the **ZEPHYR-LILIES** (605) . . . Continuing with the warm-country bulbs, we come to the unusually picturesque **MEXICAN SHELL-FLOWERS** (606).

neat foliage and heads of often fragrant blossoms in a wide range of colors and color combinations. The clusters are two inches or so across and each contains a number of much smaller individual blossoms. Some kinds grow in a rather sprawling yet attractive fashion, while others are definitely upstanding and well over a foot tall.

The best of these inborn characteristics have been intensified by many years of skillful crossbreeding and selection. As an illustration of these improvements it is now possible to obtain Verbena plants which spread more than two feet and bear heads of so many one-inch blossoms that they form almost perfect globes. It hardly needs to be added that their present-day variety of colors is fairly bewildering.

Out of that intriguing tropical land which stretches southward from Mexico to Guatemala comes a race of bulblike plants whose six-inch blossoms are utterly fantastic in their brilliance and dramatic markings. Some call them Tiger-flowers and others Mexican Shell-flowers. Yet even these names only faintly suggest their full beauty. The best part of it is that they can be enjoyed year after year in our own gardens, whether northern or southern.

600 ↓

602 ↓

603 605 604 606

The foliage of these willing and easily satisfied plants is quite similar to that of the Gladiolus, although it is on a smaller scale. Their flower stalks, however, are much more slender and branching. Out of their tips, in summer, come sets of three broad, flaring segments perfectly framing cuplike centers of gaudily spotted reds, oranges, yellows, and buffs. Their symmetry is reminiscent of the Trilliums', but no Trillium ever approaches their degree of tropical drama and magnificence.

From our Southeastern states, in addition to Mexico, South America, and the West Indies, we have a group of bulbs above whose grasslike leaves rise dainty, flaring flower funnels in a variety of pinks, yellows, coppers, and white. In width they run from one to four inches apiece and, from the smallest to the largest, they amply justify the names Zephyr-lilies and Fairy-lilies, which have been given to them.

As yet these delightful autumn-flowering New World bulbs are familiar to relatively few American gardeners. Nevertheless their day of popularity is sure to come, for beauty like theirs is too rare to miss.

The name Mexican Sunflower may perhaps arouse suspicions of those mighty state flowers of Kansas which may grow almost high enough to look

607

610

608

611

Perhaps the day will come when the plant-hybridizing wizards will be unable to produce new types of **ZINNIAS** (607, 608, 609, 610, 611, 612, 613, 614), but certainly we have not yet reached that point. Ten years ago most gardeners thought that they had seen the end of the expansion, only to realize a little later that they had been wrong. Perhaps history will repeat itself ten years hence! This much, at least, seems to be certain: Zinnias evidently have an inexhaustible ability to grow well almost anywhere that their seeds are planted. Within a few weeks those tiny particles of latent vigor will be forming buds of their own, and soon a new flood of color will spread across the garden spaces.

609 ↓

612 ↓

613

614

into one's bedroom windows. In this instance, however, it is only a substitute for the botanical title of Tithonias, which are somewhat shrubby annuals from Mexico southward and into the West Indies. One of the cultivated varieties is only about four feet tall and its flowers are not unlike those of single Dahlias.

Only a few generations ago the Zinnia was little more than a dull, weedy plant out of Mexico. It had received its name as a sort of memorial to one Johann Zinn, a German professor of medicine who died in 1759. But most American gardeners called it Youth-and-Old-Age and let it go at that.

Today that once mediocre wildflower is one of our most popular garden leaders. Its face and form have been transformed into an astounding variety of colors, contours, and sizes by the skill of hybridizers. There are prim little one-footers with flowers the size of silver quarters and giants three times their size whose blooms reach a width of nearly six inches. In variety of petal shapes and arrangements they remind one of modern Dahlias and Chrysanthemums. So many colors and blends are present among them that if Zinnias were to appoint a spokesman he might well say to the general public, "Just name your preference and we'll get it out of the stock room."

This incredible transformation was initiated by the late Luther Burbank about sixty years ago. A little later Mr. Bodger, the same Californian who put new life into the Nasturtium tribe, introduced the Dahlia-flowered type and really launched the Zinnias on their fabulous career toward the top of the annual flower ladder in this country and far beyond it.

In every experienced flower enthusiast's life there are times when he feels that the best regions in which to ride his hobby are the lands where the blossoms themselves have always lived. There all the natural influences which directed their ancestors are still at work—the winds, the rains, the all-important soil. It is a little like visiting the childhood home of an old friend and seeing the background out of which he came.

That is what you are doing as you enjoy this view of Verbenas and Yuccas in their native New Mexico. Their forebears have made this place their

home for countless centuries. From it they have gone out beyond the horizons, carrying some touch of freshness and perhaps of novelty to all they met along the way.

As we approach the conclusion of this book about the flowers of the world, we feel something of that same mood. The photographs you have seen and the words you have read are no more than samplings of a scene too vast for human comprehension. After all, plants are one of earth's earliest forms of life. Without them the very air would have brought quick death to any creature that breathed it in those vanished aeons when only the leaves and the alchemy of plants could nullify its poisons.

And then, when flowers came, beauty began to walk side by side with service. It took many forms, as such things always do. We cannot understand them all, nor is there any reason why we should. But they are good to see, and that alone makes them well worth knowing.

ACKNOWLEDGMENTS We are deeply indebted to a large number of helpful assistants in the preparation of this volume, in particular Roy Goin for his expert close-up photography and painstaking care in designing the page layouts; Charles Todd for his tasteful suggestions on typography; Paul E. Genereux for his many beautiful, full-page garden photos (1, 9, 29, 57, 221, 269, 338, 409, 429, 437, 461, 508, 522, 557, 572) and F. W. Cassebeer for his lovely garden shots (2, 170, 226, 235, 498); Peggy Mann (345, 348, 351, 523, 541, 564, 589) and Edward R. Darvill (192) for their stunning European garden photos; the late Charles S. Foster for his rare close-ups (153, 435, 500, 606); Chuck Abbott and Rapho-Guillemette, Inc. (530, 615) for their unusual photographic contributions and George Kalmbacher, taxonomist of the Brooklyn Botanic Garden, for his invaluable aid in checking the authentic names of the flower specimens. Our sincere gratitude also goes to all who have graciously opened their gardens to us for photographing purposes, especially the Long Island Agricultural and Technical Institute; the Fairchild Tropical Garden, Coconut Grove, Florida; Mr. Edwin R. Menninger, Stuart, Florida; Mr. Lowell Christman, Delray Beach, Florida; Mrs. Jack Hall and Mrs. Aubrey Snelling of Hull, England; Wadley & Smythe, New York; Mrs. D. Bonham; Mrs. Adolph Breiner Jr.; Mrs. George R. Brown; Mrs. Wilbur Down; Mrs. M. R. Dworin; Mrs. Robert H. Gay; Mr. Sallo Kahn; Mrs. William C. Meissner; Mrs. M. Piggott; Mrs. H. Platte; Mr. J. C. Portelroy; Miss Elizabeth Snyder; Mrs. J. Tesar; Mrs. Fred W. Wettlaufer; Miss Clara Danberry; Mrs. Carl L. Otto and to many unknown gardeners in countries all over the world who grew the specimen flowers snapped by our wandering photographers and unwittingly contributed to the beauty of this book.

This book was printed by offset lithography on Warren's 70 lb. Offset Enamel by the Case-Hoyt Corporation, Rochester, New York, and bound at the Berryville, Virginia, plant of Doubleday & Co.

Out of the seemingly arid stretches of the desert at White Sands, New Mexico the marvels of **YUCCAS** and **VERBENAS** (615) rise dauntlessly as if to prove Nature's resourcefulness for all the world to see.

Index

This index is by popular name followed by the Latin botanical name in *italics,* then the Plate number and lastly the Page number, in **bold face type.**

C

D

E

F

G

Q

R

S